THE BIG BOOK OF
RHYMING
SLANG

THE BIG BOOK OF
RHYMING SLANG

JONATHON GREEN

CASSELL

Cassell

Wellington House, 125 Strand, London WC2R 0BB

First published 2000
This edition first published 2002

© Text copyright Jonathon Green 2000

The right of Jonathon Green to be identified as author of this
work has been asserted by him in accordance with the
Copyright, Designs and Patents Act, 1988.

A CIP record for this book is available from the British Library.

ISBN 0 304 35513 5

Design Gwyn Lewis
Printed and bound by Aubin, France

CONTENTS

Introduction

Rhyming Slang is perhaps the best known of all the many varieties of words and phrases that make up the larger slang vocabulary. It may represent but a tiny subset, some 3000 examples out of the 90,000-plus that make up a comprehensive slang dictionary, but for many people, it remains the one that counts. It is, in vocabulary terms, a relatively modern invention. Unlike canting or criminal slang, which can be traced back to the early 16th century, it emerged only around 1810. Where did it come from? There are various 'creation myths'. One suggests that the language was deliberately covert and was created by street 'patterers' (sellers of ballads, dying speeches and melodramatic reports of major events) to confuse the police. Another theory ascribes the original rhyming slang to thieves, whose varieties of slang had by necessity always been at the cutting edge of 'counter-language' coinage. Julian Franklyn, in his *Dictionary of Rhyming Slang* (1960, 1984), notes the criminal input, but suggests that the villains, while proficient in the new slang, were not its creators, but rather picked it up from roving vagabonds. Peter Wright, in *Cockney Dialect and Slang* (1981), adds bricklayer's slang (his source describes it as 'the most picturesque, involved and unintelligible' of all rhyming slangs); and also suggests a large input from the Irish navvies recently imported to England to build railways and canals. According to Franklyn it was the linguistic rivalry between these navvies, and similarly recruited Cockneys (who worked alongside them and like them revelled in language), that created rhyming slang. But wherever its origins, rhyming slang is first and foremost a London phenomenon. The metropolis remains the great source of the vocabulary. But it has spread, first through Britain and in time to the coastal cities of America, brought there by visiting sailors, and to Australia, where first immigrants and later natives have contributed many terms.

In the terse definition offered by the OED, rhyming slang is 'a variety of (orig. Cockney) slang in which a word is replaced by a phrase which rhymes with it'. And there is nothing that very mysterious – nothing, for instance, on the scale of the endlessly questionable etymologies of 'cant' or criminal slang – about it. It can, of course, defeat the untutored listener. Like all slangs it originated in the desire to create a 'secret' language – a secrecy that was helped by its generally 'clipped' form, i.e. *Barnet* for 'hair' (rather than the full-out *Barnet Fair*), but the basic principle is an undaunting one. One takes a word one wishes to describe, and in its place provides a brief phrase, usually of two but often of three words, of which the last word rhymes with the word for which it is a synonym. *Round the houses*, means 'trousers', *Alan Whickers*, 'knickers', *Artful Dodger*, 'lodger', thus the pattern.

There are – this is slang, after all, and works on a seditious principle – greater complexities, usually originating from the layers of rhyme through which the 'translator' has to pass. Thus *ala* meaning 'buttocks', makes its way through *ala* which abbreviates *alabaster* = 'plaster', which clips *plaster of Paris* = 'arris', which abbreviates *aristotle* = 'bottle', which clips *bottle and glass* = standard slang 'arse' = Standard English 'buttocks'. There are also examples that, to non-Cockney ears, seem devoid of rhyme: *Charing Cross* does not immediately offer 'horse', not until one recalls the Cockney pronunciation 'crorss'; similarly, once 'Cocknified', *cold potato* ('pertater') is a waiter, *Max Miller* is a pillow ('piller'), *burnt cinder* a window ('winder') and so on. And that pretty much is it. As for secrecy: in the words of the 19th-century lexicographer John Camden Hotten, 'if there is any secrecy about the rhyming slang it is this – the rhyme is left out.'

There are approximately 3000 examples of rhyming slang in the pages that follow. Some, inevitably, are obsolete, but a suprisingly large number have lasted since their coinage a century and half ago. As in Standard English, if the linguistic cap fits, who should toss it aside. Slang of any sort tends towards ephemerality, and one might imagine that rhyming slang fitted that bill, yet one need but look at the numbers of otherwise long-forgotten sportsmen and show business stars still enshrined in the lexicon to undermine that assumption. *Apples and pears*, the ultimate, or at least most clichéd, of the type, was there in the first ever dictionary to include the rhymes, published in 1857: it shows no sign of fading. I doubt, however, that these words make up the entire rhyming slang vocabulary. Even as I put these entries together, I was still unearthing new material. Such is the lot of the lexicographer, and such is the nature particularly of rhyming slang, which seems to thrive on human inventiveness. As I have said elsewhere, I remain open to suggestion.

Jonathon Green / slang@blueyonder.co.uk

April 2002

Abbreviations

adj	adjective	phr.	phrase
adv.	adverb	pl.	plural
Antg.	Antigua, Antiguan	r.	reigned
Aus.	Australia, Australian	ref.	reference, referring
b.	born	S Afr.	South Africa
c.	circa	Scot.	Scotland, Scots
Can.	Canada, Canadian	sing.	singular
derog.	derogatory	sl.	slang
dial.	dialect, dialectal	UK	United Kingdom
esp.	especially	Und.	Underworld
excl.	exclamation	US	United States
ext.	extension, extended	usu.	usually
fig.	figurative	var.	variant
imper.	imperative	v.	verb
lit.	literally	W.I.	West Indies
n.	noun	WWI	First World War
N.Z.	New Zealand	WWII	Second World War
orig.	original, originally		

How to enjoy
The Big Book of Rhyming Slang

The Big Book of Rhyming Slang is divided into
two sections: the Dictionary, containing the full
rhyming slang lexicon of around 3000 words and
phrases, and the Thesaurus, a thematic listing of
most of the rhyming slang words and phrases
under Standard English headwords.

The Dictionary

The layout of the Dictionary follows standard
lexicographical conventions. Headwords are given
in their most frequently used form with variants
indicated where appropriate. Each headword is
followed by a date of use and a definition.
Definitions are given in Standard English. If the
word on which the headword rhymes is not
Standard English (e.g. *Brahms and Liszt* = pissed),
the full rhyme will be given in square brackets
after the definition along with any relevant
etymological notes.

The Thesaurus

This section takes the form of a thematic listing of categories with alphabetical listings of Standard English words and their rhyming slang counterparts. Where rhymes are formed on slang words rather than Standard English, these are indicated by italics.

busy bee n. [1]

... hire. [busy bee ...

butcher's (hook
...a930s.] a w...

butcher's ...
... and ...
... [will, ja...

butcher's look

buttered bread

buttered bun ...

buttered scone ...

butter flap n. [

buttons and ...

THE DICTIONARY

a

Aberdeens *n*. [20C] beans.

Abergavenny *n*. [19C] a penny.

abraham (*also* **abram**) *v*. [19C] to malinger, to sham, to fake illness. [*abram* = sham, or nautical sl. *abram* a malingerer]

abraham's willing *n*. [19C] a shilling (five pence).

abram *v*. *see* ABRAHAM

Adam (and Eve) *v*. **1** [late 19C+] to leave. **2** [1920s+] to believe, esp. in the phrase *would you Adam and Eve it?* [from the biblical Adam and Eve; the images of leaving the Garden of Eden and the requirement of belief in such myths may be coincidental]

Adrian (Quist) *adj*. [1970s+] (*Aus*.) drunk. [*Adrian Quist* = pissed; from the Aus. tennis player Adrian Quist (b.1913)]

After Eight Mint *adj*. [1980s+] penniless. [*After Eight Mint* = skint]

aggravation *n*. [1920s] a station.

a.i.f. *adj*. [1960s+] deaf. [A.I.F. stands for the Australian Imperial Forces]

ain't it a treat *n*. [late 19C+] a street.

airs and graces *n.* [20C] **1** faces. **2** braces. **3** horse races.

ajax *n.* [1950s+] tax, esp. the tax disk displayed on a car windscreen.

ala *n.* [20C] the buttocks, the behind. [*alabaster* = PLASTER OF PARIS]

alacompain (*also* **allacompain**) *n.* [mid-19C] rain. [perversion of Standard English *all complain*]

Alan Ladd *adj.* [1940s–60s] sad. [from the Hollywood film star Alan Ladd (1913–64)]

Alan Whickers *n.* [1960s] knickers. [from the BBC TV personality Alan Whicker (b.1925)]

Al Capone *n.* [1930s] (*Aus.*) the telephone. [from the Chicago gang-boss Alphonse 'Al' Capone (1899–1947)]

Alderman's nail *n.* [19C] an animal's tail.

Alf Garnett *n.* [1960s–70s] the hair. [*Alf Garnett* = BARNET (FAIR); from the TV character Alf Garnett, cockney anti-hero of the 1960s sitcom *Till Death Us Do Part*; Garnett, played by Warren Mitchell, was bald]

'alfpenny dip *n.* [mid-19C+] a ship. [a halfpenny dip was a small candle made by dipping a wick into melted tallow]

Alfred (the Great) *n.* [20C] weight. [from Alfred the Great, King of Wessex (849–99)]

ali oop *n.* [20C] excrement. [*ali oop* = poop]

alive or dead *n.* [late 19C+] the head.

allacompain *n. see* ALACOMPAIN.

all afloat *n*. [mid-19C] a coat.

Allied Irish *n*. [1990s+] (*Irish*) an act of masturbation. [*Allied Irish Bank* = wank]

alligator! *excl*. [1950s] later [from the jazz salutation *see you later, alligator*; *alligator* itself was a Black pejorative, coined to describe White musicians who 'swallowed up' original Black ideas]

all quiet *n*. [1930s+] the vagina. [*all quiet on the western front* = cunt; from the 1929 book *All Quiet on the Western Front* by Erich Maria Remarque]

all stations *n*. [20C] (*Aus*.) an Alsatian dog. [*all stations* = Alsatian or jocular mispronunciation]

Alma Gray *n*. [20C] (*Aus*.) a threepenny piece. [*Alma Gray* = trey (sl. 'threepenny piece')]

almond *n*. [late 19C+] the penis. [*almond rock* = cock]

almond rocks (*also* **almonds**) *n*. [late 19C+] socks.

almonds *n. see* ALMOND ROCKS.

alphonse *n*. [1950s+] (*UK Und*.) a pimp. [*alphonse* = ponce; the French name underlines the stereotyping of France as a land of corrupt sexuality]

Amos and Andy *n*. [1940s–50s] brandy. [from the *Amos and Andy* radio show, highly popular in the US in the 1930s–40s, which featured two White actors, Freeman Gosden (1899–1982) and Charles Correll (1890–1972), faking it as 'dumb but happy darkies', one of the last interpretations of the old 'minstrel show']

ampster *n. see* AMSTER.

amster (*also* **ampster**) *n.* [1940s+] (*Aus.*) one who works outside a carnival, sideshow, strip club etc., touting the pleasures inside and pulling in the customers. [*Amsterdam* = ram (Aus. sl. 'work as a confidence trickster's accomplice')]

Andy Cain *n.* [late 19C+] rain.

Andy Capp *n.* [1960s+] (*Aus.*) an act of defecation. [*Andy Capp* = crap; from the well-known strip cartoon character Andy Capp, created in 1956 by Reg Smythe for the London *Daily Mirror*]

Andy Capp *v.* [1960s] (*Aus.*) to defecate. [*see* ANDY CAPP *n.*]

Andy Maguire (*also* **Barney Maguire**) *n.* [20C] (*Aus.*) a fire.

Andy McGinn *n.* [1930s–50s] the chin.

Andy McNish *n.* [20C] fish.

Andy Pandy *n.* [1990s+] brandy. [from the puppet Andy Pandy, which featured in the children's television programme *Watch with Mother* in the 1950s–70s]

angel's kiss *n.* [20C] (*Aus.*) an act of urination. [*angel's kiss* = piss]

Anna Maria (*also* **Aunt Maria**) *n.* [late 19C+] a domestic fire. [note pronunciation of Maria as *mar-eye-a*]

Anna May Wong *n.* [1920s+] a stink, a smell. [*Anna May Wong* = pong; from the film star Anna May Wong (1907–61)]

Annie Louise *n.* [20C] (*Aus.*) cheese.

Anthea (Turner) *n.* [1990s+] any job or plan that pays well, almost invariably criminal. [*Anthea Turner* = earner; from the UK TV personality Anthea Turner (b.1960)]

any racket *n.* [mid-19C–1900s] a penny faggot.

any Wee Georgie? *phr.* [1930s+] any good? [WEE GEORGIE WOOD]

apple and pears *n. see* APPLES (AND PEARS).

apple and pip *v.* [late 19C+] **1** to sip. **2** to urinate. [**2** *apple and pip* = sip (backslang 'piss')]

apple core *n.* [1950s] 20 pounds (sterling). [*apple core* = a score]

apple fritter *n.* [20C] bitter beer.

applejack *n.* [1980s+] (*drugs*) crack cocaine.

apple pie *n.* [20C] the sky.

apple-pips *n.* [1900s–20s] the lips.

apples *adj.* [1940s+] (*Aus./N.Z.*) satisfactory, as required, esp. in the phrase *she'll be apples* it will be fine. [APPLES AND SPICE or from the phrase *apple-pie order*; although primarily associated with Australians, *apples* is used by the residents of Brooklyn, New York, to mean the same thing]

apples (and pears) (*also* **apple and pears**) *n.* [19C+] **1** stairs. **2** (*UK Und.*) an appearance in court. [**2** *apples and pears* = (*fig.*) stairs, i.e. those that lead from the cells to the dock in the Old Bailey; possibly underpinned by the arrangement of fruit in ascending 'stairs' on a coster-monger's stall]

apples and rice *adj.* [20C] (*usu. ironic*) nice.

apples and spice *adj.* [1940s+] (*Aus.*) satisfactory. [*apples and spice* = nice; *see* APPLES *adj.*]

apple sauce *n.* [20C] (*Aus.*) a horse. [possibly linked to the sl. *apple sauce* something either easy or ridiculous, both of which could refer to betting on the horse races]

apple tart *n.* [20C] (*Aus.*) a breaking of wind. [*apple tart* = fart]

apple tart *v.* [20C] (*Aus.*) to break wind. [*see* APPLE TART *n.*]

apricot (and peach) *n.* [20C] the beach.

April fools *n.* [20C] **1** stools (for sitting). **2** tools. **3** implements for burglary. **4** football pools. [**3** *April fools* = tools (sl. 'implements for burglary')]

April in Paris *n.* [1950s+] the buttocks, the behind. [*April in Paris* = ARRIS]

April showers *n.* [20C] flowers. [underpinned by an image of springtime]

Archbishop Laud *n.* [1950s] fraud. [from William Laud (1573–1645), Archbishop of Canterbury; the term (used in Robin Cook's lowlife novel *The Crust on Its Uppers* (1962)) may, like a number of similar citations, be a nonce-word]

ari *n. see* ARRIS.

aristotle *n.* [late 19C+] **1** the buttocks, the behind. **2** a bottle. [**1** *aristotle* = BOTTLE; from the Greek philosopher Aristotle (384–322 BC)]

army and navy *n.* [20C] gravy.

army rocks *n.* [late 19C+] socks.

arris (*also* **ari**, **arry**, **harris**) *n.* [20C] the buttocks, the behind. [ARISTOTLE]

arry *n. see* ARRIS.

arse over header *n.* [20C] (*Aus.*) the *varsovienne*, a dance, which has a possible French origin and resembles some of the Polish national dances. [the name comes from French *Varsovien*, i.e. from *Varsovie* Warsaw; the underlying image is of couples falling over]

artful dodger *n.* [mid-19C+] a lodger. [from the character Artful Dodger, who appears in Charles Dickens's *Oliver Twist* (1838); 'artful' here implies the lodger's traditional interest in his landlady]

artful fox *n.* [late 19C–1900s] a box in the theatre.

arthur *n.* [20C] a bank. [*j. arthur rank* = bank; from J. Arthur, later Lord, Rank (1888–1972), the UK flour producer turned film magnate who dominated the UK film business during the 1930s–40s]

artichoke (ripe) *v.* [mid–late 19C] to smoke a pipe.

Arty Roller *n.* [1910s+] (*Aus.*) a collar.

Ascot races (*also* **Ascots**) *n.* [20C] **1** the horse races. **2** braces.

Ascots *n. see* ASCOT RACES.

Aston Villa *n.* [20C] **1** a pillow. **2** a pillar. [from the Birmingham-based Premier League football team Aston Villa; note pronunciation of pillow as *piller*]

Auntie Ella *n.* [1940s+] an umbrella.

Auntie Flora *n.* [20C] (*W.I./Antg.*, *St Lucia*) the floor, esp. in the phrase *knock/take Auntie Flora* to sleep on the floor. [partial rhyming slang]

Auntie Meg *n.* [20C] (*Aus.*) a keg (of beer).

Auntie Nelly *n.* [20C] the stomach. [*Auntie Nelly* = belly]

Aunt Maria *n. see* ANNA MARIA.

Aylesbury (Duck) *n.* [20C] (*euphemistic*) a damn. [*Aylesbury duck* = fuck]

Aylesbury'ed *adj.* [20C] exhausted. [*Aylesbury ducked* = fucked]

ayrton *n.* [1990s+] ten pounds (sterling), a ten-pound note. [*ayrton senna* = tenner; from the champion Grand Prix racing driver Ayrton Senna (1960–94)]

b

bab *n. see* BABBLER

babbler (*also* **bab**, **babbling brook**) *n.* (*Aus./N.Z.*) **1** [1910s+] a cook, esp. in an institution, mining camp or farm. **2** [1920s–60s] a criminal, a villain. [*babbling brook* = **1** cook **2** crook]

babbling brook *n. see* BABBLER.

baby pap (*also* **baby's pap**) *n.* [mid-19C] a cap.

baby's cries *n.* [1920s+] the eyes.

baby's pap *n. see* BABY PAP.

baby's pram *n.* [20C] jam.

backseat driver *n.* [1920s+] a lazy person, a shirker. [*backseat driver* = skiver]

back-wheel skid *n. see* FRONT-WHEEL SKID.

bacon and eggs *n.* [1950s+] (*orig. Aus.*) the legs.

bacon-bonce *n.* [1970s+] a child molester. [*bacon-bonce* = nonce (sl. 'paedophile')]

bacon (rind) *adj.* [20C] blind.

Baden-Powell *n.* [late 19C+] a trowel. [from Robert Baden-Powell (1857–1941), the founder of the Boy Scouts]

bag of coke *n.* **1** [1940s+] (*Aus.*) a man, a person. **2** [20C] sexual intercourse. [*bag of coke* = **1** bloke **2** poke]

bag of flour *n.* [1970s+] a (bathroom) shower.

bag of fruit (*also* **box of fruit**) *n.* [1960s+] (*Aus./S.Afr./US*) a suit of clothes.

bag of sand *n.* [1940s+] a thousand, usu. a thousand pounds (sterling). [*bag of sand* = grand]

baked bean *n.* [1990s+] a sexual encounter. [*baked bean* = scene]

baker's dozen *n.* [late 19C+] a cousin.

balaclava *v.* [20C] to have sexual intercourse. [*balaclava* = charver (sl. 'have sexual intercourse')]

ball (and/of chalk) *n.* [20C] **1** a walk. **2** a talk.

ball (and/of chalk) *v.* [20C] **1** to walk. **2** to talk.

ball and bat *n.* [1900s–10s] a hat.

ball of dirt *n.* [late 19C] (*US*) the earth. [*ball of dirt* = earth and/or fig. use of Standard English]

ball of lead *n.* [1900s–10s] the head.

ball of twine *n.* [20C] (*Aus.*) a railway line.

balloon *n.* [20C] the saloon bar of a pub. [*balloon car* = bar]

balmy breeze *n.* [20C] cheese.

banana fritter *n.* [1980s+] a lavatory. [*banana fritter* = shitter]

banana (splits) *n*. [1950s+] **1** diarrhoea. **2** (*sing*.) an act of defecation. [*banana splits* = the shits]

bander *n*. [20C] (*Aus*.) soap. [BAND OF HOPE]

band in the box *n*. [1960s+] venereal disease. [*band in the box* = pox]

band of hope *n*. [late 19C+] soap. [from the temperance society Band of Hope, formed in Leeds in 1847]

bang and biff *n*. [20C] syphilis. [*bang and biff* = syph]

bangers (and mash) *n*. [1930s+] an act of urination. [*bangers and mash* = slash]

bang the plank *v*. [1990s+] to masturbate. [*bang the plank* = wank; note also the many other sl. terms for masturbation based on beating or slapping]

barclay's *n*. [1930s+] an act of masturbation. [*barclay's bank* = wank; from the high-street banking chain Barclays]

bark and growl *n*. [mid-19C+] a trowel.

barker's *adj*. [mid-20C] naked, nude. [*barker's* = starkers; from the former department store, Barker's, based in High Street Kensington, London, until *c*.1970]

barley *n*. [1990s+] (*drugs*) cocaine. [*oats and barley* = charlie (sl. 'cocaine')]

barmaid's blush *n*. [20C] (*Aus*.) in poker, a flush.

Barnaby Rudge *n*. [20C] a judge. [from Charles Dickens's 1841 novel *Barnaby Rudge*; the eponymous Barnaby is not in fact a judge but a halfwit, swept up in the anti-Catholic Gordon Riots that form the background of the novel]

barnet (fair) *n.* [mid-19C+] the hair. [from the country's former major horse fair, Barnet Fair, *fl.* 16C–18C; so important was the town's position on a main northbound thoroughfare that it became known as 'the town of inns']

Barney Dillon *n.* [1930s] (*Scot.*) a shilling (five pence).

Barney Maguire *n. see* ANDY MAGUIRE.

Barney Moke *n.* [1930s–50s] a pocket. [*Barney Moke* = poke (sl. 'pocket')]

Barney (Rubble) *n.* [1960s+] trouble. [from Barney Rubble, a character in the TV cartoon (and latterly the film) *The Flintstones*]

bar of soap *n.* [1970s+] drugs. [*bar of soap* = dope]

barrel of fat *n.* [20C] (*Aus.*) a hat.

basin of gravy *n.* [20C] a baby.

bat and ball *n.* [20C] (*Aus.*) a wall.

bat and wicket *n.* [20C] a ticket.

bath bun *n.* **1** [late 19C+] a son. **2** [1970s+] the sun.

battle and cruiser *n. see* BATTLE-CRUISER.

battle-cruiser (*also* **battle and cruiser**, **battleship and cruiser**) *n.* [1940s+] a pub. [*battle-cruiser* = boozer]

battle of the Nile *n.* [mid-19C–1900s] a hat. [*battle of the Nile* = tile (19C sl. 'hat'); from the Battle of the Nile

(1 August 1798), in which Nelson defeated Napoleon's fleet, thus wrecking the French expedition to Egypt]

battle of Waterloo *n.* [mid-19C+] **1** a stew. **2** a queue. [from the Battle of Waterloo, which took place on 18 June 1815]

battleship and cruiser *n. see* BATTLE-CRUISER.

bazaar *n.* [late 19C+] a bar (in a pub).

bear's paw *n.* [20C] a saw. [the aptness of the rhyme is heightened by the idea of woodland as the traditional habitat of bears as well as the workplace of the logger]

beattie and babs *n.* [1930s+] body lice. [*beattie and babs* = crabs]

Beecham's pill *n.* **1** [1920s+] a bill. **2** [1930s] (*pl.*) hand-bills, i.e. any form of sign denoting one's qualifications for begging ('blind', 'ex-soldier' etc.). **3** [1950s+] a still (photograph). **4** [1950s+] (*Aus.*) a fool, a simpleton. [**4** *Beecham's pill* = dill (Aus./N.Z. sl. 'fool'); from Beecham's Pills, a late-19C–early-20C indigestion remedy; Beecham's Pills were among the many items advertised by sign-carrying 'sandwich-men' in the early 20C]

beef-heart *n.* [late 19C] a breaking of wind. [*beef-heart* = fart]

beehive *n.* [1920s+] **1** the number five. **2** a five-pound note.

beery buff *n.* [20C] a fool. [*beery buff* = muff (early-20C sl. 'fool')]

bees (*also* **beesum**) *n.* [late 19C+] money. [BEES AND HONEY]

bees and honey *n.* [late 19C+] money. [the term evokes the industriousness of the bee and the 'sweetness' of wealth]

beesum *n. see* BEES.

bees wingers *n.* [1960s+] the fingers.

beggar boy's (arse) *n.* [1940s–60s] **1** money. **2** a bottle of Bass ale. [*beggar boy's arse* = **1** brass **2** Bass]

beggar my neighbour *phr.* [1920s+] visiting the labour exchange/unemployment office to draw unemployment benefit. [*beggar my neighbour* = on the labour]

beg your pardon *n.* [late 19C] a garden.

bell ringers *n.* [20C] the fingers.

below Nathaniel *adj.* [late 19C–1910s] exceedingly evil, i.e. metaphorically even lower than hell. [either from *Nathaniel* = hell (Partridge) or *Nathaniel* as a synonym for Satan (Ware)]

be my Georgie Best *phr.* [1960s+] (*orig. US*) a phrase of encouragement (esp. in response to a request to borrow something), 'go ahead', 'feel free', 'help yourself', 'make yourself at home' etc. [*be my Georgie Best* = be my guest; *see* GEORGIE BEST]

bended knees *n.* [20C] cheese.

ben-flake *n.* [mid-19C–1900s] a cheap beefsteak, 'used at a slap-bang, i.e. a low cook-shop or eating house' (Ducange Anglicus).

Benny Hill *n.* [1960s+] **1** a drill. **2** a till, i.e. a cash register. [from the UK comedian Benny Hill (1925–92)]

berk (*also* **burk, burke**) *n.* [1930s+] a fool, an incompetent. [BERKELEY HUNT]

Berkeley hunt (*also* **Berkshire hunt, Burlington hunt**) *n.* [1930s+] **1** the vagina. **2** a fool, an incompetent. [*Berkeley hunt* = cunt]

Berkshire hunt *n. see* BERKELEY HUNT.

bet on the Mary Lou *v.* [1920s+] (*Aus.*) to bet on credit. [*bet on the Mary Lou* = bet on the blue (Aus. sl. 'bet on credit')]

Betty Grable *n.* [1950s+] (*Aus.*) a table. [from the US film star and WWII pin-up Betty Grable (1916–73)]

Betty Lea (*also* **Betty Lee**) *n.* [20C] tea.

Betty Lee *n. see* BETTY LEA.

Bexley Heath *n.* [late 19C+] the teeth. [from Bexley Heath in Kent; originally an open heath, the area was built over in the 19C]

bib and bub *n.* [20C] (*Aus.*) a bath. [*bib and bub* = tub]

big and bulky *n.* [late 19C] (*Aus.*) a sulky (a horse-drawn carriage). [far from 'big and bulky' the sulky is a light two-wheeled carriage or chaise seated for one person, now used principally in America for trials of speed among trotting-horses; the vehicle is so called because it 'refuses' to seat more than one passenger]

Big Ben *n.* [20C] **1** the number ten. **2** ten pounds (sterling). [from Big Ben, the clock in the tower of the Houses of Parliament in London]

big bloke *n.* [1940s+] (*drugs*) cocaine. [*big bloke* = coke]

big hit *n.* [1920s+] (*Aus.*) an act of defecation. [*big hit* = shit]

big mac *n.* [1980s+] dismissal from a job. [*big mac* = the sack; underpinned by the image of McDonalds, vendor of the Big Mac hamburger, as tough employers]

Billie Hoke *n.* [1980s+] (*drugs*) cocaine. [*Billie Hoke* = coke]

Billy Bunter *n.* [1990s+] a member of the public, a customer. [*Billy Bunter* = punter; from the fictional schoolboy Billy Bunter, created by Frank Richards]

Billy Button *n.*[1] [mid-19C] mutton. [note standard mid-19C sl. *billy button* a journeyman tailor]

Billy Button *n.*[2] [20C] (*W.I.*) a gullible fool, esp. one who performs a job of work without first making sure that they will be paid. [*Billy Button* = (gets) nutten, i.e. 'nothing', plus jocular use of a 'proper name']

billy goat *n.* [20C] a coat. [var. on NANNY (GOAT)]

Billy Liar *n.* [1960s+] a tyre. [from the book (and subsequently the film) *Billy Liar* (1959) by Keith Waterhouse]

Binnie Hale *n.* [20C] a story used for begging or for a confidence trick. [*Binnie Hale* = tale; from the UK actress Binnie Hale (1899–1984)]

birch broom *n.* [mid-19C] a room. [note the colloquial phrase 'birch broom in a fit' used of messy hair]

Birchington hunt (*also* **Burchington hunt**) *n.* [1930s+] the vagina. [var. on BERKELEY HUNT plus possible overtones of sado-masochism, i.e. the birch]

bird (lime) *n*. **1** [mid-19C] a prison sentence; hence *birded (up)* imprisoned, *in bird* in prison, *do bird* serve a sentence. **2** [1920s–30s] previous convictions. **3** (*fig.*) any form of constraint, responsibility. [*bird lime* = time]

biscuits and cheese *n*. [1940s+] the knees.

bit of blink (*also* **blink**) *n*. [late 19C–1900s] drink.

bit of tripe *n*. [late 19C] a wife. [possibly a loose rhyme; the reference may be to the *tripe* she talks or that which she cooks]

bit on the cuff *adj*. [1930s+] (*Aus./N.Z.*) excessive, severe, 'over the top'. [*bit on the cuff* = a bit rough]

Black and Decker *n*. [1950s+] the penis. [*Black and Decker* = pecker; from the Black and Decker range of DIY equipment; neatly equating with such general sl. terms for the penis as a 'tool']

black and white *n*. [late 19C–1900s] (*UK Und.*) night.

blackbird and thrush *v*. [late 19C] to clean one's boots or shoes. [*blackbird and thrush* = brush]

black man kissed her *n*. [20C] a sister. [presumably underpinned by an inference of racist dislike of such an embrace occurring]

Blackwall Tunnel *n*. [20C] a ship's funnel. [from the 4410-foot-long Blackwall Tunnel, running under the River Thames connecting Blackwall to Greenwich, which was completed in 1897; a second tunnel was added in 1967]

bladder of fat *n*. [1900s–10s] a hat.

bladder of lard *n.* **1** [20C] a playing card. **2** [1910s] in WWI, a bingo card. **3** [1920s–50s] Scotland Yard, the former headquarters of London's Metropolitan Police.

blindman's buff *n.* [1960s+] snuff.

blink *n. see* BIT OF BLINK.

block and tackle *n.* [20C] handcuffs. [*block and tackle* = shackle]

blood blister *n.* [20C] (*Aus.*) a sister.

blueberry (hill) *n.* [1950s+] the police. [*blueberry hill* = Old Bill; there is a possible link to the force's traditional blue uniforms and the Fats Domino hit 'Blueberry Hill']

blue de hue *n.* [1970s] (*drugs*) marijuana from Vietnam. [internal rhyme (*hue* pronounced *hoo-ay*); from Hue, a major city in Vietnam]

blue moon *n.* **1** [late 19C] a spoon. **2** [1970s+] (*Aus.*) a pimp. [**2** *blue moon* = hoon (Aus. sl. 'procurer of prostitutes')]

blue moon *v.* [late 19C–1930s] to romance, to 'chat up'. [*blue moon* = spoon]

blue o'clock in the morning *n.* [late 19C–1900s] the last minutes of proper night-time, when darkness is gradually giving way to dawn. [weak rhyme on *blue* = two]

board and plank *n.* [1940s+] an American. [*board and plank* = Yank]

boat *n. see* BOAT-RACE.

boat and oar (*also* **broken oar**) *n.* [1950s] a prostitute. [*boat and oar* = whore]

boat-race (*also* **boat**) *n.* [1940s+] the face.

bob and dick *n.* [1970s] the penis. [*bob and dick* = prick]

bob and dick *adj.* [1960s+] sick, esp. after drinking.

bob and hit *n.* **1** [19C] the vagina. **2** [1990s+] excrement. [*bob and hit* = **1** pit **2** shit]

Bobby Martin *n.* [20C] (*Aus.*) a carton.

Bobby Moore *n.* [1970s+] a door. [from the UK footballer Bobby Moore (1941–93)]

Bobby Rocks *n.* [20C] (*Aus.*) a pair of socks. [plus a presumed reference to US *bobby sox* socks reaching just above the ankle, esp. those worn by girls in their teens]

bob, harry and dick *adj.* [late 19C–1900s] sick, usu. from drinking. [a play on sl. *Tom, Dick and Harry*].

Bob Hope *n.* [1960s] **1** (*drugs*) cannabis. **2** (*Aus.*) soap. [**1** *Bob Hope* = dope; from the US comedian Bob Hope (b.1903)]

bob my pal (*also* **bob's my pal**) *n.* [mid-19C] a girl. [*bob my pal* = gal]

Bob Powell *n.* [20C] (*Aus.*) a towel.

bob's my pal *n. see* BOB MY PAL.

Bob Squash *n.* [20C] **1** a wash. **2** a public convenience, hence *work the bob* (of a pickpocket) to rob jackets and coats that have been hung up while people wash their hands.

boiled rag *n.* [1940s] (*US*) an old, unattractive woman. [*boiled rag* = old hag]

◆◆

Dishonourable Members

Douglas Hurd	turd/third
enoch	towel
Harold Macmillan	villain
House of Lords	cords
John Prescott	waistcoat
John Selwyn	bummer
Lord Sutch	clutch/crutch
Ted Heath	thief/teeth
Tony Benn	ten (pounds)
Tony Blair	hair

◆◆

bona fide *adj.* [20C] (*Aus.*) terrified.

bonnets so blue *n.* [mid-19C+] (*Irish*) stew.

bonny fair *n.* [1940s] (*US*) the hair. [var. on BARNET (FAIR)]

booed and hissed *adj.* [1980s] drunk. [*booed and hissed* = pissed]

boots and socks *n.* [20C] (*Aus.*) venereal disease. [*boots and socks* = pox]

bo-peep *n.* [late 19C+] **1** sleep. **2** a peep, i.e. a look. [from the nursery rhyme tale of *Little Bo-Peep* who, while sleeping, 'lost her sheep, and didn't know where to find them']

boracic (*also* **brassick**, **brassic (lint)**) *adj.* [1950s+] out of funds, impoverished. [*boracic lint* = skint; note pronunciation is always *brassik*]

borrow and beg *n*. [late 19C+] an egg.

Botany Bay *n*. [1940s+] the bed; hence *hit the Botany Bay* to go to bed. [*Botany Bay* = hay; from Botany Bay, New South Wales, where Captain Cook made his first landing in Australia in 1770]

Botany Bay *v*. [1940s+] (*Aus.*) to run away, hence *do a Botany*. [possibly linked to the role of Botany Bay as the first ever Aus. penal colony (late 18C–mid-19C); prisoners would naturally wish to escape]

bottle *n*. [1950s+] **1** the buttocks, the posterior; hence ON THE BOTTLE. **2** courage, bravery. **3** (*fig., usu. derog.*) a person. [BOTTLE AND GLASS]

bottle *v*.[1] [20C] **1** to sodomize. **2** of a man, to have sexual intercourse. **3** (*gay*) to lick the anus. [BOTTLE AND GLASS]

bottle *v*.[2] [20C] to stink, to smell badly. [probably from *bottle of drink* = stink]

bottle and glass *n*. **1** [20C] (*Aus.*) the posterior. **2** [1950s+] courage, bravery, 'spirit' [*bottle and glass* = arse; **2** plays on 18C Standard English *bottom* character]

bottle (and stopper) *n*. [1950s–70s] a policeman. [*bottle and stopper* = copper]

bottle of beer *n*. [20C] the ear.

bottle of cola (*also* **bottle of Kola**) *n*. [1940s–50s] a bowler hat. [not from Coca Cola but from the UK soft drink Kola, which pre-dated the US product]

bottle of fizz *n.* [20C] pickpocketing. [*bottle of fizz* = whiz (US Und. sl. 'pickpocket')]

bottle of Kola *n. see* BOTTLE OF COLA.

bottle of sauce *n.* [late 19C+] a horse.

bottle of scent *adj.* [1950s+] of a man, homosexual, effeminate. [*bottle of scent* = bent]

bottle of scotch *n.* [mid–late 19C] a watch, specifically a Waterbury watch; *see* WATERBURY WATCH.

bottle of spruce *n.* [mid-19C] twopence. [*bottle of spruce* = deuce (17–19C sl. 'twopence')]

bottle of water *n.* **1** [1920s–30s] a daughter. **2** [1960s+] (*drugs*) a quarter (of an ounce).

bottle of wine *n.* [20C] a judicial fine.

bottles of booze *n.* [1940s–50s] (*US*) shoes.

bottletop *n.* [20C] a gain, a benefit, something good. [*bottletop* = cop]

bottletop *v.* [20C] to catch, to take in. [*bottletop* = cop]

bow and arrow *n.* [20C] **1** a sparrow. **2** a charabanc, a coach. [**2** *bow-and-arrow* (pronounced *arrer*) = chara(banc); in **1** note the reference to the poem 'Who Killed Cock Robin?': '"I," said the sparrow, "with my bow and arrow"']

bow and quiver *n.* [20C] the human liver.

bowl the hoop *n.* [mid-19C] soup.

box of glue *n.* [1950s] (*US*) a Jew.

box of fruit *n. see* BAG OF FRUIT.

box of toys *n.* [late 19C–1930s] noise. [the noise, presumably, of children playing]

boy in blue *n.* [20C] (*Irish*) stew (the food).

boys on ice *n.* [late 19C+] lice.

brace and bits *n.* [20C] (*US*) the female breasts, esp. the nipples. [*brace and bits* = tits, plus a pun on Standard English *brace* a pair]

brad *n.* [1990s+] **1** excrement. **2** an act of defecation. [*brad pitt* = shit; from the US film star Brad Pitt (b.1964)]

Bradford cities *n.* [1990s+] the female breasts. [*Bradford cities* = titties]

bradleys *n.* [1990s+] the female breasts. [*bradley pitts* = tits; *see* BRAD]

Brahms and Liszt *adj.* [1920s+] drunk. [*Brahms and Liszt* = pissed; from the composers Johannes Brahms (1833–97) and Franz Liszt (1811–86)]

brandy snap *n.* [1940s] (*US*) a slap.

brass *n.* [1980s+] (*drugs*) cannabis. [probably *brass* = grass]

brass band *n.* [20C] the hand.

brassick *adj. see* BORACIC.

brassic (lint) *adj. see* BORACIC.

brass (nail) *n.* [1930s+] a prostitute. [*brass nail* = tail (sl. 'woman', 'prostitute')]

brass tacks *n*. [20C] (*orig. US*) the facts, i.e. the central issues or heart of a matter, esp. in the phrase *get down to brass tacks* (or *nails*). [now almost Standard English]

brave and bold *adj*. [late 19C–1920s] cold.

bread *n*. [1930s+] money. [probably from Yiddish *broyt* money, but note Partridge's suggestion of a link to BREAD AND HONEY; the over-riding image is of something basic to daily life, as bread is]

bread and butter *n*. [20C] **1** the gutter. **2** an eccentric or mad person. **3** a golf putter. [**2** *bread and butter* = nutter]

bread and cheese *n*. [late 19C+] a sneeze.

bread and honey *n*. [20C] money. [var. on BEES AND HONEY]

bread and jam *n*. [20C] a tram.

bread and lard *adj*. [20C] hard.

Brenda Frickers *n*. [20C] knickers. [from the Irish character actress Brenda Fricker (b.1944)]

Brian O'Flynn *n*. [20C] gin; hence QUARTERN O' BRY.

Brian O'Linn *n*. [mid-19C+] gin.

bricks and mortar *n*. [20C] a daughter. [note use in theatre to describe a heavy, dull style of acting]

bride and groom *n*. [late 19C–1950s] **1** a broom. **2** a room.

brigg's rest *n*. [20C] a vest.

Brighton line *n*. [1940s+] (*bingo*) the number nine.

Brighton pier *n*. **1** [mid-19C+] sick, ill. **2** [mid-19C+]

peculiar, strange. **3** [1950s+] homosexual. [*Brighton pier* = **1**, **2** (Standard English) queer **3** (sl.) queer; Brighton has always had a raffish reputation, whether for its long-time popularity as a site for 'dirty weekends' for Londoners or for its more recent thriving gay community]

Brighton pier *v.* [1990s+] to leave, to run away. [*Brighton pier* = disappear]

Brighton rock *n.* [1940s+] a courtoom dock. [popularized by the film *Brighton Rock* (1947), based on Graham Greene's novel]

Bristol bits (*also* **Bristols**) *n.* [1960s] the female breasts. [*Bristol bits* = tits]

Bristol City *n.* [1960s+] a female breast. [*Bristol City* = titty]

Bristols *n. see* BRISTOL BITS.

Britney Spears *n.* [1990s+] beers. [from the US pop singer Britney Spears (b.1981)]

broken heart *n.* [20C] a breaking of wind. [*broken heart* = fart]

broken mug *n.* [1940s] (*US*) a hug.

broken oar *n. see* BOAT AND OAR.

Bromley (by Bow) *n.* [20C] money. [*Bromley by Bow* = dough]

bronze figure *n.* [20C] a kipper. [a loose rhyme; also from the bronze colour of a kipper, i.e. a smoked or 'kippered' herring]

brother and sister *n.* [20C] a blister.

brothers and sisters *n.* [1920s+] (*US*) whiskers.

brown bess *adv.* [mid-19C] yes.

brown bread *adj.* [1990s+] dead.

brown hat *n.* [late 19C–1920s] a cat.

brown joe *v.* [1930s–40s] (*Aus.*) to know, hence *brown joe* in the know.

brown joe *adv.* [mid-19C] no.

brown paper *n.* [1970s] a trick, a pursuit, a profession, a 'game'. [*brown paper* = caper]

brussel sprout *n.* [1910s+] a Boy Scout. [note sl. *sprout* a young person]

bryant and mays *n.* [1900s–10s] stays (a form of light underbodice that preceded the corset). [from the Bryant & May match factory founded in London's East End in 1839; the company was a major employer of female labour, the workers themselves known in sl. as *Bryant and May's chuckaways* a blackly humorous reference to the dangers of their job]

bubble (*also* **old bubble**) *n.* [1930s+] a wife. [*bubble* = TROUBLE AND STRIFE]

bubble and squeak *n.* **1** [late 19C+] a schoolmaster. **2** [1950s+] a Greek. **3** [1970s] a week. **4** [20C] (*Aus.*) an act of urination. [*bubble and squeak* = **1** beak **4** leak]

bubble and squeak *v.* [mid-19C+] to speak, esp. to inform to the police. [note sl. *squeak* to inform]

bubble gum *n.* [1940s+] the buttocks, the behind. [*bubble gum* = bum]

bubbly jock *n.* [19C] **1** a turkey. **2** an excessive talker. **3** a foolish braggart. [*bubbly jock* = turkey cock; **2** and **3** imply a turkey's characteristics, strutting and making too much noise; note military jargon *the Bubbly Jocks* the Royal Scots Greys, whose rival regiments equate them with the farmyard bird]

buccaneer *n.* [1950s+] a male homosexual. [*buccaneer* = queer, plus an added, pejorative inference of predatory sex]

bucket afloat (*also* **bucket and float**) *n.* [19C] a coat.

bucket and float *n. see* BUCKET AFLOAT.

bucket (and pail) *n.* [1930s+] (*Can./US Und.*) a county or local prison. [*bucket and pail* = jail]

buckle my shoe *n.* [late 19C+] **1** a Jew. **2** (*bingo*) the number two. [**2** recalls the counting rhyme 'one, two, buckle my shoe']

bugs and fleas *n.* [1940s] (*US*) the knees.

Bugs Bunny *n.* [1950s+] (*Aus.*) money. [from the Warner Bros. cartoon character *Bugs Bunny*, created 1940, itself a blend of sl. *bugs* crazy and Standard English *bunny*]

bull and cow (*also* **pantomime cow**) *n.* [mid-19C+] a row, i.e. an argument.

bull-ants *n.* [1920s–30s] (*Aus.*) trousers. [*bull-ants* = pants]

bullaphants *adj.* [20C] (*Irish*) drunk. [var. on ELEPHANT'S (TRUNK)]

bullock's heart *n.* [late 19C] a breaking of wind. [*bullock's heart* = fart]

bullock's horn *v.* [late 19C–1900s] to pawn.

bullock's liver *n.* [late 19C] a river.

bull's aunts *n.* [1940s] (*US*) trousers. [*bull's aunts* = pants]

bully beef *n.* [1950s+] (*UK prison*) a chief officer. [the rhyme is augmented by the negative assessment of the officer's mentality and physique]

bulrush *n.* [20C] a paintbrush.

bundle of socks *n.* [late 19C+] (*Aus.*) the head. [*bundle of socks* = thinkbox (late 19C–1900s Aus. sl. 'head')]

bung it (in) *n.* [1920s+] gin. [the *bunging* is presumably into the glass and thence the mouth]

bunny *n.* **1** [1950s+] a chat, a conversation. **2** [1950s–60s] a talkative person. [RABBIT]

bunsen burner *n.* [20C] any job or plan that pays well, almost invariably criminal. [*bunsen burner* = earner]

Burchington hunt *n. see* BIRCHINGTON HUNT.

burdetts *n.* [1920s+] boots. [*burdett coutts* = boots; from Burdett Coutts the bankers, specifically the 19C philanthropist and friend of Charles Dickens, Baroness Burdett Coutts; among her charitable donations were pairs of boots, given to the 'deserving poor']

burglar alarm *n.* [20C] the arm.

burk *n. see* BERK.

burk *v.* [late 19C–1910s] (*orig. N.Z.*) to avoid work. [*burk* = shirk or from Standard English *burk* to smother, to 'hush up'; both are from *burke* to strangle, named for the early-19C 'resurrectionists' or grave-robbers William Burke (1792–1829) and his partner William Hare (1790–*c*.1860), who murdered people in order to sell their corpses to the medical school for surgical dissection. Burke was hanged; Hare, who turned King's evidence, escaped the noose]

burke *n. see* BERK.

Burlington Bertie *n.* [20C] (*bingo*) the number 30. [from the music-hall hit song 'Burlington Bertie from Bow']

Burlington hunt *n. see* BERKELEY HUNT.

burnt (cinder) *n.* [1940s+] a window. [*burnt cinder* = window; note pronunciation of window as *winder*]

burton *n.* [1960s–70s] a male prostitute. [*burton-on-trent* = rent (boy), from BURTON-ON-TRENT]

Burton-on-Trent *n.* [late 19C+] the rent. [from the UK town Burton-on-Trent]

bus and tram *n.* [20C] jam.

bushel and peck *n.* [late 19C+] the throat. [*bushel and peck* – neck]

bushel of coke *n.* [20C] a man, a person. [*bushel of coke* = bloke]

Bushey Park *n. see* BUSHY PARK.

Bushy Park (*also* **Bushey Park**) *n.* [mid-19C–1900s] a lark, i.e. a joke. [from Bushy Park, near Hampton Court Palace in West London, the former hunting ground of Henry VIII, which was opened to the public after his death in 1547]

busy bee *n.* [1970s+] (*drugs*) the hallucinogen phencyclidine. [*busy bee* = PCP]

butcher's (hook) (*also* **butcher's look, docker's hook**) *n.* [1930s+] a look, a glance. [*butcher's hook* = look]

butcher's hook *adj.* (*Aus.*) **1** [20C] ill, sick. **2** [1940s+] angry, annoyed, hence *go butcher's hook* lose one's temper (with). [*butcher's hook* = crook (Aus. sl. 'ill', 'out of sorts')]

butcher's look *n.* see BUTCHER'S (HOOK).

buttered bread *adj.* [20C] dead.

buttered bun *n.* [20C] (*bingo*) the number one.

buttered scone *n.* [1950s+] (*bingo*) the number one.

butter flap *n.* [mid-19C] **1** a trap or light carriage. **2** a cap.

buttons and bows *n.* [20C] (*Aus.*) toes.

C

cabbage-tree *v.* [20C] (*US*) to flee.

cabbage-tree hat *n.* [20C] (*Aus.*) an informer. [*cabbage-tree hat* = rat; the actual hat is made of woven cabbage-tree or cabbage-palm leaves]

cabman's rests *n.* [late 19C–1960s] the female breasts.

cab rank *n.* [20C] a bank.

Cain and Abel (*also* **Cain and Able**) *n.* [mid-19C+] a table.

Cain and Able *n. see* CAIN AND ABEL.

Calcutta *n.* [20C] butter.

calf *n.* [1940s+] 50 pence. [*cow and calf* = half, i.e. half a pound sterling, originally ten shillings, now 50 pence]

Calvin Klein *n.* [1980s+] **1** a judicial fine. **2** wine. [from the US clothes designer Calvin Klein (b.1942)]

Camden Town *n.* [19C] a halfpenny. [*Camden Town* = brown (19C sl. 'halfpenny'); from Camden Town, London NW1]

camerer cuss *n.* [1920s–30s] a London bus. [from the clockmakers Camerer Cuss, founded in 1788; the reference is to the 'works' that powered the then new motor-buses, successors to the horse-driven originals]

Camilla Parker (Bowles) *n.* [1990s+] a Rolls Royce car.

[from Camilla Parker Bowles, the long-term partner of Prince Charles]

canal boat *n.* [20C] the totalizator. [*canal boat* = tote]

C&A *adj.* [1950s–60s] homosexual. [*C∂A* = gay; from the UK clothing store chain C&A]

candle (*also* **candle-sconce**) *n.* [1920s+] a pimp. [*candle-sconce* = ponce; the image is of the greasy smoothness of the pimp]

candle-sconce *n. see* CANDLE.

can of coke *n.* [20C] a joke.

can of oil (*also* **canov**) *n.* [late 19C+] a boil.

canov *n. see* CAN OF OIL.

can't-keep-still *n.* [mid–late 19C] a prison treadmill. [underpinned by the endless movement of the machine and necessity for constant 'walking' by those thus punished]

cape kelly *n.* [1940s] (*Aus.*) the stomach. [*cape kelly* = belly]

Cape of Good Hope *n.* [1900s–10s] soap.

Captain Bligh *n.* [1930s+] a pie. [from Captain William Bligh (1754–1817) of HMS *Bounty* and the celebrated mutiny of 1789, popularized through the film *Mutiny on the Bounty* (1935)]

Captain Bloods *n.* [20C] (*Aus.*) potatoes. [*Captain Bloods* = spuds; from the Irish adventurer Captain Thomas Blood (1618–80), best known for a failed attempt to steal the British Crown Jewels in 1671]

Captain Cook n. [1930s+] (*Aus.*) **1** a look. **2** a book. [from the navigator and explorer Captain James Cook (1728–79), whose 'look' at Australia in 1769 rendered him its European discoverer]

Captain Cook adj. [1950s] (*Aus.*) ill, sick. [*Captain Cook* = crook (Aus./N.Z. sl. 'ill'); *see* CAPTAIN COOK *n.*]

Captain Grimes n. [1980s] *The Times* newspaper. [possibly from Evelyn Waugh's character Captain Grimes, the raffish schoolmaster in *Decline and Fall* (1928)]

Captain Hicks n. [1930s–40s] in craps dice, six points, made with a pair of threes.

Captain Kettle v. [late 19C–1940s] to settle (after some energetic dispute). [from the character Captain Kettle, created by Cutliffe Hyne, who appeared in stories published 1893–1938]

Captain Kirk n. [1960s+] a Turk. [from the character Captain James T. Kirk, master of the Starship *Enterprise* in the cult TV series *Star Trek*]

captain's log n. [1960s+] a lavatory. [*captain's log* = bog; presumably linked to the cult TV series *Star Trek*, each episode of which began with the intonation 'Captain's Log, Stardate …']

cardboard box n. [1970s+] venereal disease. [*cardboard box* = pox]

careless talk n. [1940s] a stick of chalk, usu. as used by darts players for scoring. [from the legend 'Careless talk costs lives' featured on WWII posters]

carlo *adj.* [1900s–30s] eccentric, mad. [*carlo gatti* = batty; from the firm of Carlo Gatti, suppliers of ice to London restaurants pre-refrigeration]

Carl Rosa *n.* [1960s+] a poser, anyone pretending to be something that they are not; hence *old carl rosa* a fraud. [from the popular Carl Rosa Operatic Society, founded in London in 1875]

carpark *n.* [1960s+] an informer. [*carpark* = nark]

carpet *n.* [late 19C+] (*UK prison*) **1** a three-month sentence. **2** three pounds or 30 pounds (sterling). [*carpet-bag* = drag (sl. 'three-month jail term') or from the earlier assumption that prison workshops took just 90 days to produce a particular type of regulation-size carpet; **2** is an extension of **1**; but note the remark by the anonymous prisoner 'No. 77' in *Mark of Broad Arrow* (1903): 'Your "Auto-leyne" cares little about a "drag" (three months), a sixer (a "carpet" it is generally called), or a "stretch"']

carried *adj.* [late 19C+] married.

carving knife *n.* [1910s] a wife. [the inevitable negative sterotyping of the domineering wife; note CHARMING WIFE]

cash and carry *v.* [late 19C+] to marry; hence *cash and carried* married. [the wife gets her husband's cash after being, traditionally, carried across the doorstep]

cast a net *v.* [20C] (*Aus.*) to have a bet. [a presumed inference of the random hopefulness of such a cast]

castle rag *n.* [19C] (*UK Und.*) fourpence. [*castle rag* = flag (sl. 'groat')]

cat and kitty *n*. [20C] a female breast. [*cat and kitty* = titty; aside from the convenience of the rhyme, feline attributes are more usually linked to the female genitals]

cat and mouse *n*. [mid-19C] a house.

cat cuff *n*. [1940s] (*US*) a bluff.

cats and kitties *n*. [1940s] (*US*) the female breasts. [*see* CAT AND KITTY]

cats and mice *n*. [20C] (*Aus.*) dice.

cat's face *n*. [1940s+] in cards, the ace. [especially, perhaps, that of hearts]

cattle dog *n*. [20C] (*Aus.*) a catalogue. [as well as the rhyme, a jocular mispronunciation]

cattle ticks *n*. [20C] (*Aus.*) Catholics. [as well as the rhyme, a jocular mispronunciation]

cattle truck *v*. [20C] **1** to copulate. **2** to destroy, hence *cattled* ruined, hurt, destroyed, beaten etc. [*cattle truck* = fuck]

cauliflower *n*. [1970s] (*US*) cowardice, fear. [*cauliflower ear* = fear, plus a possible reference to the 'white heart' of the vegetable]

Cecil Gee *n*. [1950s+] the knee. [from the Cecil Gee chain of men's tailoring stores]

cellar-flap *n*. [late 19C] a tap-dance. [the image is of a dance performed on a space no larger than the trap-door leading to a cellar]

cellar-flap *v*. [20C] to borrow. [*cellar-flap* = tap, i.e. on the shoulder, preparatory to asking for money]

center lead *n.* [20C] (*US*) the forehead.

centre half *n.* [20C] a scarf.

chain and crank *n.* [20C] a bank.

chain and locket *n.* [20C] a pocket.

chair and cross *n.* [mid-19C+] (*US*) a horse. [var. on CHARING CROSS]

chalfonts *n.* [1970s+] haemorrhoids. [*chalfont st giles* = piles; from the Buckinghamshire village of Chalfont St Giles]

chalk boulder *n.* [1920s] (*US*) a shoulder.

Chalk (Farm) *n.* **1** [mid-19C–1910s] an arm. **2** [1920s] harm. [from Chalk Farm, London NW1]

champagne glass *n.* [20C] a prostitute. [*champagne glass* = BRASS (NAIL)]

channel fleet *n.* [20C] (*Irish*) a street.

Charing Cross *n.* [mid-19C+] a horse. [from Charing Cross, London WC1, best known for its railway station and Charing Cross Road, home of many booksellers; note Cockney pronunciation of cross as *crorss*]

Charles Dance *n.* [1980s+] a chance. [from the UK actor and film star Charles Dance (b.1946)]

Charles James *n.* [late 19C–1930s] **1** a box in the theatre. **2** in hunting, a fox. [*Charles James Fox* = **1** box **2** fox; from the politician Charles James Fox (1749–1806)]

Charley Brady *n.* [late 19C–1940s] a hat. [*Charley Brady* = cady (sl. 'hat')]

Charley Chalk *n.* [1940s] (*US*) talk.

Charley Dilke *n.* [late 19C–1930s] milk. [from the radical politician Sir Charles Dilke (1843–1911)]

Charley Frisky *n.* [mid-19C–1900s] whisky.

Charley Howard *n.* [1930s] a coward.

Charley Lancaster *n.* [mid-19C] a handkerchief. [*Charley Lancaster* = 'handkercher']

Charley Mason *n.* [late 19C+] **1** a basin. **2** a great deal. [**2** *Charley Mason* = (*fig.*) basin, i.e. a basinful]

Charley Pope *n.* [1910s] soap.

Charley Randy *n.* [mid-19C–1900s] brandy. [underpinned by the amorous effects of alcohol]

Charley Sheard *n.* [1970s+] a beard.

Charley Skinner *n.* [mid-19C–1900s] dinner.

Charley Wiggins *n.* [late 19C+] (*orig. theatre*) lodgings. [*Charley Wiggins* = diggings (19C sl. 'lodgings')]

charlie *n.* [1940s+] a fool, esp. in the phrases *a proper charlie, a right charlie.* [*charlie hunt* = cunt; given the popularity of the term among otherwise 'clean' radio and TV comedians, one must assume their (and their audiences') ignorance of the etymology]

Charlie Beck *n.* [1940s] (*US*) a (forged or bouncing) cheque.

Charlie Britt *n.* [20C] (*Aus.*) a fit; hence *throw a Charlie* have a fit. [possibly linked to a fig. use of JIMMY BRITTS]

Charlie Chase *n.* [20C] (*Aus.*) a race; hence *not in the charlie* not worthy of consideration.

Charlie Clore *n.* [1960s] the floor, i.e. the ground. [from the UK property developer Charles Clore (1904–79)]

Charlie Cooke *n.* [1970s] a look, a glance. [from the UK footballer Charlie Cooke (b.1942)]

Charlie Drake *n.* [1950s–60s] **1** a brake (on a car). **2** a break (for tea etc.). [from the UK comedian Charlie Drake (b.1925)]

Charlie Freer *n.* [late 19C–1900s] beer.

Charlie Horner *n.* [1940s] (*US*) a corner.

Charlie Prescott (*also* **Colonel Prescott**) *n.* [mid–late 19C] a waistcoat.

Charlie Rawler *n.* [1940s] (*US*) a collar.

Charlie Rocks *n.* [1940s] (*US*) socks.

Charlie Roller *n.* [1920s–40s] (*US*) **1** a dollar. **2** a collar.

Charlie Ronce (*also* **Harry Ronce**) *n.* [1930s+] a pimp. [*Charlie Ronce* = ponce]

charlies *n.* [mid-19C+] the female breasts. [probably from CHARLIE WHEELER; Ware attributes the term to the predilection of King Charles II (r.1660–85) for décolletage, which would seem fanciful but for the date, which well precedes the Aus. rhyme *Charlie Wheeler* = sheila; Partridge suggests Romani *chara* to touch, to meddle with]

Charlie Smirke *n.* [1970s+] a fool. [*Charlie Smirke* = BERK;

from the jockey Charlie Smirke, who claimed three Derby wins and the St Leger among other successes during his career 1922–53]

Charlie Wheeler *n.* [1940s+] (*Aus.*) **1** a woman. **2** (*pl.*) the female breasts. [*charlie wheeler* = sheila; thus **2** her distinguishing characteristics; from the painter Charles Wheeler (1881–1977), who specialized in nudes]

charming mottle *n.* [late 19C–1900s] (*Aus.*) a bottle.

charming wife *n.* [20C] a knife. [note CARVING KNIFE]

chatham and dover *v.* [late 19C] to stop, to cease. [*chatham and dover* = give over; from the two Kentish towns Chatham and Dover; given their positions, respectively on the Thames Estuary and on the south coast, the inference may be that the land itself must stop]

cheap and nasty *n.* [20C] (*Aus.*) a meat pasty.

cheerful giver *n.* [20C] the human liver. [possibly linked to organ donations]

cheese and crackers *n.* [20C] the testicles. [*cheese and crackers* = knackers]

cheese (and kisses) *n.* [late 19C+] (*chiefly Aus.*) a wife. [*cheese and kisses* = missus]

cheese and spices *n.* [1940s] (*US racing*) the starting prices.

cheese grater *n.* [20C] a waiter.

cheesy kiss *n.* [20C] (*Aus.*) a miss, esp. a missed catch at cricket.

Chelsea bun *n*. [20C] **1** a son. **2** the sun. [a Chelsea bun is a kind of rolled currant bun originally made in Chelsea, London SW3]

Cheltenham (bold) *adj*. [late 19C+] cold. [from the racing calendar's Cheltenham Gold Cup]

cherries *n*. [1970s] greyhound racing tracks. [*cherry hogs* = the dogs]

cherry ace *n*. [1940s–50s] the face.

cherry hog *n*. [mid-19C+] a dog.

cherry oggs *n*. [1920s+] greyhound racing. [*cherry oggs* = the dogs]

cherry-picker *n*. [1970s] one pound (sterling). [*cherry-picker* = nicker]

cherry-pipe *n*. [late 19C] a woman. [*cherry-pipe* = cherry-ripe (sl. 'woman')]

cherry red *n*. [20C] the head.

cherry-ripe *n*. **1** [mid-19C] a tobacco pipe. **2** [20C] nonsense. [**2** *cherry-ripe* = tripe; **1** was linked to the popular, and cheap, cherry-wood pipe]

chesapeake shad *phr*. [1940s] (*US*) not bad. [the shad is a common fish in the Chesapeake Bay]

chevy chase *n*. [mid-19C–1950s] the face. [from Chevy Chase, the site of a celebrated 17C border skirmish and thus the subject and title of a popular ballad]

chew one's ear (*also* **chew one's lug**) *v*. [1900s–10s] to drink, esp. beer. [*chew one's ear* = drink one's beer; note sl. *lug* ear]

chew one's lug *v. see* CHEW ONE'S EAR.

chews and molasses *n.* [1940s] (*US*) glasses, i.e. spectacles.

chew the fat *v.* [late 19C+] **1** to converse, to talk something over. **2** to complain. [*chew the fat* = have a chat]

chicken and rice *adj.* [1990s+] nice.

chicken-perch *n.* [late 19C+] a church. [the image is presumably of the vicar in his pulpit]

chicken's neck *n.* [20C] a cheque.

china (plate) *n.* [late 19C+] a (best) friend. [*china plate* = mate]

chips and chase *n.* [1920s–40s] (*US*) the face.

chips and peas *n.* [20C] the knees.

chirrup and titter *n. see* GIGGLE AND TITTER.

chock and log *n.* [20C] (*Aus.*) a dog.

chocolate *n.* [20C] (*derog.*) a Black person; hence *chocolate to the bone* referring to a very dark skin. [*chocolate frog* = wog, or purely a link to the colour]

chocolate frog *n.* [1970s+] (*Aus.*) **1** an informer. **2** influenza. [*chocolate frog* = **1** dog **2** wog (Aus. sl. 'illness')]

chopping sticks *n.* [late 19C+] (*bingo*) the number six.

chopsticks *n.* [1960s+] (*bingo*) the number six.

chorus and verse *n.* [20C] the anus, the rectum. [*chorus and verse* = erse, i.e. arse]

Christmas card *n.* [20C] a guard; usu. a guard on the railway, but uses include a Grenadier Guard or a fireguard.

Christmas crackered *adj.* [1970s+] utterly exhausted. [*Christmas crackered* = knackered]

Christmas crackers *n.* [1970s+] the testicles. [*Christmas crackers* = knackers]

Christmas Eve *v.* [20C] to believe.

Christmas log *n.* [1970s] a dog.

Christmas tree *n.* [20C] the knee.

Christopher Lee *n.* [1960s+] an act of urination. [*Chrisopher Lee* = pee/wee; from the UK actor and film star Christopher Lee (b.1922)]

chuck me in the gutter *n.* [20C] (*Aus.*) butter.

chump of wood *phr.* [mid-19C] no good.

chunder *v.* [1950s+] (*Aus.*) to vomit. [according to Barry Humphries (b.1934), the great popularizer of the word in his 'Barry Mackenzie' strip in *Private Eye* and on film, the term comes from the nautical shout of warning 'watch under!'; thus Humphries (1988) 'Jeez I'm sorry lady – I forget to yell watch under'; he also suggests the rhyme *Chunder Loo of Akim Foo* = spew. Chunder Loo featured in a long-running series of advertisements for Cobra boot polish (*c.*1910–29), drawn by Norman Lindsay (1879–1969) and featured in the Sydney *Bulletin*; thence the term moved from public school sl. to surf jargon to popular use; Moore (1993) suggests a possible link to UK dial. *chounter/chunter/chunder* to grumble]

chunka beef *n. see* CHUNK OF BEEF.

chunk of beef (*also* **chunka beef**) *n.* [20C] (*Aus.*) the chief, i.e. the boss.

chunk of wood *adj.* [mid-19C] good; esp. in phrase *no chunk of wood*.

cigarette (holder) *n.* [20C] a shoulder.

cinder shifter *n.* [1930s–40s] (*US*) a drifter, a tramp.

Cisco Kid *n.* [1950s+] (*derog.*) a Jew. [*Cisco Kid* = Yid; from the popular US-originated children's TV show *The Cisco Kid*]

city tote *n.* [20C] a coat.

Claire (Rayner) *n.* [1990s+] (*esp. pl.*) a trainer, i.e. a gymshoe. [from the agony aunt and novelist Claire Rayner (b.1931)]

◆◆

The Cockney Riviera

Brighton pier	queer
Brighton rock	dock
Isle of Wight	light/all right/tight
Margate sands	hands
Ramsgate sands	hands
Southend-on-Sea	pee/wee
Southend pier	ear

◆◆

Clark Kent *adj.* [1960s+] corrupt. [*Clark Kent* = bent; from the character Clark Kent, the mild-mannered reporter on the *Daily Planet* who is, in fact, Superman and is, of course, anything but corrupt]

clever Mike *n.* [20C] a bicycle. [*clever Mike* = bike]

clickety-clicks *n.* [20C] women's underpants. [*clickety-clicks* = knicks]

clickety-click *n.* [20C] **1** (*bingo*) the number six or 66. **2** (*Aus.*) a stick.

clink and blank *n.* [1940s] (*US*) a bank.

clod *n.* [1930s] (*UK tramp*) (*usu. pl.*) a penny or any copper coin. [*clodhopper* = copper]

clodhopper *n.* [mid-19C+] a policeman. [*clodhopper* = copper; note standard sl. *clodhopper* a peasant; the reference is to the policeman's large, and thus ploughman-like, boots]

clothes-peg *n.* [20C] an egg.

clothes-pegs *n.* [20C] the legs. [including a possible reference to the shape]

cloven hoofter *n.* [20C] (*Aus.*) a male homosexual. [*cloven hoofter* = poofter]

club and stick *n.* [1930s–40s] a policeman. [*club and stick* = dick (sl. 'detective', 'policeman'); the implements are, of course, apposite]

coachman on the box *n.* [20C] venereal disease. [*coachman on the box* = pox]

coal and coke (*also* **coals and coke**) *adj.* [late 19C+] penniless, impoverished. [*coal and coke* = broke]

coal heaver *n.* [late 19C] a penny. [*coal heaver* = stiver (sl. 'thing of little value')]

coals and coke *adj. see* COAL AND COKE.

coat and badge *v.* [mid-19C+] to cadge, esp. in the phrase ON THE C AND B. [from Doggett's Coat and Badge, awarded to Thames watermen, who, with this prize, had the right to charge higher fares in their mid-19C heyday]

Cobar shower *n.* [1950s] (*Aus.*) **1** a flower. **2** a shower of rain. [from the copper-mining town of Cobar, New South Wales; in **2** other Aus. names can be substituted according to local geography; a late-19C standard sl. use of *Cobar* means copper or a copper, i.e. a penny]

cobblers *n.*[1] [late 19C] the past. [*cobbler's last* = past]

cobblers *n.*[2] *see* COBBLER'S.

cobbler's (*also* **cobblers, cobblers' awls, cobbler's stalls**) *n.* [1930s+] **1** the testicles. **2** rubbish, nonsense, esp. as an exclamation *cobblers!* [*cobbler's awls* = balls]

cobblers' awls *n. see* COBBLER'S.

cobbler's stalls *n. see* COBBLER'S.

cob o' coal *n.* [1920s–50s] the dole.

Coca-Cola *n.* [1950s+] (*Aus.*) in cricket, a bowler.

cockaleekie *adj.* [20C] cheeky. [the reference to cockaleekie soup – a cock boiled with leeks – seems purely coincidental]

cock and hen *n*. **1** [mid-19C+] ten pounds (sterling).
2 [20C] (*bingo, gambling*) the number ten. **3** [20C] a pen.

cocked hat *n*. [1940s] (*US*) an informer. [*cocked hat* = rat]

cockies' clip *n*. [late 19C+] (*Aus.*) **1** a pickpocket. **2** a dip,
i.e. a swim. [**1** *cockies' clip* = dip (sl. 'pickpocket')]

cockle (and hen) *n*. [mid-19C+] the number ten, usu. ten
pounds (sterling).

cock linnet *n*. [late 19C+] a minute. [popularized by the
music-hall hit 'My Old Dutch']

cockroach *n*. [1940s+] a motor (rather than railway)
coach.

cock sparrow *n*. [late 19C+] an arrow. [note BOW AND
ARROW]

cock-sparrow *adj*. [1960s+] (*Aus.*) mad, insane. [*cock-
sparrow* = yarra (Aus. sl. 'insane'); note pronunciation of
sparrow as *sparrer*]

cocky's clip *n*. [1920s+] (*Aus.*) sheep dip. [in Aus. sl. a
cocky is a small farmer while *clip* refers to the shearing of
sheep that accompanies the dip]

cocoa *v*. [1930s+] to speak. [COFFEE AND COCOA]

cod's roe *n*. [20C] money. [*cod's roe* = dough]

coffee and cocoa *phr*. [20C] say so; hence I SHOULD
COCOA!

coffee stalls *n*. [1940s–60s] the testicles. [*coffee stalls* = balls]

coffs harbour *n*. [20C] (*Aus.*) a barber.

cold potato *n.* [20C] a waiter. [note Cockney pronunciation of potato as *pertater*]

collar and cuff *n.* [mid-20C] a male homosexual. [*collar and cuff* = puff]

collar and tie *n.* [20C] a lie.

Colleen Bawn *n.* [19C] an erection [*colleen bawn* = horn; from the anglicized version of Irish *cailín bán* the white or fair woman]

Collie Knox *n.* [1960s+] venereal disease. [*Collie Knox* = pox]

colney *n.* [1930s] a match. [*colney hatch* = match; from the once celebrated Hertfordshire lunatic asylum, Colney Hatch]

Colonel Prescott *n. see* CHARLIE PRESCOTT.

colonial puck *n.* [1940s] (*US*) sexual intercourse. [*colonial puck* = fuck]

comb and brush *n.* [late 19C] a drink. [*comb and brush* = lush]

come a clover *v.* [1910s–20s] to fall or trip over.

comical chris *n.* [1970s–80s] an act of urination. [*comical chris* = piss]

comical farce *n.* [late 19C–1910s] a glass.

comic cuts (*also* **comics**) *n.* [1940s+] (*Aus.*) **1** the stomach. **2** in the game of two-up, the 'guts', i.e. the centre of the betting circle into which betted money is tossed. [*comic cuts* = guts]

comics *n. see* COMIC CUTS.

con and coal *n.* [20C] the dole.

Conan Doyle *n.* [late 19C+] a boil (on the neck). [from Sir Arthur Conan Doyle (1859–1930), novelist and creator of Sherlock Holmes]

Conan Doyle *v.* [late 19C+] to boil (a kettle). [*see* CONAN DOYLE *n.*]

conger (eel) *v.* [20C] (*UK Und.*) to inform to the police. [*conger eel* = squeal]

constant screamer *n.* [19C] a concertina. [possibly more a jocular mispronunciation than actual rhyming slang]

cook *n.* [1940s+] (*Aus.*) a look, a glance. [as well as the rhyme note Yiddish *guck* a look, a glance, esp. in the phrase *geb a guck* have a look]

cop a flower-pot *v.* [1930s] to be severely reprimanded, punished or beaten. [*cop a flower-pot* = cop it hot; the image is of a flower-pot dropping from an upper window-ledge]

cop deuces *v.* [20C] (*US prison*) to make excuses. [underpinned by slang *cop* get + *deuce*, a possible reference to the losing roll of two in craps dice, which one might blame on bad luck]

corned beef *n.* **1** [20C] a thief. **2** [1950s+] (*UK prison*) a chief officer.

corns and bunions *n.* [late 19C+] onions.

cotton wool *v.* [20C] to seduce. [*cotton wool* = pull]

cough and choke *v.* [20C] to smoke.

cough and sneeze *n.* [late 19C+] cheese.

cough and stutter *n.* [20C] butter.

council gritter *n.* [1990s+] the anus; hence GO UP THE COUNCIL. [*council gritter* = shitter]

council houses *n.* [1920s+] trousers.

country cousin *n.* [late 19C+] a dozen.

cousin sis *n.* [20C] an act of urination. [*cousin sis* = piss]

couple of bob *n.* [1940s–50s] a damp swab, as used in wiping the blackboard clean when scoring a game of darts.

Covent Garden *n.* [mid-19C] a farthing. [from Covent Garden, London's former central market, now re-created as the city's major tourist zone; note pronunciation of farthing as *farden*]

cow and calf *n.* [20C] (*orig. sporting*) a half, usu. as a half-pound, i.e. ten shillings or 50 pence.

cow and calf *v.* [mid-19C] to laugh.

Cow and Gate *adj.* [20C] late; esp. in the context of a woman missing her period. [from Cow and Gate, a manufacturer of baby food, the need for which arises when a missed period indicates pregnancy]

cow-and-kisses *n.* [mid-19C] a wife. [*cow-and-kisses* = missus]

cowclap *n.* [1940s] (*Irish*) cow dung. [possibly *cowclap* = crap]

cowhide *adj.* [20C] (*Irish*) aware, knowledgeable. [*cowhide* = wide (sl. 'sharp')]

cows and kisses *n.* [mid-19C] a woman or women. [*cows and kisses* = mistress/misses]

cow's (calf) *n.* [20C] ten shillings (50 pence). [*cow's calf* = half (a pound)]

cow's lick *n.* [1960s] prison. [*cow's lick* = nick]

cow's licker *n.* [1930s+] one pound (sterling). [*cow's licker* = nicker]

crackers on toast *n.* [1940s] (*US racing*) the winning post.

cream crackered *adj.* [1990s+] exhausted, tired out. [*cream crackered* = knackered]

cream crackers *n.* [1940s–60s] the testicles. [*cream crackers* = knackers]

cream puff *n.* [20C] a bad temper, a rage. [*cream puff* = huff]

cribbage-peg *n.* [1920s] a leg.

cricket bats *n.* [20C] (*Aus.*) the teeth. [*cricket bats* = tats (Aus./N.Z. sl. 'teeth')]

cries and screeches *n.* [20C] (*Aus.*) leeches.

crimea *n.* [late 19C+] beer.

Crocodile Dundee *n.* [1980s] a flea. [from the film *Crocodile Dundee* (1986) starring the Aus. actor Paul Hogan (b.1939)]

crouton *n.* [1990s+] an erection. [*crouton* = (blue-veined) root-on]

crowded space *n.* [20C] a suitcase.

crust of bread *n.* [20C] the head. [var. on sl. *crumpet*, *loaf* and *scone*]

cry and laugh *n.* [20C] (*Aus.*) a scarf.

cucumber *n.* [20C] (*Aus.*) a number.

cuddle and kiss *n.* [1930s+] **1** a woman. **2** an act of urination. [*cuddle and kiss* = **1** miss **2** piss]

cuff link *n.* [20C] (*Aus.*) a drink.

curly locks *n.* [20C] (*Aus.*) socks.

currant bread *adj.* [20C] dead.

currant bun *n.* **1** [late 19C+] the sun. **2** [1980s+] the *Sun* newspaper. [**1** refers to the mutually circular shapes]

currant-cakey *adj.* [1900s–30s] shaky, esp. in the context of a hangover.

currants and plums *n.* [mid-19C] threepence. [*currants and plums* = thrums (sl. 'threepence')]

curry and rice *n.* [1950s+] (*Aus.*) a price.

custard and jelly *n.* [1960s+] television. [*custard and jelly* = telly]

cut and carried *adj.* [20C] married.

cuts and scratches *n.* [late 19C+] matches.

d

dad and dave *v.* [20C] (*Aus.*) to shave. [from the popular 1930s radio serial *Dad and Dave* concerning various aspects of rural Aus. life. The show was based 'somewhat remotely' (Wilkes, 1985) on characters in the novel *On Our Selection* by Steele Rudd (Arthur Hoey Davis, 1868–1935), itself taken from his columns in the *Sydney Bulletin*, starting in 1895]

dad and mum *n.* [20C] (*Aus.*) rum or the cordial Bonox and rum.

daffadown dilly (*also* **daffydown dilly**, **daffy-down-dilly**) *adj.* [20C] silly.

daffydown dilly *adj. see* DAFFADOWN DILLY.

daffy-down-dilly *adj. see* DAFFADOWN DILLY.

daft and barmy *n.* [1960s+] the army.

daily bread (*also* **daily breader**) *n.* [late 19C–1940s] the head of the family. [as well as the rhyme the reference is to the Lord's Prayer 'Give us this day our daily bread ...']

daily breader *n. see* DAILY BREAD.

Daily (Mail) *n.* [1930s+] **1** the buttocks; hence *up one's daily* following close behind. **2** a lie. **3** ale. **4** nail. **5** bail. [*Daily Mail* = **1** tail **2** tale; from the newspaper the *Daily Mail*]

daisy beat *v.* [late 19C+] to cheat, i.e. to swindle.

daisy recroots *n. see* DAISY ROOTS.

daisy recruits *n. see* DAISY ROOTS.

daisy roots (*also* **daisy recroots, daisy recruits**) *n.* [mid-19C+] boots.

Damon (Hill) *n.* [1990s+] (*drugs*) a pill, esp. an amphetamine. [from the UK Grand Prix motor racing driver Damon Hill (b.1960)]

Dan Dares *n.* [1960s+] flared trousers. [*Dan Dares* = flares; from the comic-based space hero Dan Dare, created by Frank Hampson and featured in the *Eagle* comic of the 1950s and beyond]

Danny la Rue *n.* [1990s+] a clue, i.e. an idea, a suspicion. [from the female impersonator Danny la Rue, real name Daniel Patrick Carroll (b.1927)]

Danny Rucker *n.* [1940s] (*US*) butter.

Dan O'Leary *adj.* [1940s] (*US*) weary.

Dan Tucker *n.* [mid-19C] butter. [possibly anecdotal]

darby and joan *n.* **1** [late 19C+] the telephone. **2** [1940s+] (*Aus.*) a loan. [from the phrase *Darby and Joan*, a synonym for an elderly, possibly impoverished, but long-married couple, which first appeared in the *Gentleman's Magazine* (vol. V, 1735) in a verse titled 'The joys of love never forgot, a song'. The third verse runs: 'Old Darby, with Joan by his side,/You've often regarded with wonder,/He's dropsical, she is sore-eyed,/Yet they're never happy asunder.' Whether the names refer to real-life characters (*Darby* is not a common UK name) or are taken from some earlier fiction remains unknown]

darby and joan *adj.* [20C] alone; hence *on one's darby* by oneself. [*see* DARBY AND JOAN *n.*]

Darby Kelly (*also* **Derby Kelly**) *n.* [late 19C+] the stomach, esp. abbreviated as *darby kel*. [*Darby Kelly* = belly; the rhyme was hugely popularized by the music-hall song 'Boiled Beef and Carrots', sung by Harry Champion, which contained the line 'That's the stuff for your derby kel / Makes you fat and keeps you well']

dark and dim *n.* [20C] (*Aus.*) a swim. [presumably beneath the surface of the waves]

dark felt *n.* [20C] (*Aus.*) a belt.

darling it hurts *n.* [20C] (*Aus.*) Darlinghurst, a rough inner-city area of Sydney. [the image is of wife-beating or rough sex]

Darren Gough *n.* [1990s+] a cough. [from the England cricketer Darren Gough (b.1970)]

date *n.* [1910s+] (*Aus./N.Z./UK*) **1** the anus, the backside as a whole. **2** the vagina. **3** a general term of contempt or abuse. [*date and plum* = bum]

David Gower *n.* [1980s+] a shower of rain. [from the England cricketer David Gower (b.1957)]

Davy Crockett *n.* [1950s] a pocket. [from the frontiersman and US Congressman Davy Crockett (1786–1836), who died defending the Alamo; his UK fame came with the children's TV series of the 1950s]

Davy Large *n.* [late 19C] a barge.

Dawn Frazer *n.* [1960s+] (*Aus.*) a razor. [from the 1960s Aus. swimming star Dawn Fraser (b.1937)]

day and night *n.* [late 19C–1900s] light ale.

day's a-dawning *n. see* DAY'S DAWNING.

day's dawning (*also* **day's a-dawning**) *n.* [20C] morning.

dead horse *n.* [1940s+] (*Aus.*) tomato sauce.

dead spotted ling of *phr.* [1910s+] (*Aus.*) the absolute image of. [*dead spotted ling of* = dead ring of]

dead wowsers *n.* [20C] (*Aus.*) trousers. [in Aus. sl. a *wowser* is a puritan or censor]

deaf and dumb *n.* [1910s+] (*Aus.*) inside information, as in *I'll give you the deaf and dumb*. [*deaf and dumb* = drum (Aus. sl. 'piece of information')]

deep-sea diver *n.* [1970s+] a five-pound note. [*deep-sea diver* = fiver]

Derby Kelly *n. see* DARBY KELLY.

derby winner *n.* [20C] (*Aus.*) a dinner. [the dinner is purchased with one's winnings, although the reference may be to the possible use of horsemeat]

Derry and Toms *n.* [1940s] bombs. [from the department store Derry and Toms, in High Street Kensington, London W8, plus a possible reference to Aus. sl. *have a derry on* to dislike]

desmond *n.* [1980s+] a 2:2, i.e. a lower second-class

degree. [*desmond tutu* = 2:2; from the Cape Town Arch-bishop and Nobel Peace Prize winner Desmond Tutu (b. 1931)]

deuce and ace *n*. [late 19C–1940s] the face.

Diana Dors *n*. [1960s+] (*bingo*) the number 44. [*Diana Dors* = all the fours; from the UK actress and personality Diana Dors (1931–84)]

dibs and dabs *n*. [20C] (*Aus.*) body lice. [*dibs and dabs* = crabs]

Dick Dunn *n*. [late 19C+] the sun. [from the well-known 'ready-money' bookmaker Richard 'Dick' Dunn (d.1905); there might have been an additional nod to the shine of the diamonds with which this 'Leviathan' of the turf adorned himself]

dickery *n*. **1** [late 19C+] a clock. **2** [20C] the penis. [DICKORY DOCK]

dickey-bird *n. see* DICKY-BIRD.

Dickey (Dirt) *n. see* DICKY (DIRT).

dickory dock *n*. **1** [late 19C+] a clock. **2** [20C] the penis. [**2** *dickory dock* = cock; the nursery rhyme from which this comes ('Hickory, dickory dock, / The mouse ran up the clock') is itself a Romani creation. According to the Romani expert Gerald Denley, 'Hickory' is derived from the Romani *ek ore* meaning one o'clock. The word for one in Romani varies according to the tribe, so it is either *ek*, *yek* or *ik*. The stress is on the first vowel, so that *ek ore* is pronounced as one word. *Dickory Dock* is often described as London rhyming slang, but it could mean the *dock* where the *dick* puts you when you are caught *choring* or stealing. The word for a Gypsyman is either a *rom* or a *mush*; this last word derives from the Sanskrit and means a mouse or a thief]

Dick Turpin *n.* [1930s] the number 13. [from England's best-known highwayman Dick Turpin (1705–39)]

dicky-bird (*also* **dickey-bird**) *n.* [1930s+] **1** a word; hence *not a dicky-bird* not a word, i.e. nothing at all; also in the context of an oath, as in *I'll give you my dicky-bird on that*. **2** an informer, one who 'gives the word'.

Dicky Diddle *v.* [20C] to urinate. [*Dicky Diddle* = piddle, plus *dick* the penis]

Dicky (Dirt) (*also* **Dickey (Dirt)**) *n.* [19C+] a shirt. [despite obvious links to *dicky* a detachable shirt front, this appears to be a discrete coinage; note the cut-price shirt and jeans chain store Dickie Dirts in late 1970s London]

Dicky Lee *n.* [20C] (*Aus.*) tea.

didn't ought *n.* [late 19C–1940s] port (wine).

didn't oughter *n.* **1** [late 19C–1910s] water. **2** [1970s+] a daughter.

dieu et mon droit *phr.* [1910s] a general phrase of self-satisfied dismissal, 'doesn't bother me', 'I don't care'. [*dieu et mon droit* (pronounced *dright*) = I'm all right; *Dieu et mon droit* ('God and my right') was the motto of Richard I at the battle of Gisors (1198) and was adopted as that of the British Royal Family]

dig a grave *v.* [1910s+] (*Aus.*) to have a shave.

dig and dirt *n.* [1940s+] (*US*) a shirt.

dig in the grave *n.* [1910s+] (*orig. Aus.*) a shave.

dillydonce *n.* [1950s] (*US*) a pimp. [*dillydonce* = ponce]

dillypot *n.* [1940s–60s] (*Aus.*) **1** the vagina. **2** a fool. [*dillypot* = twat; note also sl. *dilly* a penis, plus Standard English *pot*, i.e. a container, thus a play on sl. *cunt* a fool, which is also synonymous with *twat*]

dime a pop *n.* [20C] (*US*) a policeman. [*dime a pop* = cop; *dime a pop* literally means 'ten cents a go', thus a reference to the notorious corruptability of the US police]

dingaling (*also* **ding-a-ling**) *n.* [20C] (*Aus.*) the king.

ding-a-ling *n. see* DINGALING.

ding-dong *n.* **1** [late 19C+] a (domestic) sing-song. **2** [1920s–40s] (*US*) a bell, a gong. **3** [1920s+] a serious argument, a fight, esp. in the phrase *a right old ding-dong.* **4** [1930s+] a noisy party or other gathering. [**3** and **4** are extensions of the proper rhyme in **1**]

ding-dong bell *n.* [1940s+] (*euphemistic*) hell.

ding the tot! *excl.* [late 19C] run off with/steal the lot! [sl. *ding* to steal + Standard English *tot*]

dink-do (*also* **dinky-doo**) *n.* [1940s+] (*bingo*) the number two.

dinky dirt *n.* [20C] (*Aus./US*) a shirt. [var. on DICKY (DIRT)]

dinky-dong *n.* [1940s] (*US*) a song. [echoic as well as rhyming]

dinky-doo *n. see* DINK-DOO.

dip and chuck it *n.* [20C] (*Aus.*) a bucket.

dip south *n.* [1940s] (*US*) the mouth.

dirt, grime and dust *n.* [20C] (*Aus.*) a crust (on a pie).

dirty daughter *n.* [20C] water. [note the lyrics of the once popular song 'Wash me in the water / In which you wash your dirty daughter']

dirty dish *n.* [20C] (*Aus.*) a fish.

dirty face *n.* [20C] a shoelace.

dirty old Jew *n.* [20C] (*bingo*) the number two. [presumably no longer extant]

dirty whore *n.* [20C] (*bingo*) the number 34.

dish ran away with the spoon *n.* [1970s+] (*Aus.*) a pimp. [*dish ran away with the spoon* = hoon (Aus. sl. 'procurer of prostitutes'); from the nursery rhyme 'Hey Diddle Diddle']

Divine Brown *n.* [1990] fellatio. [*Divine Brown* = go down; from the LA prostitute Divine Brown, who, in 1995, was found fellating the UK film star Hugh Grant (b.1960)]

dixie lid *n.* [1920s+] a child. [*dixie lid* = kid]

do and dare *n.* [1920s+] (*US*) underwear.

do as you like *n.* [late 19C+] a bicycle. [*do as you like* = bike]

docker's hook *n.*[1] [20C] (*Aus.*) a book; hence *make a docker's hook* to lay the odds or make a book.

Fantasy Football

Bobby Moore	door
Bradford cities	titties
Bristol City	titty
Don Revie	bevvy
Gary Ablett	tablet
Gary Lineker	vinegar
Geoff Hurst	first
Georgie Best	guest/pest
gianluca	charlie
Glasgow Rangers	strangers
Glenn Hoddle	doddle
Ian Rush	brush
Jimmy Logie	bogey
Manchester cities	titties
Millwall Reserves	nerves
Nicky Butts	nuts
Nobby Stiles	piles
Partick Thistle	whistle
Plymouth Argyll	file
Queen of the South	mouth
Queens Park Rangers	strangers

Roger Hunt	cunt
Ruud Gullit	bullet
Ryan Giggs	digs
Tom Finney	skinny
West Hams	nerves

◆◆

docker's hook *n*.[2] *see* BUTCHER'S (HOOK).

doctor and nurse *n*. [20C] a purse. [a possible reference to the cost of pre-National Health Service medicine]

Doctor Cotton *adj. see* DOLLY COTTEN.

Doctor Crippen *n*. [1940s–50s] dripping, rendered fat. [from the celebrated murderer Dr Hawley Harvey Crippen (1862–1910)]

Doctor Legg *n*. [20C] an egg.

dodge and shirk *n*. [20C] (*Aus.*) work.

dog (and bone) *n*. [1940s+] the telephone.

doggo *adj.* [1980s+] intoxicated by a drug. [*dog and boned* = stoned]

dogs *n*. [1920s+] the feet. [*dog's meat* = feet]

dog's eye *n*. [1960s] (*Aus.*) a meat pie. [underpinned by a negative assessment of its ingredients]

Dolly Cotten (*also* **Doctor Cotton**, **Dolly Cotton**) *adj.* [20C] rotten.

Dolly Cotton *adj. see* DOLLY COTTEN.

Dolly Gray *n.* [1910s+] (*Aus.*) a threepenny piece. [*Dolly Gray* = trey (sl. 'threepenny piece'); from the song 'Goodbye Dolly Gray', popularized during the Boer War]

dolly mixtures *n.* [20C] the cinema. [*dolly mixtures* = pictures]

dollypot *n.* [1920s+] (*Aus.*) a fool. [*dollypot* = twat]

Dolly Varden *n.* [late 19C+] the garden. [from the character Dolly Varden, the coquettish daughter of the upright locksmith Gabriel Varden, in Charles Dickens's novel *Barnaby Rudge* (1841)]

do me a favour *n.* [20C] a neighbour.

do-me-dags (*also* **do my dags**) *n.* [late 19C+] cigarettes. [*do-me-dags* = fags; 'do my dags' was originally a children's game equivalent to 'follow my leader'; the image is of children encouraging each other to smoke]

do me good *n.* [late 19C+] **1** a Woodbine cigarette. **2** wood. **3** (*Aus.*) firewood. [**1** suggests a less informed attitude towards nicotine]

do my dags *n. see* DO-ME-DAGS.

dona highland-flinger *n.* [late 19C–1900s] a music-hall singer. [from sl. *dona* a woman, who may additionally perform a *Highland fling*]

donald *n.* (*Aus.*) **1** [1960s+] sexual intercourse. **2** [1960s+] a truck. **3** [1970s+] luck. [*donald duck* = **1** fuck **2** truck **3** luck]

Donald Trump *n.* [1990s+] an act of defecation. [*Donald Trump* = dump; from the US property developer Donald Trump (b.1946)]

donkey (*also* **donkey's**) *n.* [20C] the penis. [*donkey dick* = prick; but note also sl. *donkey-dick* an especially large penis or one who has one]

donkey's *n. see* DONKEY.

Don Revie *n.* [1970s+] alcohol, a drink. [*Don Revie* = bevvy; from the UK football manager Don Revie (1928–89)]

don't be funny *n.* [20C] (*Aus.*) a lavatory. [*don't be funny* = dunny (Aus. sl. 'lavatory')]

don't make a fuss *n.* [20C] a bus.

doorknob *n.* [late 19C–1900s] **1** a shilling (five pence). **2** a job. [**1** *doorknob* = bob]

door to door *n.* [20C] (*bingo*) the number four.

Dora (Gray) *n.* [20C] (*Aus.*) a threepenny piece. [*Dora Gray* = trey (sl. 'threepenny piece')]

dot and carried *adj.* [late 19C–1910s] married.

dot and dash *n.* **1** [1940s+] (*US*) a moustache. **2** [1950s–60s] money. [**2** *dot and dash* = cash]

Douglas Hurd *n.* [1980s+] **1** a piece of excrement. **2** a third, i.e. a third-class degree. [**1** *Douglas Hurd* = turd; from the former Tory cabinet minister Douglas Hurd (b.1930), who served under Margaret Thatcher]

Dover boat *n.* [20C] a coat.

down and up *n.* [20C] (*Aus.*) a cup.

down the drains *n.* [20C] the human brains.

D'Oyly Carte *n.* [1970s–80s] a breaking of wind. [*D'Oyly Carte* = fart; from Sir Richard D'Oyly Carte (1844–1901), producer of many Gilbert and Sullivan operas]

drain Charles Dickens *v.* [1990s+] to masturbate. [*drain Charles Dickens* = choke the chicken (sl. 'masturbate'); from the novelist Charles Dickens (1812–70)]

dribs and drabs *n.* [20C] (*Aus.*) body lice. [*dribs and drabs* = crabs]

dripping (toast) *n.* [20C] a publican. [*dripping toast* = (mine) host]

drum and fife *n.* [1910s–40s] (*esp. military*) **1** a wife. **2** a knife. [drum and fife being the popular constituents of a military band]

drummond and roce *n.* [1940s–50s] a knife and fork. [despite the absence of a proper rhyme, the term works thus: DRUM AND FIFE = knife, *drum and* becomes *drummond*; ROAST PORK = fork, *roast*, 'Cocknified', becomes *roce*]

dry land? *phr.* [mid-19C] you understand?

Dublin fair *n.* [20C] (*Aus.*) the hair.

Dublin trick *n.* [20C] a brick. [from the identification of Irishmen with the building trade]

Duchess (of Fife) *n.* [20C] a wife. [best known in the song 'My Old Dutch']

duck and dive *v.* [20C] to hide. [*duck and dive* = skive]

ducks and drakes *n.* [1960s] (*Aus.*) delirium tremens. [*ducks and drakes* = the shakes]

ducks and geese *n.* [20C] (*Aus.*) the police.

duck's neck *n.* [20C] (*Aus.*) a cheque.

duke *n.* [mid-19C+] the hand. [*duke of york* = fork(s), i.e. the fingers or hands]

Duke of Fife *n.* [20C] (*esp. military*) a knife.

Duke of Kent *n.* [20C] **1** the rent. **2** a homosexual. [**2** *Duke of Kent* = bent]

Duke of York *n.* [19C+] **1** a fork. **2** a cork. **3** talk. **4** chalk. **5** pork.

Duke of York *v.* [19C+] **1** to talk. **2** to walk.

Dunlop tyre *n.* [20C] a liar.

dustbin lids *n.* [20C] children. [*dustbin lids* = kids]

Dutch pegs *n.* [20C] the legs. [var. on SCOTCH PEGS]

Dutch (plate) *n.* [1960s–70s] a friend. [*Dutch plate* = mate]

dyna *n.* [1960s] a male homosexual. [*dynamite* = catamite]

e

early bird *n.* [late 19C+] a word.

early door *n.* [20C] a whore.

early doors *n.* [19C] female underwear. [*early doors* = drawers]

eartha *n.* [1950s+] **1** excrement. **2** an act of defecation. [*eartha kitt* = shit; from the US singer Eartha Kitt (b.1928)]

earwig *v.* [20C] to understand. [*earwig* = twig]

east and south *n.* [mid-19C] the mouth. [a precursor of NORTH AND SOUTH]

east and west *n.* [20C] a vest.

Easter bunny *n.* [20C] money.

Easter egg *n.* [20C] a leg.

East India docks *n.* [20C] socks. [from London's former East India Docks, built in 1806 and closed in 1967, which specialized in trade with the Far East]

eat a fig *v.* [mid-19C] to commit burglary, to rob a house. [*eat a fig* = crack a crib (Und. sl. 'break into a house')]

eau-de-Cologne *n.* [20C] **1** (*Aus.*) the telephone. **2** a woman. [**2** *eau-de-Cologne* = polone (sl. 'young woman')]

Edgar Britt *n.* [1960s+] (*Aus.*) **1** excrement. **2** an act of defecation. **2** (*pl.*) diarrhoea. [*Edgar Britt* = shit; from the Aus. jockey Edgar Britt (b.1913)]

edmundo *n.* [1960s+] the leader, the most important person. [*edmundo ros* = boss; from the popular Latin American bandleader Edmundo Ros (b.1910)]

edna! *excl.* [20C] (*UK Und.*) a general excl. of dismissal; 'be off!', 'go away!' [*edna may* = on your way!; from the early-20C music-hall artiste Edna May (1878–1948)]

egg and spoon *n.*[1] [1960s+] (*derog.*) a Black person. [*egg and spoon* = coon]

egg and spoon *n.*[2] [1970s+] (*Aus.*) **1** a fool, a silly person. **2** a pimp. [*egg and spoon* = **1** goon **2** hoon (Aus. sl. 'procurer of prostitutes')]

egg flip *n.* [20C] (*Aus. racing*) a tip.

eggflipper *n.* [1960s] (*Aus. racing*) a tipster. [*eggflipper* = tipper]

Egon (Ronay) *n.* [1960s+] an act of defecation. [*Egon Ronay* = PONY; from the pioneer of food guide books, Egon Ronay (b.1920)]

Egyptian hall *n.* [mid-19C] a ball. [the 'Egyptian Hall' was the popular name for the London Museum, established *c.*1812 at today's 170 Piccadilly, holding 'upwards of Fifteen Thousand Natural and Foreign Curiosities, Antiques and Productions of the Fine Arts'. It featured an 'Egyptian' façade, and among the many visitors was, in 1844, General Tom Thumb. The hall was demolished in 1905]

Eiffel Tower *n.* [20C] (*Aus.*) a shower of rain.

eighteen pence *n.*[1] [19C+] sense.

eighteen pence *n.*[2] [1950s+] (*Aus.*) **1** a garden fence. **2** a receiver of stolen goods. [**2** *eighteen pence* = fence]

eight-six *v. see* EIGHTY-SIX.

eighty-six (*also* **eight-six**) *v.* (*US*) **1** [1960s+] to throw out, to get rid of. **2** [1970s+] to kill, murder. [*eighty-six* = nix; the term originally had a specific restaurant and bar use, indicating that the supply of an item is exhausted or that a customer is not to be served]

Elephant and Castle *n.* [late 19C+] the anus. [*Elephant and Castle* = arsehole; from the Elephant and Castle, named for a local smithy turned pub, which has been south London's major crossroads since the 17C]

elephant's (trunk) *adj.* [mid-19C+] drunk.

Elkie Clark *n. see* L.K. CLARK.

Ellen Terry *n.* [20C] a chamber pot. [*Ellen Terry* = jerry; from the Shakespearean actress Ellen Terry (1847–1928)]

Elton (John) *n.* [1970s+] a confidence trick. [*Elton John* = con; from the pop star Elton John (b.1947)]

emmas *n.* [1990s+] haemorrhoids. [*emma freuds* = haemorrhoids; from the UK TV presenter Emma Freud (b.1962)]

Emmerdale (Farm) *n.* [1980s+] an arm. [from the TV soap opera *Emmerdale Farm*, now abbreviated to *Emmerdale*]

Engelbert (Humperdinck) *n.* [1960s+] a drink. [from the

UK pop star Engelbert Humperdinck, real name Arnold George Dorsey (b.1936)]

engineers and stokers *n.* [19C] brokers, i.e. the bailiff's men employed to remove debtor's possessions.

English channel *n.* [1950s–70s] the National Health Service. [*English channel* = panel (of doctors)]

enoch *n.* [1990s+] a towel. [*enoch powell* = towel; from the right-wing, racist UK politician Enoch Powell (1912–98)]

Epsom races *n.* [mid-19C] **1** braces. **2** faces. [Epsom is the home of the celebrated Derby]

Ernie Marsh *n.* [20C] the grass.

Eros and Cupid *adj.* [20C] stupid. [from Eros, the Greek god of love, and Cupid, his Roman counterpart; the implication is presumably of love's blindness]

Errol Flynn *n.* [1940s+] the chin. [from the Hollywood star Errol Flynn (1909–59)]

eskimo *n.* [20C] (*US derog.*) a Jew. [*eskimo* = ikey-mo (sl. 'Jew')]

Eskimo Nell *n.* [20C] a call on the telephone. [*Eskimo Nell* = bell; Eskimo Nell is the heroine of one of the best-known (and coarsest) 'rugby songs']

Everton toffee *n.* [mid-19C] coffee. [like white coffee, this toffee is also made with cream or (later) evaporated milk; note nickname for the UK football club Everton, 'the Toffees']

f

fainting fits *n*. [1940s+] the female breasts. [*fainting fits* = tits]

fairy bower *n*. [20C] (*Aus.*) a shower of rain.

fal *n*. [late 19C] a young woman. [*fal* = gal]

false alarm *n*. [20C] (*orig. military*) the arm.

fancy sash *n*. [late 19C+] (*Aus.*) a hit. [*fancy sash* = bash/smash]

fancy sash *v*. [late 19C+] (*Aus.*) to hit. [*fancy sash* = bash/smash]

Fanny Blair *n*. [mid-19C] the hair.

far and near *n*. [20C] (*mainly US*) beer.

farmer Giles (*also* **farmers, Johnny Giles**) *n*. [1950s] (*Aus.*) haemorrhoids. [*farmer Giles* = piles]

farmers *n*. *see* FARMER GILES.

fat and wide *n*. [20C] a bride.

Feargal Sharkey *n*. [1980s+] (*derog.*) a Black person. [*Feargal Sharkey* = darkie; from the Northern Irish rock singer Feargal Sharkey (b.1958)]

feather (and flip) *n*. [20C] (*tramp*) **1** a bed. **2** sleep. [*feather and flip* = kip]

feather-plucker *n.* [1940s+] (*euphemistic*) a general term of abuse, usu. used to refer to someone unpleasant. [*feather-plucker* = fucker]

fellow-feeling *n.* [late 19C+] a ceiling.

fiddle and flute *n.* [1930s+] (*US*) a suit.

fiddles and flutes *n.* [20C] (*Aus.*) boots.

fiddley-did *n.* [1920s–70s] (*Aus.*) one pound [*fiddley-did* = quid]

field of wheat *n.* [20C] a street.

fife and drum *n.* [20C] the buttocks, the posterior. [*fife and drum* = bum]

fifteen and seven *n.* [1940s] (*US*) heaven.

fifteen and two (*also* **fifteen-two**) *n.* [1940s+] (*US*) a Jew.

fifteen-two *n. see* FIFTEEN AND TWO.

fifth gear *n.* [20C] an ear.

fillet of cod *n.* [1970s] a mild pejorative. [*fillet of cod* = sod]

fillet of veal *n.* [mid-19C] **1** the treadwheel. **2** a prison. [**2** *fillet of veal* = treadwheel (used metonymically)]

fine and dandy *n.* [20C] brandy. [with a nod to its positive effects both as alcohol and as an occasional 'medicine']

finger and thumb *n.* [mid–late 19C] **1** rum; hence QUARTERN O' FINGER. **2** a road. **3** a friend. **4** a mother. **5** a drum. [*finger and thumb* = **2** drum (Romani 'road') **3** chum **4** mum]

fire-alarms *n*. [20C] the arms.

first of May *n*. [mid–late 19C] the tongue. [*first of May* = say]

fish and shrimp *n*. [1940s–60s] a pimp.

fish and tank *n*. [20C] (*UK Und.*) a bank.

fisherman's daughter *n*. [late 19C] water (for drinking).

five-acre farm *n*. [mid-19C] an arm.

five by two *n*. [1920s+] a Jew.

five star nap *n*. [20C] a Japanese person. [*five star nap* = Jap]

five to two *n*. [20C] a Jew. [the reference is to book-making odds rather than time]

five to twos *n*. [1930s] shoes. [presumably referring to the angle formed by the feet wearing them]

flag unfurled *n*. [mid–late 19C] a man of the world. [with overtones of imperial conquest]

flash of light *n*. [1970s+] a sight.

flea and louse *n*. [mid-19C] a house, esp. a house with a bad reputation, i.e. a brothel.

fleas and ants *n*. [20C] trousers. [*fleas and ants* = pants]

fleas and itches (*also* **flies and itchers**) *n*. [1960s] (*Aus.*) the cinema. [*fleas and itches* = the pictures; the infestation of mid-20C cinemas is also implied by the more common standard slang *fleapit*]

fleas and scratches *n.* [20C] (*Aus.*) matches.

Flemington races *n.* [1920s+] (*Aus.*) braces. [from the Flemington racecourse, home of the Melbourne Cup]

flies and itchers *n. see* FLEAS AND ITCHES.

florin *n.* [1990s+] excrement. [var. of TWO-BOB BIT; a florin is equal to two shillings or ten pence]

flounder (and dab) *n.* [mid-19C+] a horse-drawn and subsequently taxi-cab.

flour mixer *n.* [20C] a non-Jewish woman. [*flour-mixer* = shikse (Yiddish 'Gentile woman')]

flowers and frolics *n. see* FUN AND FROLICS.

flowery dell *n.* [1920s+] a prison cell.

flue *n.* [1940s–50s] (*UK prison*) a warder. [*flue* = screw]

fly-by-nights *n.* [1970s] tights.

fly flat *n.* [1940s] (*US*) a gun. [*fly flat* = gat (from Gatling gun)]

flying sixty-six *n.* [20C] oral sex. [*flying sixty-six* = French tricks, employing the stereotyping that inevitably accompanies references to France and sex]

flying trapeze *n.* [late 19C+] cheese.

fly my kite *n.* [mid-19C] a light, i.e of a cigarette or cigar.

fly (tipper) *n.* [20C] a child. [*fly tipper* = nipper]

forgive and forget *n.* [20C] (*Aus.*) a cigarette.

fork and knife *n.* [late 19C+] **1** life. **2** a wife.

Forrest Gump *n.* [1990s+] **1** an act of defecation. **2** (*fig.*) an unpleasant place. [*Forrest Gump* = dump; from the hit film *Forrest Gump* (1994) starring Tom Hanks]

Forsyte Saga *n.* [1970s] lager. [from John Galsworthy's early-20C literary saga of UK business and social life, launched in 1922 with *The Forsyte Saga*]

Fortnum and Mason *n.* [20C] **1** a basin. **2** a pudding-basin haircut, a 'short back and sides'. [from Fortnum and Mason, the celebrated provisioners of Piccadilly, London, founded in 1707 by William Fortnum, a former royal footman, and Hugh Mason, a small shopkeeper]

forty-four *n.* [20C] **1** a whore. **2** a door-to-door salesman.

forty-four *adv.* [20C] door-to-door.

four by two *n.* **1** [1930s+] a Jew. **2** [1930s+] (*N.Z.*) a prison warder. [**2** *four by two* = screw; in Standard English a *four-by-two* is a small piece of rag used with a 'pull-through' (a small cord with an eyehole through which the rag is threaded) to clean a rifle]

fourpenny one *n.* [20C] a sharp blow, 'a clip round the ear-hole'. [*fourpenny bit* = hit]

fourth of July *n.* [20C] a tie. [an English usage, but presumably imported by WWI US servicemen]

four-wheel skid (*also* **three-wheel skid**) *n.* [1930s+] (*derog.*) a Jew. [*four-wheel skid* = Yid]

fowl roost *n.* [1940s] (*US*) a pickpocket. [*fowl roost* = boost, i.e. booster (US sl. 'thief')]

fox and badger *n.* [1990s+] the penis. [*fox and badger* = tadger]

France and Spain *n.* [late 19C+] rain.

frank and hank *n.* [1940s] (*US*) **1** a bank. **2** one's savings. [**2** *frank and hank* = (*fig.*) bank]

Frank and Pat *n* [1990s+] a chat. [from the characters Frank Butcher and his one-time wife Pat, who feature in the popular BBC soap opera *Eastenders*; underpinned by a play on *frank*, implying a 'frank' conversation]

Frank Bough *adj.* [1970s+] (of food or drink) off, i.e. stale, sour. [from the UK sportcaster and TV personality Frank Bough (b.1933)]

Frankie Fraser *n.* [1960s+] a razor. [from the London gangster 'Mad' Frankie Fraser (b.1923)]

Frank Thring *n.* [1970s] (*Aus.*) a (wedding) ring.

Frank Zappa *n.* [1970s+] a lavatory. [*Frank Zappa* = crapper; from the US rock star and experimental musician Frank Zappa (1940–93)]

Frazer Nash *n.* [1970s] an act of urination. [*Frazer Nash* = slash; from the Frazer-Nash sports car manufactured in the UK until 1940]

Fred Astaire *n.* [1940s+] (*Aus.*) **1** a chair. **2** the hair. **3** a dandy. [**3** *Fred Astaire* = lair (Aus sl. 'person who dresses flashily'); from the film star and dancer Fred Astaire (1899–1987)]

Fred Astaires *n.* [1940s] stairs. [*see* FRED ASTAIRE *n.*]

French loaf *n.* [20C] four pounds (sterling). [*French loaf* = rouf/roaf (backslang 'four')]

Friar Tuck *n.* [1950s+] **1** sexual intercourse. **2** luck. **3** a general expletive or used in combinations, as in *I don't give a Friar Tuck* or *what the Friar Tuck!* [**1, 3** *Friar Tuck* = fuck; from the mythical Robin Hood's corpulent clerical sidekick Friar Tuck]

fridge freezer *n.* [20C] a man, a person. [*fridge freezer* = geezer]

fried bread *adj.* [20C] dead. [var. on BROWN BREAD]

fried eggs *n.* [20C] (*Aus.*) the legs.

fried rice *n.* [20C] (*Aus.*) a price.

frisk and frolic *n.* [late 19C–1910s] carbolic (soap).

frisky *n.* [late 19C+] whisky. [underpinned by its effects on the drinker]

frock and frill *n.* [late 19C–1900s] a chill. [possibly noting the effects of insufficiently warm clothes]

frog (*also* **frogskin**) *n.* [late 19C–1960s] (*Aus.*) a one-pound note. [*frogskin* = sovereign]

frog and feather *n.* [1940s] (*US*) a wallet. [*frog and feather* = leather (sl. 'wallet')]

frog (and toad) *n.* [mid-19C+] the road.

frog in the throat *n.* [1910s–50s] a boat.

frogskin *n. see* FROG.

frog (spawn) *n.* [20C] an erection. [*frog spawn* = horn]

front-wheel skid (*also* **back-wheel skid**) *n*. [1960s+] (*derog.*) a Jew. [*front-wheel skid* = Yid]

froth and bubble *n*. [1960s+] (*Aus.*) **1** (*racing*) a double, the 'daily double'. **2** trouble.

frying pan *n*. [20C] an old man.

fuck a duck! *excl.* [1940s+] an excl. of surprise, disbelief, dismissal or rejection. [cited occasionally as rhyming slang, but only by reduplication, and not a genuine version]

full-blown stallone *n*. [1990s+] an erection. [*full-blown stallone* = bone; from the US film star Sylvester Stallone (b.1946), known for his macho 'hard' roles]

fun and frolics (*also* **flowers and frolics**) *n*. [20C] the testicles. [*fun and frolics* = bollocks]

g

gah damn *n. see* GOR DAMN.

Gamble and Proctor *n.* [20C] a doctor. [from the manu-facturing firm of Proctor and Gamble]

game of nap *n.* [20C] **1** a cap. **2** excrement. [**2** *game of nap* = crap; from nap, a card game, in which each player receives five cards, and calls the number of tricks he expects to win]

gammon rasher *n.* [1970s] anything excellent, first-rate. [*gammon rasher* = smasher]

garden gate *n.* **1** [mid-19C+] a magistrate. **2** [1940s+] (*bingo*) the number eight. **3** [1940s+] eight pounds (sterling). **4** [1950s+] a friend. [**4** *garden gate* = mate]

garden (gate) *v.* [20C] to fellate. [despite the obvious rhyme, the link is *garden gate* = PLATE]

garden gates *n.* [20C] rates, i.e. taxes.

garden gnome *n.* [1980s+] a comb.

garden hop *v.* [20C] (*UK Und.*) to inform against, to betray. [*garden hop* = shop]

garden plant *n.* [20C] an aunt.

Garibaldi biscuit *v.* [20C] to risk it. [from the Garibaldi or 'squashed flies' biscuit, whose name comes from the Italian nationalist Giuseppe Garibaldi (1807–82)]

Gary Ablett *n.* [1980s+] (*drugs*) a tablet. [from the footballer Gary Ablett (b.1965); the term is thus a pun on Standard English *pill* and sl. *pill* a ball]

Gary Glitter *n.* **1** [1980s] (a pint of) bitter. **2** [1990s+] the anus. [**2** *Gary Glitter* = shitter; from the pop singer Gary Glitter, real name Paul Gadd (b.1940)]

Gary Lineker *n.* [1980s+] vinegar. [from the UK football star Gary Lineker (b.1960)]

gasp and grunt *n.* [1940s–60s] the vagina. [*gasp and grunt* = cunt; underpinned by a reference to the sounds of intercourse]

gates of Rome *n.* [20C] home.

gavel and wig *v.* [20C] to scratch (an itchy anus). [*gavel and wig* = twig, i.e. the image of using a twig to do the scratching]

gay and frisky *n.* [20C] whisky.

gay (and hearty) *n.* [1960s] (*Aus.*) a party.

gay gordon *n.* [20C] (*US*) a traffic warden. [from the gay gordons, a Scottish dance]

gear *adj.* [1930s+] homosexual. [*gear* = queer]

General Booth *n.* [20C] a tooth. [from the founder of the Salvation Army 'General' William Booth (1829–1912)]

general election *n.* [20C] an erection.

General Smuts *n.* [20C] the testicles. [*General Smuts* = nuts; from the S Afr. General Jan Christian Smuts (1870–1950)]

Gene Tunney *n.* [1960s] (*N.Z.*) money. [from the US boxer Gene Tunney (1898–1978)]

Geoff Hurst *n.* [1970s+] a first, i.e. a first-class degree. [from the UK footballer Sir Geoff Hurst (b.1941), who scored a hat-trick to take England to victory in the 1966 World Cup]

Geoffrey Chaucer *n.* [20C] a saucer. [from Geoffrey Chaucer (*c.*1343–1400) author of *The Canterbury Tales* (*c.*1386)]

George and Ringo *n.* [1960s] bingo. [from the Beatles members George Harrison (1943–2001) and Ringo Starr (b.1940)]

george and zippy *adj.* [1980s] very cold. [*george and zippy* = nippy; from the puppets George, a pink hippopotamus, and Zippy, an obnoxious and non-specific creature with a zip for a mouth, on the children's TV show *Rainbow*]

George Bernard Shaw *n.* [1940s–50s] a door. [from the Irish-born playwright George Bernard Shaw (1856–1950)]

George Blake *n.* [1960s] a snake. [from the Soviet spy George Blake (b.1922)]

George Bohee *n.* [1900s–50s] tea. [from the once well-known banjo player George Bohee; but note *bohea* the best variety of black tea, from the Wu-i hills in north Fukien, China]

George Moore *n.* [1970s+] (*Aus.*) in cricket, a four. [possibly from the Aus. jockey George Moore (b.1923)]

George Raft *n.* [1950s–60s] **1** a draught. **2** a banker's draft. **3** hard work. [**3** *George Raft* = graft; from the film star George Raft (1895–1980)]

George Robey *n.* [1910s–30s] (*tramp*) the road. [*George Robey* = toby (sl. 'road'); from the comedian Sir George Robey (1869–1954)]

George the Third *n.* [1980s+] a third, i.e. a third-class degree. [from King George III (1738–1820)]

Georgie Best *n.* [1960s+] **1** a guest; hence BE MY GEORGIE BEST. **2** a (drunken) pest. [from the football star and fabled drinker George Best (b.1946)]

Germaine Greer *n.* [1980s+] (*Aus.*) a beer. [from the Aus. feminist writer Germaine Greer (b.1939)]

German bands *n.* [20C] the hands.

German flutes *n.* [mid-19C] a pair of boots.

Gerry Riddle *n.* [1930s+] (*Aus.*) an act of urination. [var. on JIMMY RIDDLE]

gert and daisy *adj.* [20C] lazy. [from characters created on BBC radio in the 1930s by comediennes Elsie (d.1990) and Doris Waters (d.1978)]

Gertie Gitana *n.* [20C] (*Aus.*) banana. [from the music-hall star Gertie Gitana (1888–1957)]

Gertie Lee *n.* [1910s] (*bingo*) the number 33.

get on someone's wick *v.* [1940s+] to irritate or annoy someone. [*see* HAMPTON (WICK)]

◆◆

What the Dickens?

artful dodger	lodger
Barnaby Rudge	judge
Dolly Varden	garden
drain Charles Dickens	choke the chicken
Little Nell	bell
Oliver Twist	pissed
tale of two cities	titties
Tiny Tim	flim (five-pound note)
Uriah Heep	creep

◆◆

get the tom-tits *v.* [1960s+] to become frightened. [*get the tom-tits* = get the shits]

gezunter *n.* [20C] a bettor. [*gezunter* = punter]

gianluca *n.* [1990s+] cocaine. [*gianluca vialli* = charlie (sl. 'cocaine'); from the Italian footballer and manager Gianluca Vialli (b.1965)]

giddy goat *n.* [1920s+] (*Aus.*) the totalizator. [*giddy goat* = tote]

giddy gout *n.* [20C] (*Aus.*) a Boy Scout. [note the popular juvenile rhyme 'Giddy, giddy gout, your shirt is hanging out!']

giggle and titter (*also* **chirrup and titter**) *n.* [20C] bitter beer.

gigglestick *n.* [20C] (*orig. US*) the penis. [*gigglestick* = prick; the word may be equally placed among the various terms that equate penis with 'weapon' as well as something that supposedly induces 'giggles' in those who are having sex]

Gilbey's gin *n.* [20C] the chin.

Gillie Potters *n.* [1950s+] **1** pig's trotters. **2** the feet. [**2** *Gillie Potters* = trotters (sl. 'feet'); from the comedian Gillie Potter (1887–1975)]

ginger ale *n.* [20C] **1** a jail. **2** (*N.Z.*) bail.

ginger beer *n.* **1** [20C] (*mainly naval*) an engineer. **2** [1940s] (*US*) a tear (that one weeps).

ginger (beer) *n.* [1920s+] a male homosexual. [*ginger beer* = queer]

gingerbread *n.* [20C] the head. [plus a possible reference to the sweetmeat, a gingerbread man]

ginger-pop *n.* [late 19C] a policeman. [*ginger-pop* = (orig.) slop (backslang 'police'); latterly influenced by US *cop*]

Giorgio Armani *n.* [1980s+] a sandwich. [*Giorgio Armani* = sarnie; from the Italian couturier Giorgio Armani (b.1935)]

gipsy's (kiss) *n. see* GYPSY'S (KISS).

gipsy's warning *n. see* GYPSY'S WARNING.

girl abductor *n.* [late 19C–1910s] (*Aus.*) a tram conductor.

girl and boy *n.* **1** [mid-19C] a saveloy. **2** [20C] a toy.

girls and boys *n.* [20C] noise.

give and get *n*. [20C] a bet.

give and take *n*. [mid-19C+] **1** a cake. **2** a bundle of notes. [**2** *give and take* = (*fig.*) cake, i.e. a 'cake' of notes]

give someone the loaf of bread *v*. [1940s+] to hit someone with one's head. [*see* LOAF (OF BREAD)]

Glasgow boat *n*. [late 19C+] (*Anglo-Irish*) a coat.

Glasgow Rangers (*also* **Glasgows**) *n*. [1920s+] strangers, esp. used as a warning by look-out men working with unlicensed street pitchmen.

Glasgows *n*. *see* GLASGOW RANGERS.

glass case *n*. [mid-19C] a face.

glass of beer *n*. [late 19C+] an ear.

glass of plonk *n*. [20C] the nose. [*glass of plonk* = conk]

Glenn Hoddle *n*. [1970s+] something very easy. [*Glenn Hoddle* = doddle; from the former football star and England team manager Glenn Hoddle (b.1957)]

glimmie glide *n*. [20C] (*Anglo-Irish*) the other side, i.e. of a road, a field etc.

Gloria Gaynors *n*. [1980s+] trainers. [from the US singer Gloria Gaynor (b.1947)]

glorious sinner *n*. [mid-19C] dinner.

glory be *n*. [20C] tea.

gluepot *n*. [20C] the vagina. [*gluepot* = twat; as well as the rhyme, this is one of a number of terms that define the vagina as a repository for semen]

goanna *n.* [1910s+] (*Aus.*) a piano. [play on JOANNA and Standard Aus. English *goanna* a type of lizard]

gobstopper *n.* [20C] the penis. [*gobstopper* = chopper; possibly underpinned by an image of oral sex]

God almighty *n.* [20C] a nightdress. [*God almighty* = nightie]

God damn *n.* [20C] jam.

goddess Diana [mid-19C] a sixpence (2¹/₂ pence). [*goddess Diana* = tanner (early 19C–1970s sl. 'sixpence')]

God forbid *n.* [20C] a hat. [*God forbid* = lid (sl. 'hat')]

God-forbids *n.* [late 19C+] **1** children. **2** (*derog.*) Jews. [*God-forbids* = **1** kids **2** Yids; **1** refers ironically to the problems of offspring; **2** to the supposed popular Jewish exclamation, 'God forbid I should…']

God in heaven (*also* **God's in heaven**) *n.* [20C] (*bingo*) the number seven.

God love her *n.* [1970s] a mother.

God save the queens *n.* [20C] greens, i.e. vegetables.

God's in heaven *n. see* GOD IN HEAVEN.

go for a Burton *v.* [1940s+] (*orig. military*) **1** to die. **2** to fail, to malfunction. [the precise etymology remains unknown but there are a number of suggestions: first is the elision of Standard English *burnt 'un*, i.e. a burning aircraft (and its pilot); Partridge (1970) and Beale (1984) suggest: (1) a euphemism, going for a glass of Burton ale; (2) the rhyming slang *Burton-on-Trent* = went, as in 'went west'; (3) the heaviness of Burton ale, equivalent to that of a burning aircraft as it crashes to the ground; (4) the tailors Montague Burton; (5) the billiard halls, invariably sited above Burton shops, used as medical centres in WWII, i.e. those who attended such centres had *gone for a Burton*; other suggestions include the inter-war advertising campaign for Burton ales, bearing the copy line: 'He's gone for a Burton' and the use of Burton's halls for Morse aptitude tests, rather than medical check-ups, thus the phrase meant failing such a test; a final possibility is the seafarers' jargon *burton* the notoriously unsafe stowing of a barrel athwart rather than fore-and-aft, thus *going for a Burton* means risking death]

go for a leslie *v.* [1990s+] of a woman, to urinate. [*go for a leslie ash* = go for a slash; from the UK actress Leslie Ash (b.1960)]

golden gate *n.* [20C] 800 pounds (sterling).

golden hind *adj.* [20C] blind. [from the ship *Golden Hind*, in which Francis Drake circumnavigated the globe (1577–80)]

Goldie Hawn *n.* [1970s+] a prawn. [from the US film star Goldie Hawn (b.1945)]

goldilocks *n.* [20C] venereal disease. [*goldilocks* = pox]

gold ring *n.* [20C] a king.

gold watch *n.* [19C+] Scotch whisky. [the original reference was to the Waterbury watch; *see* BOTTLE OF SCOTCH]

go like the clappers *v.* [1940s+] (*euphemistic*) to run very fast. [*clappers* conjures up *bell* = hell, thus 'go like hell'; note RAF jargon *like the clappers of hell* very fast]

golliwog *n.* [1910s] **1** a dog. **2** (*pl.*) greyhound racing. **3** fog. [**2** *golliwogs* = the dogs]

gone and forgotten *n.* [20C] (*Aus.*) rotten.

gone to bed *adj.* [20C] dead.

Gonzo (the Great) *n.* [1970s+] a state (usu. of drunken excess). [from the puppet character Gonzo the Great in the TV series *The Muppet Show*, the puppet itself named for sl. *gonzo* eccentric, bizarre, out of control]

good and bad *n.* [20C] a father. [*good and bad* = dad]

goodie and baddie *n.* [20C] an Irish person. [*goodie and baddie* = paddy]

goodnight kiss *n.* [20C] an act of urination. [*goodnight kiss* = piss]

good ship Venus *n.* [20C] the penis. [from the coarse and popular rugby song 'The Good Ship Venus']

go on the cousin sis *v.* [1920s+] to get drunk. [*go on the cousin sis* = go on the piss]

goose and duck *n.* **1** [late 19C+] sexual intercourse. **2** [20C] a truck. [**1** *goose and duck* = fuck]

gooseberry pudden *n. see* GOOSEBERRY PUDDING.

gooseberry pudding (*also* **gooseberry pudden**) *n.* [mid-19C+] a woman, esp. in the phrase *the old gooseberry* one's wife. [such an old woman is possibly linked to *gooseberry* an unwanted chaperone or third party; note pronunciation of pudding as *pudden*]

gooseberry tart *n.* [mid-19C–1930s] **1** the heart. **2** a breaking of wind. [**2** *gooseberry tart* = fart]

goose's neck *n.* [20C] a cheque; hence SAUSAGE (A GOOSE'S).

gor damn (*also* **gah damn**) *n.* [late 19C–1910s] jam.

Gordon and Gotch *n.* [20C] a watch. [from the once well-known firm of book and periodical importers Gordon and Gotch]

Gordon Hutter *n.* [1930s–40s] (*N.Z.*) butter. [from the contemporary racing and wrestling commentator Gordon Hutter]

Gospel Oak *n.* [20C] a joke. [from the London suburb of Gospel Oak, on the borders of Hampstead and Kentish Town; the name comes from the ancient practice of 'beating the parish bounds', an event accompanied by a reading from a gospel under a large, usually oak tree]

got out of pawn *adj.* [20C] born. [the 'pawnshop' being the womb]

go up the council *v.* [1990s+] to have anal intercourse. [*see* COUNCIL GRITTER]

grandfather (clock) *n.* [20C] the penis. [*grandfather clock* = cock]

granite boulder *n.* [late 19C+] a shoulder. [both can be leaned on]

granny grunt *n.* [20C] a fussy, irritating person, although not necessarily female or old. [*granny grunt* = cunt]

granny's wrinkle *n*. [20C] a winkle, i.e. the crustacean.

grapevine *n*. [20C] a washing-line.

grass *n*. [1930s+] an informer. [*grasshopper* = shopper]

grasshopper *n*. [late 19C+] a policeman. [*grasshopper* = copper]

grass in the park *n*. [20C] an informer. [*grass in the park* = nark]

grave digger *n*. [20C] (*derog.*) a Black person. [*grave digger* = nigger, plus a pun on Standard English *spade* (for digging graves) and sl. *spade* a Black person]

greasy (mop) *n*. [20C] (*Aus.*) a policeman. [*greasy mop* = cop]

greengages *n*. [late 19C+] wages.

greens *n*. [1930s+] wages. [from GREENGAGES]

greens and brussels *n*. [20C] muscles. [reflecting the parental cry of 'Eat your greens' as a way of 'growing big and strong']

green tea *n*. [1980s+] (*drugs*) the hallucinogen phencyclidine or PCP. [the rhyme is possibly on phencycli*dine*; but note the common mixing of the drug with parsley, which may resemble marijuana, i.e. *tea*]

Gregory Peck *n*. [1950s+] the neck. [from the US actor Gregory Peck (b.1916)]

Gregory Pecks *n*. [1950s+] (*Aus.*) spectacles, glasses. [*Gregory Pecks* = specs; *see* GREGORY PECK]

Gregory Peg *n.* [20C] (*Aus.*) the leg. [pun on the name Gregory Peck and Standard English *peg-leg*]

Greville Starkey *n.* [1980s+] (*derog.*) a Black person. [*Greville Starkey* = darkie; from the UK horse-racing trainer Greville Starkey (b.1939)]

grey mare *n.* [20C] a fare, e.g. on a bus.

grey nurse *n.* [20C] (*Aus.*) a purse.

griddle *n.* [late 19C–1900s] a violin. [*griddle* = fiddle]

grim and gory *n.* [20C] (*Aus.*) a story. [presumably of a 'blood-and-thunder' variety]

Grimsby Docks *n.* [20C] socks. [from Grimsby Docks, near Hull, Lincolnshire, the site of one of Britain's major fishing ports]

groan and grunt *n. see* GRUMBLE AND GRUNT.

grocer's cart *n.* [20C] (*Aus.*) the heart.

grocer's shop *n.* [1970s] (*derog.*) an Italian. [*grocer's shop* = wop]

grocery store *n.* [20C] (*US*) a door.

Grosvenor Squares *n.* [1970s] flared trousers. [*Grosvenor Squares* = flares; from Grosvenor Square, London, home of the US Embassy – and site of a variety of anti-US demonstrations from 1967–71]

groucho *n.* [20C] an electrician. [*groucho marx* = sparks; from the US comedian Groucho Marx (1890–1977)]

growl and grunt *n. see* GROWL AND GRUNT.

gruesome and gory *n.* [20C] the penis. [*gruesome and gory* = corie (sl. 'penis')]

grumble and grunt (*also* **groan and grunt**, **growl and grunt**) *n.* [1930s+] **1** the vagina. **2** sexual intercourse. [*grumble and grunt* = cunt]

grumble and mutter *n.* [20C] a bet. [*grumble and mutter* = flutter; the inference is that the bettor has lost]

guinea pig *n.* [20C] a wig.

Gunga Din *n.* [20C] the chin. [from the Rudyard Kipling poem 'Gunga Din' (1892), which features the famous last line *You're a better man than I am, Gunga Din*]

guy *n.* [late 19C+] a walk, thus an expedition or journey. [*guy fawkes* = walk; from the Catholic revolutionary Guy Fawkes, who was executed in 1605 for his part in the 'Gunpowder Plot', an attempt to blow up the Houses of Parliament]

Gypsie Lee *n.* [1930s+] (*Aus.*) tea. [var. on ROSIE (LEA); Lee is one of the best-known Romani families, but note the celebrated US striptease artiste Gypsy Rose Lee (1914–70)]

gypsy's (kiss) (*also* **gipsy's (kiss)**) *n.* [20C] an act of urination. [*gypsy's kiss* = piss]

gypsy's warning (*also* **gipsy's warning**) *n.* [mid-19C+] morning.

h

Hackney Marsh *n.* **1** [late 19C–1950s] a glass (of alcohol).
2 [20C] (*pl.*) glasses, i.e. spectacles. [from Hackney
Marsh, London E9, once home of field sports, now of
Sunday morning football]

Hackney Wick *n.* [20C] the penis. [*Hackney Wick* = prick]

haddock and bloater *n.* [20C] a motor-car. [*haddock and
bloater* = motor]

haddock and cod *n.* [20C] an irritating person, also
used as an affectionate name for a child. [*haddock and
cod* = sod]

hail and rain *n.* [1920s–70s] a train.

hail smiling morn *n.* [1970s+] an erection. [*hail smiling
morn* = horn; referring to the propensity of men to awake
with erections]

hair and brain *n.* [1940s] (*US*) a chain

hairy goat *n.* [1940s] (*US*) the throat.

hale and hearty *n.* [1970s+] a party.

half-a-cock *n.* [mid-19C+] five pounds (sterling). [Standard
English *half* + COCK AND HEN]

half-a-dollar *n.* [20C] a collar.

half-an-hour *n.* [late 19C–1930s] (*Aus.*) flour.

half-a-nicker *n. see* HALF-NICKER.

half an Oxford (scholar) *n.* [late 19C] half a crown ($12^1/_2$ pence). [*see* OXFORD SCHOLAR]

half a peck *n.* [late 19C–1950s] the neck.

half-hitch *v.* [1970s+] (*N.Z.*) to steal. [*half-hitch* = snitch]

half-inch *v.* [1920s+] to steal. [*half-inch* = pinch]

half-nicker (*also* **half-a-nicker**) *n.* [20C] a vicar.

half of marge *n.* [20C] (*UK Und.*) a police sergeant. [*half of marge* = sarge]

half-ounce *v.* [20C] **1** to beat up. **2** to cheat, to short change. [*half-ounce* = bounce]

half-ounce of baccy *n.* [1970s+] (*derog.*) a British Asian. [*half-ounce of baccy* = paki]

half-ouncer *n.* [20C] a security man at a nightclub, dance-hall or similar place. [*half-ouncer* = bouncer]

half past two *n.* [20C] a Jew.

halfpenny dip *n.* [mid-19C+] a ship.

halfpenny stamp (*also* **half-stamp**) *n.* [20C] a tramp.

half-stamp *n. see* HALFPENNY STAMP.

half-track *n.* [1980s+] (*drugs*) 125 dollars-worth of crack cocaine. [*half-track* = crack]

ham and beef *n.* [mid-19C+] (*UK prison*) the chief officer.

ham and bone *n.* [20C] home.

ham and eggs *n.* [1950s+] (*orig. Aus.*) the legs.

hambone *n.* **1** [20C] a telephone. **2** [1930s] (*US*) a trombone.

hammer and discus *n.* [20C] whiskers. [the hammer and the discus are two athletic field events]

hammer (and nail) *v.* [20C] to follow. [*hammer and nail* = tail]

hammer and saw *n.* [1920s] (*US*) a policeman. [*hammer and saw* = officer of the law]

hammer (and tack) *n.* (*Aus./N.Z.*) **1** [late 19C+] a sixpence. **2** [1920s+] a road. **3** [1950s+] the back. **4** [1980s+] (*drugs*) heroin. [*hammer and tack* = **1** zac (Aus/N.Z. sl. 'sixpence') **2** track **4** smack]

hamps *n. see* HAMPSTEADS.

hampsteads (*also* **hamps**) *n.* [mid-19C+] the teeth. [*hampstead heath* = teeth; from Hampstead Heath, North London's major area of rough park and woodland]

Hampton Court *n.* [20C] salt. [from Hampton Court Palace, built for Cardinal Wolsey in 1514 and passed on to the royal family; note Cockney pronunciation of salt as *sort*]

Hampton rock *n.* [late 19C+] the penis. [*Hampton rock* = cock]

Hampton (Wick) *n.* [late 19C+] 1 the penis. 2 a fool. [*Hampton Wick* = prick; from the London suburb of Hampton Wick]

hamshank *n.* [1940s–60s] an American. [*hamshank* = Yank]

ham shank *n.* [1990s+] an act of masturbation. [*ham shank* = wank]

ham shanker *n.* [1990s+] 1 a masturbator. 2 an unpleasant, stupid, despised person. [*ham shanker* = wanker]

hand and fist *adj.* [20C] drunk. [*hand and fist* = pissed; never truncated]

handicap *n.* [20C] venereal disease. [*handicap* = clap]

handicap chase *n.* [20C] the face.

hands *n.* [20C] (a piece of) meat. [*hands and feet* = meat]

Hanger Lane *n.* [20C] pain. [from the West London suburb of Hanger Lane; possibly referring to the notorious traffic problems of the Hanger Lane Gyratory System]

hang bluff *n.* [mid-19C] snuff.

hangnail *n.* [20C] a snail, i.e. a slow, shambling person.

Hank Marvin *adj.* [1960s+] starving. [from the guitarist Hank B. Marvin (b.1941), best known as a member of Cliff Richard's band The Shadows]

Hannibal Lecter *n.* [1990s+] a ticket inspector. [from the cannibalistic and murderous fictional Dr. Hannibal Lecter, 'star' of the novel *The Silence of the Lambs* (1990) and its sequel *Hannibal* (1999) by Thomas Harris]

hansel and gretel *n.* [20C] a kettle. [from the fairy-tale characters Hansel and Gretel]

hansom cab *n.* [20C] (*Aus.*) a non-unionist. [*hansom cab* = scab]

hansom cabs *n.* [20C] body lice. [*hansom cabs* = crabs]

happy hour *n.* [1950s+] (*Aus.*) a shower of rain.

happy hours *n.* [1940s+] flowers.

harbour light *phr.* [late 19C+] all right, esp. in the phrase *all harbour.*

hard and flat *n.* [1940s] (*US*) a hat.

hard hit *n.* [1970s] an act of defecation. [*hard hit* = shit]

hard labour *n.* [20C] a neighbour.

hare and hound *adj.* [20C] round.

haricot *n.* **1** [1960s+] (*Aus.*) a male homosexual. **2** [late 19C–1900s] the penis. [*haricot bean* = **1** queen **2** bean (late 19C–1900s sl. 'penis')]

Harold Holt *n.* [1970s+] (*Aus.*) **1** salt. **2** an act of absconding; hence *do a Harold Holt* to abscond. [**2** *Harold Holt* = bolt; from the former Aus. Prime Minister Harold Holt (1908–67), who died in mysterious circumstances, apparently drowned in the Bass Strait]

Harold Lloyd *n. see* LLOYD.

Harold Macmillan *n.* [1950s–60s] a villain. [from the former Prime Minister Harold Macmillan (1894–1986)]

Harold Pinter *n.* [1960s+] a splinter. [from the dramatist Harold Pinter (b.1930)]

harolds *n.* [20C] **1** trousers. **2** (*Aus.*) knickers. [*Harry Taggs* = bags]

harris *n. see* ARRIS.

Harris Tweed *n.* [20C] a weakling. [*Harris Tweed* = weed; from Harris Tweed, the proprietary name of a superior brand of tweed cloth]

harry *adj.* [1990s+] foolish. [*harry and billy* = silly]

Harry Bluff *n.* [late 19C–1920s] snuff.

Harry Dash *adj.* [20C] showy, ostentatious. [*Harry Dash* = flash]

Harry Huggins *n.* [20C] a fool, an idiot. [*Harry Huggins* = muggins]

Harry Lauder *n.* [20C] a prison warder. [from the Scottish music-hall star Harry Lauder (1870–1950)]

Harry Lime *n.* [1950s–70s] time. [from the character Harry Lime, the anti-hero (played by Orson Welles) in the film *The Third Man* (1949)]

Harry Monk *n.* [20C] semen. [*Harry Monk* = spunk]

Harry Nash *n.* [20C] cash.

Harry Randall *n.* [20C] **1** a handle. **2** a candle. [from the music-hall comedian Harry Randall (1860–1932)]

Harry Ronce *n. see* CHARLIE RONCE.

Rogues Gallery

Al Capone	telephone
Dick Turpin	13
Doctor Crippen	dripping
Frankie Fraser	razor
Hannibal Lecter	ticket inspector
Jack the Ripper	kipper/slipper
Jekyll and Hyde	snide
Ned Kelly	belly/telly
reggie and ronnie	johnnie
Ronnie Biggs	digs
Yorkshire rippers	slippers

Harry Tate *n.* [20C] **1** (*bingo*) the number eight. **2** a condition of emotional stress. **3** a plate. **4** (*pl.*) Weights, i.e. Player's Weights cigarettes. [**2** *Harry Tate* = state; from the comedian Harry Tate (1872–1940); note also the WWI military use *Harry Tate's Cavalry* the Yeomanry, *Harry Tate's Navy* the Royal Naval Volunteer Reserve, the Fleet Auxiliary and the Motor Boat Reserve]

Harry Tate *adj.* [20C] late. [*see* HARRY TATE *n.*]

harry, tom and dick *adj.* [20C] sick. [play on the generic *Tom, Dick and Harry*]

Harry Wragg *n.* [20C] a cigarette. [*Harry Wragg* = fag; from the jockey and trainer Harry Wragg (*fl.*1930s)]

harvest moon *n.* [20C] (*derog.*) a Black person. [*harvest moon* = coon]

Harvey Nichol *n.* [1920s+] a problem, a difficult situation. [*Harvey Nichol* = pickle; *see* HARVEY NICHOLS]

Harvey Nichols *n.* [20C] pickles. [from the Harvey Nichols store in Knightsbridge, London SW3]

has-beens *n.* [20C] (*chiefly UK prison*) greens, i.e. vegetables.

hash-me-gandy *adj.* [1940s] (*US*) handy, i.e. convenient. [note the Aus./N.Z. *hashmagandy* a basic form of stew]

hat and cap *n.* [1940s] (*US*) venereal disease [*hat and cap* = clap]

hat and coat *n.* [20C] a boat, esp. a refrigerated cargo ship.

hat and feather *n.* [20C] weather.

hat and scarf *n.* [20C] a bath.

have a cook *v.* [20C] to have a look. [a semi-rhyming phrase; it may equally well stem from the Yiddish *geb a guck* have a look]

have the Richard *v.* [1960s+] (*Aus.*) to be finished or exhausted, to be irreparably damaged. [*have the Richard the Third* = get the bird; *see* RICHARD (THE THIRD)]

have the stick *v.* [1950s+] (*Aus.*) to be finished, to be permanently damaged. [*have the stick* = have the dick (Aus. sl. 'be finished')]

Hawkesbury rivers *n.* [20C] (*Aus.*) the cold shivers. [from the Hawkesbury River, north-west of Sydney]

hawk one's pearly *v.* [1970s+] to act in a promiscuous manner, to offer one's body for sexual enjoyment. [Standard English *hawk* + PEARLY KING]

hay lee *n.* [1940s–50s] tea.

haystack *n.* [20C] the back, i.e. of a building etc.

heap o' coke (*also* **heap of coke**, **heapy**) *n.* [20C] a man, a person. [*heap o' coke* = bloke]

heap of coke *n. see* HEAP O' COKE.

heapy *n. see* HEAP O' COKE.

heart and dart *n.* [mid-19C–1920s] a breaking of wind. [*heart and dart* = fart]

heart and lung *n.* [1920s] (*US*) **1** talk, conversation. **2** the tongue. [**1** *heart and lung* = (*fig.*) tongue]

hearth rug *n.* [1910s–50s] **1** a fool, a simpleton. **2** a bed-bug. [**1** *hearth rug* = mug]

heart of oak (*also* **hearts of oak**) *adj.* [20C] penniless, impoverished. [*heart of oak* = broke]

hearts of oak *adj. see* HEART OF OAK.

heaven and hell *n.* **1** [20C] a smell. **2** [1940s] a projectile shell.

heavenly bliss *n.* [20C] (*orig. US*) a kiss.

heavenly plan *n.* [late 19C–1900s] (*Aus.*) a man.

heavens above *n*. [20C] love.

heaver *n*. [1910s–20s] a coin of small value, esp. a penny. [*coal-heaver* = stiver (sl. 'thing of little value')]

hedge and ditch *n*. [late 19C+] **1** a market pitch. **2** a cricket or football pitch.

hedgehog *n*. [20C] (*derog.*) a foreigner, esp. a Black or Asian person. [*hedgehog* = wog]

helter-skelter *n*. **1** [1940s] an air-raid shelter. **2** [1950s+] a bus shelter.

Henley Regatta *n*. [1950s+] a chat, a gossip. [*Henley Regatta* = natter; from the regatta held annually at the Berkshire town of Henley-on-Thames, which is a highlight of both the social and the sporting calendars]

Henrietta *n*. [20C] a letter.

Henry Fonda *n*. [1970s+] a Honda 90 motorcycle, esp. as used by trainee taxi-drivers or 'knowledge boys'. [from the US film star Henry Fonda (1905–82)]

Henry Halls *n*. [1950s+] the testicles. [*Henry Halls* = balls; from the popular UK bandleader Henry Hall (1898–1989)]

Henry III (*also* **Henry the Third**) *n*. [1950s+] a piece of human excrement. [*Henry the Third* = turd; from the English King Henry III (r.1216–72)]

Henry Melville *n*. [late 19C] (*euphemistic*) the devil. [from the G.R. Sims ballad 'Tottie' (1887): 'What the Henry Melville / Do you think you're doing there?'; presumably an elision of '*H*enry' and '*Me*lville' that makes *hell* and thus 'the devil']

Henry Nash *n.* [20C] cash.

Henry the Third *n. see* HENRY III.

Herbie Hides *n.* [1990s+] trousers. [*Herbie Hides* = strides; from the heavyweight boxer and former WBO champion Herbie Hide (b.1973)]

here and there *n.* **1** [20C] a chair. **2** [1930s] (*Aus.*) hair. [never truncated]

herring and kipper *n.* [20C] a stripper.

hers and hims *n.* [20C] (*Aus.*) hymns.

hey-diddle-diddle (*also* **hi-diddle-diddle**) *n.* [1950s] **1** an act of urination. **2** (the) middle. **3** a violin. [*hey-diddle-diddle* = **1** piddle **3** fiddle; from the nursery rhyme 'Hey Diddle Diddle, the cat and the fiddle']

hickey hockey *n.* [20C] (*Aus.*) a jockey.

hickory-dickory *n. see* HICKORY-DOCK.

hickory-dock (*also* **hickory-dickory**) *n.* [20C] a clock. [*hickory-(dickory-)dock* = clock; from the nursery rhyme 'Hickory, dickory dock, / The mouse ran up the clock'; *see* DICKORY DOCK]

hide and seek *n.* [20C] cheek. [never truncated]

hi-diddle-diddle *n. see* HEY-DIDDLE-DIDDLE.

hi-diddle-diddle *v.* [20C] (*Aus.*) to urinate. [*hi-diddle-diddle* = piddle; *see* HEY-DIDDLE-DIDDLE]

high as a kite *adj.* [1930s+] very drunk. [*high as a kite* = tight]

highland fling *n.* (*Aus.*) **1** [20C] string. **2** [1960s+] in cards, the king.

highland fling *v.* [1950s] to sing; hence *highland flinger* a singer.

highland frisky *n.* [late 19C] whisky. [var. on CHARLEY FRISKY]

high noon *n.* [1950s] a spoon. [from the film *High Noon* (1952)]

high seas *n.* [1920s] (*US*) the knees.

high-stepper *n.* [20C] pepper.

hi jimmy knacker *n.* [20C] tobacco. [from the name of an old street game; note Cockney pronunciation of tobacco as *terbaccer*]

hill and dale *n.* [1940s+] a story used for begging or for a confidence trick. [*hill and dale* = tale]

hillman hunter *n.* [20C] a customer. [*hillman hunter* = punter; from the defunct Hillman Hunter motor-car]

hipsy hoy *n.* [20C] a boy.

hit (and miss) *n.* [1960s+] **1** a kiss. **2** urine. **3** an act of urination. [**2**, **3** *hit and miss* = piss]

hit and missed *adj.* [1960s+] drunk. [*hit and missed* = pissed; never truncated]

hit and run *n.* [20C] the sun.

hit and run *adj.* [20C] cheated, deceived. [*hit and run* = done]

hit or miss *n.* [late 19C+] **1** urine. **2** an act of urination. [*hit or miss* = piss]

hit the deep *n.* [20C] (*Aus.*) sleep.

hobson's choice *n.* [20C] the voice. [from the Standard English phrase *Hobson's choice* no choice at all; named for Tobias Hobson or Jobson (d.*c.*1630), the Cambridge carrier (commemorated by John Milton (1608–74) in two epitaphs), who let out horses and is said to have compelled customers either to take the horse that happened to be next to the stable-door or to go without; orig. *Hodgson's choice* and cited as such by Ernest Weekley as occurring in 1617, 13 years before Hobson's death]

hock *n.* [20C] a male homosexual. [*hock* = cock (used generically)]

hod of mortar *n.* [mid-19C] a pot of porter.

hokey *n.* [late 19C–1910s] a prison. [*hokey* = chokey/pokey]

hokey cokey *n.* [1980s+] karaoke. [from the popular dance the *hokey-cokey* (originally *cokey-cokey*): 'You do the Hokey Cokey and turn around / That's what it's all about']

hole in the ground *n.* [20C] one pound (sterling).

holla (boys) *n. see* HOLLER (BOYS).

holler (boys) (*also* **holla (boys)**) *n.* [19C] a (stiff) collar.

hollow log *n.* [1970s] (*Aus.*) a racing dog.

Holyfield's ear *n.* [1990s+] a year. [from the famous biting of the boxer Evander Holyfield's ear by opponent Mike Tyson during their WBA Heavyweight Championship bout in Las Vegas (June 1997)]

holy friar *n.* [20C] a liar. [never truncated]

holy ghost *n.* (*Aus.*) **1** [20C] post, i.e. mail. **2** [20C] the post, i.e. the start or finish line of a horserace. **3** [1950s+] toast.

holy ghosts *n.* [20C] (*Aus.*) fence posts.

holy nail *n.* [late 19C+] bail.

holy smoke *n.* [20C] **1** coke (the fuel). **2** Coke, i.e. Coca-Cola.

holy water *n.* [20C] a daughter.

home on the range *n.* [20C] (*Aus.*) small change.

home on the range *adj.* [20C] strange.

honey *n.* [1920s] money. [POT O' HONEY]

honeypot *n.* [early 18C+] the vagina. [Puxley (1992) suggests *honeypot* = twat, but the chronology militates against this; D'Urfey (1719) credits the lines to the poem 'To chuse a Friend, but never Marry' by the Earl of Rochester, but offers no date; in either case the term is one of a number that equate the vagina with a receptacle for semen]

Hong Kong *n.* [20C] a smell. [*Hong Kong* = pong]

Hong Kong *adj.* [20C] wrong.

honky tonk *n.* [20C] (*Aus.*) cheap wine. [*honky tonk* = plonk; *see* PLINKITY PLONK]

hook of mutton *n.* [1940s] (*US*) a button.

hoot and holler *n.* [1940s] (*US*) a dollar.

hop it and scram *n.* [20C] ham.

hopping pot *n.* [late 19C+] the lot, i.e. everything.

hopscotch *n.* [20C] a watch.

horn of plenty *n.* [20C] (*bingo*) the number 20.

hors d'oeuvres *n.* [20C] nerves.

horse *n.* [1960s+] venereal disease, specifically gonor-rhoea. [*horse and trap* = clap]

horse and carriage *n.* [20C] a garage. [note Cockney pronunciation of garage as *garridge*]

horse and cart *n.* **1** [late 19C] the heart. **2** [20C] (*Aus.*) the start. **3** [1970s+] a breaking of wind. [**3** *horse and cart* = fart]

horse and cart *v.* [1970s] to break wind. [*horse and cart* = fart]

horse and foal *n.* [20C] (*Aus.*) the dole.

horse and trap *n.* **1** [20C] excrement. **2** [1960s+] venereal disease, specifically gonorrhoea. [*horse and trap* = **1** crap **2** clap]

horse and trough *n.* [20C] a cough.

horses and carts *n*. [20C] darts.

horse's hoof *n*. [1950s+] a male homosexual. [*horse's hoof* = poof]

hot and cold *n*. [20C] gold.

hot cross bun *n*. [20C] **1** a gun. **2** [20C] (*Aus.*) the sun. **3** a son.

hot cross bun *phr.* [20C] escaping from justice or the authorities. [*hot cross bun* = on the run]

hot dinner *n*. [20C] a winner.

hot potato *n*. [late 19C] a waiter. [note Cockney pronunciation of potato as *pertater*]

hot potato *adv.* [1950s+] (*Aus.*) later. [note Aus. pronunciation of potato as *pertater*]

hot scone *n*. [1920s+] (*Aus.*) a policeman, a detective. [*hot scone* = john (sl. 'policeman')]

hot toddy *n*. [20C] the human body.

Hounslow Heath *n*. [mid-19C] the teeth. [from Hounslow Heath, West London, once home to many marauding highwaymen, plus a display of gibbets to remind them of their potential fate]

housemaid's knee *n*. [1970s] the sea. [also known as *water on the knee*, a link that may be coincidental]

House of Fraser (*also* **howser**) *n*. [20C] a razor, either as a weapon or for shaving. [from the business House of Fraser, one-time owners of, *inter alia*, Harrods]

House of Lords *n*. [20C] corduroy trousers. [*House of Lords* = cords]

house to let *n*. [20C] a bet.

housewives' choice *n*. [1950s+] a voice. [from the once popular BBC radio programme *Housewives' Choice*]

housey-housey *adj*. [20C] lousy, i.e. unwell. [*housey-housey* is a synonymous name for bingo]

howard's way *adj*. [1990s+] homosexual. [*howard's way* = gay; from the UK 1980s TV serial *Howard's Way*]

how-do-you do *n*. [mid-19C+] **1** a shoe. **2** a problem, a difficulty, a fuss, esp. in phrase *a fine how-do-you do*. [**2** *how-do-you do* = stew]

howd'ye do *n*. [19C] (*often pl.*) a shoe.

howser *n*. *see* HOUSE OF FRASER.

hubba, I am back *n*. [1980s+] (*US drugs*) crack cocaine. [from the sl. exclamation of sexual approval *hubba! hubba!* plus a jocular reference to the clichéd line 'Honey, I'm home']

Huckleberry Finn *n*. [20C] (*Aus.*) gin. [from the novel *The Adventures of Huckleberry Finn* (1884) by Mark Twain]

hugs and kisses (*also* **love and kisses**) *n*. [20C] a wife. [*hugs and kisses* = missus]

hundred to eight *n*. [20C] a plate.

hundred to thirty *adj*. [1970s] dirty.

hurricane lamp *n*. [20C] a tramp.

husband and wife *n*. [20C] a knife. [underpinned by a negative view of marriage]

hush puppy *n*. [1980s+] a yuppie. [from the shoe brand Hush Puppies, although these were not an especially yuppiesque fashion]

Hyde Park *n*. [20C] an informer. [*Hyde Park* = nark; from London's great central park, once a haunt of wild animals, latterly a royal hunting ground and, since the 17C, a public space]

hydraulics *n*. [20C] nonsense, rubbish. [*hydraulics* = bollocks]

i

I am back *n*. [1980s] (*drugs*) crack cocaine.

Ian Rush *n*. [1980s] a brush. [from the footballer Ian Rush (b.1961)]

ice-cream freezer *n*. [20C] a man, a person. [*ice-cream freezer* = geezer]

ideal home *n*. [1950s+] a comb.

I declare *n*. [1940s] (*US*) a chair.

I desire *n*. [mid-19C] a fire.

I don't care *n*. [1940s] (*US*) the electric chair.

Ilie Nastase *n*. [1970s] the lavatory. [*Ilie Nastase* = carsey; from the Romanian tennis star Ilie Nastase (b.1946)]

I'll be there *n*. [20C] a chair.

I'm afloat *n*. [20C] **1** a boat. **2** a coat.

I'm so (frisky) *n*. [1930s] whisky.

I'm willing *n*. [20C] a shilling (five pence).

in-and-out *n*. [20C] **1** the snout, i.e. the nose. **2** a cigarette. **3** a bottle of stout. **4** a tout, i.e. a racecourse tipster. **5** a spout; hence *up the in-and-out* pregnant. **6** gout [**2** *in-and-out* = snout]

in-between *n.* [20C] (*Aus.*) a male homosexual. [*in-between* = queen]

Indian charm *n.* [20C] the arm.

inky blue *n.* [1970s+] influenza. [*inky blue* = flu]

inky smudge *n.* [late 19C–1930s] a judge.

insects (and ants) *n.* [20C] **1** trousers. **2** knickers, i.e. underwear. [*insects and ants* = pants]

inside right *adj.* [20C] mean, grasping. [*inside right* = tight]

in the book *n.* [1940s] (*US*) a thief. [*in the book* = hook (sl. 'thief') plus a reference to the police *booking* of an offender]

in the lurch *n.* [20C] (*Aus.*) a church. [playing on the abandoned bride who is left *in the lurch*]

in the mood *n.* [20C] food.

in the nude *n.* [1970s] food.

Irish jig *n.* [20C] **1** a wig. **2** a cigarette. [**2** *Irish jig* = cig]

Irish Kerby *n. see* IRISH KIRBY.

Irish kirby (*also* **Irish Kerby**) *n.* [1940s] (*US*) a Derby hat.

Irish lasses *n.* [20C] glasses, i.e. spectacles.

Irish rose *n.* [20C] the nose.

Irish stew *adj.* [20C] **1** true; hence TOO IRISH STEW! **2** blue.

iron duke *n.* [late 19C+] a lucky chance. [*iron duke* = fluke; from the Duke of Wellington (1769–1852), nicknamed the 'Iron Duke']

iron girder *n*. [20C] murder; usu. in fig. phrases such as *get away with iron girder, there'll be iron girder if …*

iron (hoof) *n*. [1930s+] a male homosexual. [*iron hoof* = poof]

iron hoop *n*. [late 19C–1910s] soup.

iron horse *n*. [20C] **1** a racecourse. **2** a coin. [**2** *iron horse* = toss; note Cockney pronunciation of toss as *torss*]

iron Mike *n*. [1980s+] a bicycle. [*iron Mike* = bike; from the US boxing champion 'Iron' Mike Tyson (b.1966)]

iron tank *n*. [20C] a bank.

isabella (*also* **isabeller**) *n*. [mid-19C] an umbrella.

isabeller *n. see* ISABELLA.

I should coco! *excl. see* I SHOULD COCOA!

I should cocoa! (*also* **I should coco!**) *excl.* [1930s+] you must be joking! don't make me laugh! [*I should cocoa* = I should say so; esp. popular in BBC Radio's *Billy Cotton Bandshow* in the 1950s]

Isle of France *n*. [mid–late 19C] a dance.

Isle of Man *n*. [20C] a pan. [never truncated]

Isle of Wight *adj*. [20C] **1** light. **2** all right. **3** mean, grasping. [**3** *Isle of Wight* = tight]

I suppose (*also* **suppose**) *n*. [mid-19C+] a nose.

itch and scratch *n*. [20C] a match.

ivory float *n*. [1920s–50s] (*US*) a coat.

ivory pearl *n*. [1930s–60s] a girl.

j

jack *n.*[1] [1940s+] (*Aus.*) a non-union labourer, a strike-breaker, specifically a member of the Permanent and Casual Waterside Workers' Union. [*jack mcnab* = scab]

jack *n.*[2] [1950s+] a pill of heroin in which the drug is issued to registered addicts. [JACK AND JILL **4**]

jack *n.*[3] [1970s] a bar (in a pub). [JACK TAR]

jack, the *n.* [1950s+] (*Aus.*) venereal disease. [JACK IN THE BOX]

jack-a-dandy *n.* [late 19C+] brandy.

jack an' danny *n.* [1990s+] the vagina. [*jack an' danny* = fanny]

jack and jill *n.* [20C] **1** a hill. **2** a bill. **3** a till. **4** a pill, esp. of heroin. **5** (*Aus.*) a fool. [**5** *jack and jill* = dill]

Jack and Joan *adv.* [20C] on own's own.

jackanory *n.* [1960s+] **1** a children's story. **2** a lie. [**2** *jackanory* = story; from the BBC children's television series *Jackanory*, in which stories were read aloud in daily instalments by celebrities]

Jack Benny *n.* [20C] a penny. [from the US comedian Jack Benny (1894–1974)]

Jack Dandy *n.* [mid-19C] (*US*) brandy.

jackdaw *n.* [mid-19C+] a jaw.

Jack Dee *n.* [1990s+] an act of urination. [*Jack Dee* = pee/wee; from the UK comedian Jack Dee (b.1961)]

Jack Doyle *n.* [late 19C+] a boil (on the neck). [var. on CONAN DOYLE]

jacket and vest *n.* [1910s–30s] the West End of London.

Jack Flash *n.* [1960s+] (*Aus.*) hashish. [*Jack Flash* = hash; with a possible reference to the Rolling Stones' song 'Jumping Jack Flash' (1968)]

Jackie (Dash) *n.* [1960s+] an act of urination. [*Jackie Dash* = slash; from the UK dockers' leader Jack Dash]

Jackie Lancashire (*also* **Jacky Lancashire**) *n.* [1940s] (*Aus.*) a handkerchief. [*Jackie Lancashire* = 'handkercher']

Jackie Trent *adj.* [1990s+] corrupt, untrustworthy. [*Jackie Trent* = bent; from the UK singer Jackie Trent (b.1940)]

jack in the box *n.* [late 19C+] **1** venereal disease. **2** socks. [**1** *jack in the box* = pox]

Jack Jones *adj.* [20C] alone, esp. in the phrase ON ONE'S JACK (JONES).

Jack Ketch *n.* [mid-18C+] a jail sentence. [*Jack Ketch* = stretch; from the common executioner Jack Ketch (*c.*1663–86), whose name became widely known partly on account of his barbarity at the executions of Lord Russell, the Duke of Monmouth and other political offenders, and partly perhaps from the obvious links with the Standard English *catch*. When it was given to the hangman in the puppet-play of *Punchinello*, which arrived from Italy shortly after his death, his immortality was assured]

Jack Malone *adv.* [20C] (*Aus.*) alone. [var. on PAT MALONE]

Jack O'Brien *n. see* JOHNNY O'BRIEN.

jack of spades *n.* [20C] dark glasses. [*jack of spades* = shades]

Jack Randall (*also* **Jack Randle**) *n.* [mid-19C] a candle. [according to John Camden Hotten (1859), based on the 'noted pugilist' Jack Randle]

Jack Randle *n. see* JACK RANDALL.

Jack Rees *n.* [20C] (*Aus.*) fleas.

jack's (alive) (*also* **jax**) *n.* [1920s+] the number five, esp. a five-pound note.

jack scratches *n.* [20C] (*Aus.*) matches.

Jack Shay *n. see* JACK SHEA.

Jack Shay *v.* [20C] (*Aus.*) to stay.

Jack Shea (*also* **Jack Shay**) *n.* [late 19C] (*Aus.*) a tin container, holding a quart (3.2 litres) of liquid, used for brewing tea and, when empty, containing a smaller vessel for drinking the tea. [*Jack Shea* = tea; note Irish pronunciation of tea as *tay*)]

Jackson Pollocks *n.* [1990s+] the testicles. [*Jackson Pollocks* = bollocks; from the US artist Jackson Pollock (1912–56)]

Jack Sprat *n.* [20C] **1** fat (on meat). **2** a brat, an irritating small child.

Jack Surpass *n.* [mid-19C] a glass.

Jack Tar *n.* [20C] a bar (in a pub).

jack the dancer *n.* [20C] (*Aus.*) cancer.

jack the lad *adj.* [20C] bad.

Jack the Ripper *n.* [20C] **1** a kipper. **2** a slipper. [from the late-19C unidentified serial killer 'Jack the Ripper'; **1** like the Ripper's victims, kippers are slit open]

Jacky Lancashire *n. see* JACKIE LANCASHIRE.

Jagger's lips *n.* [1970s+] chips. [from the rock star Mick Jagger (b.1943) whose protuberant lips have always occasioned comment]

Jamaica rum *n.* [20C] a thumb.

jam duff *n.* [20C] a male homosexual. [*jam duff* = puff; possibly underpinned by the image of the soft, sticky pudding]

James Hunt *n.* [20C] audacity, cheek. [*James Hunt* = front; from the UK motor racing champion James Hunt (1947–93), notorious (and much envied) for a somewhat rackety lifestyle]

jam (jar) *n.* [1930s+] a motor-car.

jammy dodger *n.* [1990s+] an act of sexual intercourse. [*jammy dodger* = roger]

jam pies *n.* [1990s+] the eyes.

jam roll *n.* [1970s+] (*UK prison*) **1** parole. **2** the dole.

jam tart *n.* **1** [mid–late 19C] a mart (orig. in the context of the Stock Exchange). **2** [19C+] a sweetheart, a girlfriend.

3 [20C] a heart, whether anatomically or as a card suit.

Jane Russell *n.* [20C] a mussel. [from the US film star Jane Russell (b.1921)]

Jane Shore *n.* [mid–late 19C] **1** the floor. **2** a prostitute. [**2** *Jane Shore* = whore; from Jane Shore (d.1527), mistress of Edward IV]

janet *n.* [1980s+] (*drugs*) a quarter ounce of cannabis. [*janet street-porter* = quarter; from the UK media personality Janet Street-Porter (b.1944)]

jar of jam *n.* **1** [20C] a pram. **2** [1930s] a tram.

J. Arthur *n.* [1940s+] **1** a bank. **2** an act of masturbation. **3** a fool. [**2** *J. Arthur Rank* = wank; **3** is an ext. use of **2**; *see* ARTHUR]

Jasper Carrott *n.* [1990s+] a parrot. [from the UK comedian Jasper Carrott (b.1945)]

jax *n. see* JACK'S (ALIVE).

J. Carroll Naish *n.* [1970s] an act of urination. [*J. Carroll Naish* = slash; from the US actor J. Carroll Naish (1900–73)]

Jean-Claude (Van Damme) *n.* [1990s+] ham. [from the Belgian action-film star Jean-Claude Van Damme (b.1961); the reference is to food, but critics might suggest it refers to the quality of his performances]

jeckle *adj.* [1990s+] fake, counterfeit, forged. [JEKYLL AND HYDE]

jeer *n. see* JERE.

Jekyll and Hyde *adj.* [1920s+] crooked, fake, spurious, counterfeit. [*Jekyll and Hyde* = snide; from the novella *Dr Jekyll and Mr Hyde* (1886) by Robert Louis Stevenson]

Jekyll and Hydes *n.* [20C] (*Aus.*) trousers. [*Jekyll and Hydes* = strides; *see* JEKYLL AND HYDE]

jellied eels *n.* [20C] transport. [*jellied eels* = wheels]

Jem Mace *n.* [20C] face. [from the prize-fighter Jem Mace (1831–1910)]

Jemmy O'Goblin (*also* **Jimmy O'Goblin**) *n.* [mid-19C+] (*orig. theatre*) **1** a sovereign. **2** (*pl.*) a generic term for money. [**2** *Jemmy O'Goblins* = sovereigns]

Jennie Lee (*also* **Jenny Lea**) *n.* [20C] **1** a flea. **2** a key. **3** tea.

Jenny Hills *n.* [late 19C] pills, i.e drugs. [from the UK music-hall star Jenny Hill (1851–96)]

Jenny Lea *n. see* JENNIE LEE.

Jenny Lind *n.* [20C] wind, either in the context of weather or the stomach; hence *Jenny Lindy* windy. [from the Swedish soprano Jenny Lind (1820–87)]

Jenny Linda (*also* **Jenny Linder**) *n.* [mid-19C] a window. [*see* JENNY LIND; note Cockney pronunciation of window as *winder*]

Jenny Linder *n. see* JENNY LINDA.

Jenny Riddle *n. see* JIMMY RIDDLE.

Jenny Wren *n.* [20C] Ben Truman beer.

jere (*also* **jeer**) *n.* [20C] a homosexual. [*jere* = queer]

jeremiah *n.* [1930s] a fire.

Jeremy Beadle *n.* [20C] irritation, annoyance. [*Jeremy Beadle* = the needle; from the UK TV entertainer Jeremy Beadle (b.1948)]

jerry *v* **1** [mid–late 19C] to tumble, i.e. to shake about. **2** [late 19C+] to understand, to work out, to recognize, to discern. [probably from JERRYCUMUMBLE]

jerrycumumble (*also* **jerrymumble**) *v.* [late 18C–19C] **1** to tumble, i.e. to shake about. **2** to understand, to work out. [**2** *jerrycumumble* = tumble]

jerry-diddle *n.* [late 19C+] a violin. [*jerry-diddle* = fiddle]

Jerry McGinn *n.* [1940s] (*US*) the chin.

jerrymumble *v. see* JERRYCUMUMBLE.

Jerry O'Gorman *n.* [20C] a Mormon.

Jerry Riddle *n.* [mid-19C] an act of urination. [*Jerry Riddle* = piddle]

Jerry Rumble *v.* [1900s] (*N.Z.*) to discover, to understand. [*Jerry Rumble* = tumble]

Jersey city *n.* [1950s–60s] (*US*) a female breast. [*Jersey city* = titty]

jerseys *n.* [1960s+] the female breasts. [*see* JERSEY CITY]

Jerusalem artichoke *n.* [20C] a donkey. [*Jerusalem artichoke* = moke (sl. 'donkey'); note also the synonymous standard sl. *Jerusalem cuckoo*; both terms refer to Christ's arrival in that city on a donkey]

Odds On

five to two	Jew
hundred to eight	plate
hundred to thirty	dirty
six to four	whore
ten to two	Jew

Jew chum *n.* [1940s] (*US*) a tramp. [*Jew chum* = bum]

jiggle and jog *n.* [1970s] (*derog.*) *a* Frenchman. [*jiggle and jog* = frog]

Jim Britts *n. see* JIMMY BRITTS.

Jim Brown *n.* [late 19C+] the West End of London. [*Jim Brown* = town]

Jim Crow *n.* [mid-19C] a street clown. [*Jim Crow* = saltimbanco; from an early-19C Kentucky plantation song with the chorus 'Jump Jim Crow' and the 'black face' entertainer Thomas Dartmouth Rice (1808–60), who first performed it in Louisville in 1828; its popularity in the UK followed Rice's appearance at the Adelphi theatre in 1836, in a 'farcical Burletta' entitled 'A Flight to America, or, Twelve Hours in New York']

Jim Gerald *n.* [20C] (*Aus.*) the *Herald* newspaper.

jimmies *n. see* JIMMY BRITTS.

Jimmy Boyle *n.* [1990s+] (*drugs*) kitchen foil, as used for smoking heroin or to 'chase the dragon'. [from the ex-prisoner and writer Jimmy Boyle (b.1944)]

Jimmy Britts (*also* **Jim Britts, jimmies**) *n.* [1940s+] (*orig. Aus.*) **1** diarrhoea. **2** (*fig.*) nerves, fears. [*Jimmy Britts* = the shits; from the US-born boxer Jimmy Britt (1879–1940), who toured Australia during WWI]

Jimmy Dancer *n.* [20C] (*Aus.*) cancer.

Jimmy Grant *n.* [mid-19C–1940s] (*Aus./N.Z./S Afr.*) an immigrant.

Jimmy Hicks *n. see* JIMMY HIX.

Jimmy Hills *n.* [1970s+] pills, i.e. drugs. [from the UK TV football pundit Jimmy Hill (b.1928)]

Jimmy Hix (*also* **Jimmy Hicks**) *n.* **1** [1910s+] (*US gambling*) in craps dice, six points. **2** [1940s–50s] (*UK Und.*) an injection of narcotics. [**2** *Jimmy Hix* = fix]

Jimmy Hope *n.* [1910s+] (*US prison*) soap.

Jimmy Lee *n.* [20C] (*Aus.*) tea. [var. on ROSIE (LEA)]

Jimmy Logie *n.* [1950s] a piece of nasal mucus. [*Jimmy Logie* = bogey; from the Scottish footballer Jimmy Logie (1919–84)]

Jimmy Mason *n.* [20C] a basin.

Jimmy Nail *n.* [1990s+] **1** mail. **2** a sale. [from the UK actor and singer Jimmy Nail (b.1954)]

Jimmy Nail *adj.* [1990s+] stale. [*see* JIMMY NAIL *n.*]

Jimmy O'Goblin *n. see* JEMMY O'GOBLIN.

Jimmy Prescott *n*. [mid–late 19C] a waistcoat [var. on CHARLIE PRESCOTT]

Jimmy Riddle (*also* **Jenny Riddle**) *n*. [1930s+] an act of urination. [*Jimmy Riddle* = piddle]

Jimmy Rollocks *n*. [20C] the testicles. [*Jimmy Rollocks* = bollocks]

Jimmy Skinner (*also* **Jim Skinner**, **Joe Skinner**, **Johnny Skinner**) *n*. [20C] dinner.

Jimmy Wilde *n*. [1920s–40s] mild beer. [from the former world flyweight boxing champion Jimmy Wilde (1892–1969)]

Jimmy Young *n*. [20C] **1** a bribe. **2** the tongue. [**1** *Jimmy Young* = bung; from the singer turned radio personality Jimmy Young (b.1923)]

Jim Skinner *n*. *see* JIMMY SKINNER.

joanna *n*. [mid-19C+] a piano. [the single 19C citation is spelt *joano*; *joanna* appears *c*.1910]

Joan of Arc *n*. **1** [20C] a park. **2** [20C] a lark, a situation, as in *sod this for a Joan of Arc*. **3** [1940s–50s] (*Aus.*) a shark. [from the French national heroine Joan of Arc (*c*.1412–31)]

jockey's whip *n*. [1940s–60s] **1** a bed, a sleep. **2** (*pl.*) chips. [**1** *jockey's whip* = kip]

jodrell *n*.[1] [1950s+] an act of masturbation. [*jodrell bank* = wank; from the home of UK astronomy Jodrell Bank, near Manchester]

jodrell *n.*[2] [1950s+] a tired-out old prostitute. [*jodrell banker* = wanker, i.e. one who masturbates another; *see* JODRELL *n.*[1]]

joe *n.* [1960s+] (*N.Z.*) a general term of abuse. [JOE HUNT]

Joe Baxi *n.* [20C] a taxi. [from the US heavyweight boxer Joe Baksi (*fl.*1940s)]

Joe (Blake) *n.*[1] **1** [late 19C+] cake. **2** [20C] (*gambling*) a stake.

Joe (Blake) *n.*[2] [1940s+] (*Aus.*) **1** a snake. **2** a steak.

Joe Blakes *n.* (*Aus./N.Z.*) [late 19C+] delirium tremens; hence *out the joe* passed out drunk. [*Joe Blakes* = the shakes; a later meaning (1940s+) was 'snakes', i.e. the hallucinations experienced during delirium tremens]

Joe Bonce *n.* [1930s+] a pimp [*Joe Bonce* = ponce]

Joe Brown *n.* [1960s+] a town.

Joe Buck *n.* [1930s+] (*Aus.*) sexual intercourse. [*Joe Buck* = fuck]

Joe Daki *n.* [1970s+] (*derog.*) a British Asian. [*Joe Daki* = paki]

Joe Erk *n.* [20C] a fool, a general term of abuse. [*Joe Erk* = BERK; but note RAF sl. *erk* a semi-derog. term for an air mechanic]

Joe Goss *n.* [20C] (*Aus./US*) **1** the boss. **2** a policeman. [possibly from Joe Goss, a late-19C US prize-fighter; **2** is an ext. use of **1**]

Joe (Gurr) *n.* [20C] prison. [*Joe Gurr* = stir]

Joe Hoke *n. see* JOE ROKE.

Joe Hook (*also* **Joe Rook**) *n*. **1** [1930s] a criminal, a villain. **2** [1930s+] a book. [**1** *Joe Hook* = crook]

Joe Hope *n*. [20C] (*Aus.*) soap.

Joe Hunt *n*. [20C] **1** a fool. **2** a general derog. term. [*Joe Hunt* = cunt; **1** usually abbreviated to JOEY; **2** never truncated]

Joe Loss *n*. [20C] an infinitesimal amount, nothing whatsoever, as in *not give a Joe Loss* not care at all. [*Joe Loss* = toss; from the UK bandleader Joe Loss (1909–90)]

Joe MacBride *n*. [20C] sexual intercourse. [*Joe MacBride* = ride]

Joe Marks *n*. [1930s–40s] (*Aus.*) sharks.

Joe Maxi *n*. [1990s+] (*Irish*) a taxi. [var. on JOE BAXI]

Joe Morgan *n*. [1940s] (*Aus.*) an organ.

Joe O'Gorman *n*. [late 19C+] a foreman.

Joe Rocks *n*. [20C] (*Aus.*) socks.

Joe Roke (*also* **Joe Hoke**) *n*. [late 19C+] (*US*) smoke.

Joe Ronce (*also* **Johnny Ronce**) *n*. [1930s+] a pimp. [*Joe Ronce* = ponce]

Joe Rook *n. see* JOE HOOK.

Joe Rookie *n*. [20C] a bookmaker. [*Joe Rookie* = bookie; perhaps underpinned by the negative image of a rook]

Joe Rourke *n*. [20C] a fork.

joes *n.* [1910s+] **1** (*Aus.*) a fit of depression. **2** an attack of nerves. [JOE BLAKES]

Joe Savage *n.* [mid-19C] a cabbage.

Joe Skinner *n. see* JIMMY SKINNER.

Joe Soap *n.* [1930s+] **1** a self-description, as in *joe soap here* ... **2** any man. **3** a fool, a gullible individual. [*Joe Soap* = dope]

Joe Strummer *adj.* [20C] unpleasant, disappointing. [*Joe Strummer* = bummer; from the guitarist and singer Joe Strummer (b.1952), a member of the early punk band The Clash (1977–86)]

joey *n.* [20C] a weakling, a foolish, inadequate person. [JOE HUNT]

John (Bull) *n.* [20C] **1** an arrest. **2** a seduction, or the hope of it; hence *go out on the John Bull* to go out looking for sex. [*John Bull* = pull]

John Bull *adj.* [1960s+] (*Aus.*) drunk. [*John Bull* = full]

John Cleese *n.* [1970s+] cheese. [from the UK actor and comedian John Cleese (b.1939)]

John Dillon *n.* [1930s+] (*N.Z.*) a shilling (five pence).

John Hop (*also* **Johnny Hop**) *n.* [1910s+] a policeman. [*John Hop* = cop]

Johnny Bliss *n.* [20C] (*Aus.*) an act of urination. [*Johnny Bliss* = piss]

Johnny Cash *n.* [1960s+] **1** an act of urination. **2** (*Aus.*)

hashish. [*Johnny Cash* = **1** slash **2** hash; from the US country singer Johnny Cash (b.1932)]

Johnny Cotton *adj.* [20C] rotten.

Johnny Giles *n. see* FARMER GILES.

Johnny Hop *n. see* JOHN HOP.

Johnny Hopper *n.* [1910s+] a policeman. [*Johnny Hopper* = copper]

Johnny Horner *n.* [late 19C+] the corner, esp. a pub on a corner.

Johnny O'Brien (*also* **Jack O'Brien**) *n.* [1930s–50s] (*US tramp*) the railway. [*Johnny O'Brien* = iron (used metonymically)]

Johnny Rann *n.* [20C] food. [*Johnny Rann* = scran]

Johnny Raper *n.* [20C] (*Aus.*) a newspaper.

Johnny Raw *n.* [20C] (*US*) **1** a saw. **2** the jaw. [note standard sl. *Johnny Raw* a novice]

Johnny Ronce *n. see* JOE RONCE.

Johnny Rousers *n. see* JOHNNY ROWSERS.

Johnny Rowsers (*also* **Johnny Rousers**) *n.* [20C] (*US*) trousers.

Johnny Russell *n.* [late 19C] (*Aus.*) bustle, hustle, esp. in the phrase *on the Johnny Russell* bustling about. [probably from the UK politician Lord John Russell (1792–1878)]

Johnny Rutter *n.* [late 19C–1930s] butter.

Johnny Skinner *n. see* JIMMY SKINNER.

Johnny Walker *n.* [20C] **1** a talker, i.e. a garrulous person. **2** an informer. [**2** = talker, i.e. one who 'talks' to the police]

John O'Groat *n.* [20C] a coat. [from John O'Groats, the most northerly point of the British mainland]

John O'Groats *n.* [20C] sexual satisfaction. [*John O'Groats* = oats; *see* JOHN O'GROAT]

John Prescott *n.* [1980s+] a waistcoat. [var. on CHARLIE PRESCOTT; from the UK Labour politician John Prescott (b.1938)]

John Selwyn *n.* [1980s] **1** an unpleasant reaction to drugs. **2** any unpleasant experience or person. [*John Selwyn Gummer* = bummer; from the UK Conservative politician John Selwyn Gummer (b.1939)]

John Wayne *n.* [1950s+] a train. [from the US film star John Wayne (1907–79)]

joint of beef *n.* [20C] the chief, i.e. the boss.

jolly for polly *adj.* [20C] sexually available. [*jolly* + *polly* = lolly, i.e. the money paid to ensure sexual availability]

jolly joker *n.* [20C] a poker.

jolly roger *n.* [20C] a lodger. [underpinned by the amorous lodger who wishes to *roger* his landlady]

jolly rousers *n.* [20C] trousers.

Jolson story *n.* [1970s] the penis. [*Jolson story* = corie (sl. 'penis'); from *The Jolson Story* (1946), a biopic of the singer Al Jolson (1886–1950)]

jonah's whale *n.* [late 19C–1910s] a tail. [from the biblical story (Jonah i–ii)]

Jonathan Ross *n.* [1980s+] **1** a drink, specifically beer. **2** an infinitesimal amount, nothing whatsoever, as in *not give a Jonathon Ross* not care at all. [*Jonathan Ross* = **1** toss (as in *toss it back*) **2** toss; from the UK TV personality Jonathan Ross (b.1960)]

Joynson-Hicks *n.* [1920s] (*bingo*) the number six. [from the right-wing 1920s Home Secretary Sir William Joynson-Hicks (1865–1932)]

joy of my life *n.* [19C] a wife.

Judge Dread *n. see* JUDGE DREDD.

Judge Dredd (*also* **Judge Dread**) *n.* [1990s+] the head. [from the cartoon character Judge Dredd created in the comic *2000AD*]

Judi Dench *n.* [1990s+] a stench, a stink. [from the UK actress Dame Judi Dench (b.1934)]

judy and punch *n.* [20C] lunch. [from the age-old children's entertainment 'Punch and Judy']

jug and pail *n.* [20C] jail. [possibly referring to the limited washing facilities on offer in Britain's mainly Victorian jails]

juicy fruit *n.* [1950s+] (*Aus.*) sexual intercourse. [*juicy fruit* = root]

Julian Clary *n.* [1990s+] a male homosexual. [*Julian Clary* = fairy; from the outrageously camp UK gay entertainer Julian Clary (b.1959)]

Julian Clary *adj.* [1990s+] showy, ostentatious. [*Julian Clary* = lairy; *see* JULIAN CLARY *n.*]

Julius Caesar *n.* [20C] **1** a 'cheesecutter' cap. **2** a freezer. [**1** *Julius Caesar* = cheeser; from the Roman general and dictator Julius Caesar (100–44 BC)]

jumbo's trunk *adj.* [late 19C] drunk. [var. on ELEPHANT'S (TRUNK); from Jumbo, the celebrated elephant of the Regent's Park Zoo, sold to Barnum and Bailey's Circus in 1881; the Zoo had opened in 1828 and Jumbo and a female, Alice, arrived in 1863]

jumping jack *n.* [20C] in snooker, the black ball.

jungle Jim *n.* [1950s] a swim [from the late-1940s–early-1950s US TV series *Jungle Jim*, starring Johnny 'Tarzan' Weismuller (1904–1984); before turning to acting Weismuller was a highly successful Olympic swimmer]

just as I feared *n.* [20C] a beard. [from the Edward Lear limerick (1846): 'There was an old man with a beard / Who said "It is just as I feared! / Two owls and a hen / Four larks and a wren / Have all built their nests in my beard"']

k

kanga *n.*[1] [1950s+] (*Aus.*) **1** money. **2** a prison warder. [*kangaroo* = **1** screw (sl. 'wage') **2** screw]

kanga (*also* **kangar**) *n.*[2] [1940s–50s] (*UK prison*) chewing tobacco. [*kangaroo* = chew]

kangar *n. see* KANGA *n.*[2].

kangaroo *n.* **1** [1920s+] a prison warder. **2** [20C] a Jew. [**1** *kangaroo* = screw]

kate and sidney (*also* **kate and sydney**) *n.* [20C] steak and kidney.

kate and sydney *n. see* KATE AND SIDNEY.

Kate Carney (*also* **Kate Karney**) *n.* [late 19C+] the UK army. [from the music-hall singing star Kate Carney (1869–1950)]

Kate Karney *n. see* KATE CARNEY.

Kate Moss *n.* [1990s+] an infinitesimal amount, nothing whatsoever, as in *not give a Kate Moss* not care at all. [*Kate Moss* = toss; from the UK supermodel Kate Moss (b.1974)]

Kate Moss *v.* [1990s+] to toss, i.e. to throw. [*see* KATE MOSS *n.*]

Katharine Docks *n.* [20C] socks. [from the St Katharine's

Docks, London, built by Thomas Telford and opened in 1828; the docks closed in 1968 and the area has been redeveloped]

Kathleen Mavourneen *n.* [20C] (*Aus.*) the morning. [from the once popular Irish song 'Kathleen Mavourneen']

Keith Moon *n.* [20C] an eccentric, a loon. [from the notably zany rock drummer Keith Moon (1947–78)]

Kelly Ned *n.* [20C] (*Aus.*) the head. [from the bushranger Ned Kelly (1855–80)]

kembla (grange) *n.* [1950s+] (*Aus.*) small change.

Ken Dodd *n.* [20C] a large roll of banknotes. [*Ken Dodd* = wad; from the UK comedian Ken Dodd (b.1931); *see* KNOTTY ASH]

Ken Dodds *n.* [20C] the testicles. [*Ken Dodds* = cods; *see* KEN DODD]

kennedy rot *n.* [20C] (*Aus.*) a sot. [from the Standard Aus. English *Kennedy rot* a disease similar to scurvy]

Kennington Lane *n.* [20C] pain. [from Kennington Lane, London SE11]

Kentish Town *n.* [20C] a penny. [*Kentish Town* = brown (19C sl. 'halfpenny', 'copper'); from Kentish Town, north London]

Kentucky horn *n.* [1940s–50s] (*US*) corn whisky. [the reference is to the state's production of both legal and illicit whisky]

kerb and gutter *n.* [20C] (*Aus.*) butter.

Kermit the Frog *n.* [1970s] **1** a lavatory. **2** sexual caressing, stopping short of intercourse. [*Kermit the Frog* = **1** bog **2** snog; from the character Kermit the Frog, who appeared in *The Muppet Show* (1976–81)]

kerried *adj.* [1970s+] exhausted, tired out. [*kerry packered* = knackered; from the Aus. media magnate Kerry Packer (b.1937)]

kettle *n.* [20C] a nickname for a person called Robert. [*kettle on a hob* = Bob]

kettle (on a hob) *n.* [late 19C+] a shilling (five pence). [*kettle on a hob* = bob]

kewpie *n.* [1990s+] (*Aus.*) a prostitute. [*kewpie doll* = moll; the kewpie doll is a chubby doll with a curl or topknot on its head, from a design by R.C. O'Neill (1874–1944)]

Keystone cop *n.* [20C] a chop (pork, beef etc.). [from the silent films' comedy team the Keystone Cops, created at Mack Sennett's Keystone Studios and appearing in many films between 1912–20]

Khyber (Pass) *n.* **1** [late 19C] a glass. **2** [1940s+] the buttocks. [**2** *Khyber Pass* = arse; from the Khyber Pass, the chief pass in the Hindu Kush mountains between Afghanistan and north-west Pakistan]

kick and prance *n.* [20C] a dance.

kid blister *n.* [20C] (*Aus.*) a sister. [note sl. *blister* an objectionable person]

Kid Creole *n.* [1980s+] the dole. [from the 1980s pop group Kid Creole and The Coconuts]

kidney pies *n.* [1920s–40s] (*US*) the eyes.

kidney punch *n.* [20C] lunch, esp. in the phrase *a bit of kidney*.

kidstakes! *excl.* [1910s+] (*Aus./N.Z.*) nonsense! rubbish! 'fiddlesticks!'. [*kidstake* − fake, or a fig. use of *kid* a child + *stake* a wager]

kilkenny *n.* [late 19C+] a penny.

Kilkenny cats *adj.* [20C] stupid, foolish, silly. [*Kilkenny cats* = bats; from the fabled Kilkenny cats, a pair of cats who fought until only their tails remained]

King Canutes *n.* [mid-19C+] boots. [from King Canute (Cnut) (*c.*955–1035), best known for the probably apocryphal tale of his failed attempt to hold back the tides]

king death *n.* [20C] bad breath.

king dick *n.* [late 19C+] a brick.

king dick *adj.* [20C] stupid, dull. [*king dick* = thick]

king dickie *n.* [late19C+] a bricklayer. [*king dickie* = brickie]

kingdom come *n.* **1** [20C] rum. **2** [1970s] the buttocks. [**2** *kingdom come* = bum]

King Farouk *n.* [1950s] a book. [from the last king of Egypt, Farouk (1920–65), celebrated for his excessive lifestyle]

King Lear *n.* **1** [late 19C+] an ear. **2** [20C] a male homosexual. [**2** *King Lear* = queer]

King of Spain *n.* [20C] (*Aus.*) rain. [possibly linked to the elocution couplet 'The rain in Spain falls mainly on the plain']

kings (and queens) *n.* [20C] baked beans; hence *kings on holy ghost* baked beans on toast. [*see* HOLY GHOST]

king's proctor *n.* [20C] a doctor.

kipper and bloater *n.* [1970s] **1** a motor-car. **2** a photo. [**1** *kipper and bloater* = motor]

kipper and plaice *n.* [20C] the face.

kippers *n.* [20C] (a pair of) slippers.

kisky *adj.* [mid-19C] drunk, tipsy. [*kisky* = whisky or Romani *kushto* feeling good or happy]

kiss and cuddle *n.* [20C] a muddle.

kiss me hardy *n.* [20C] a measure of Bacardi rum. [from the alleged last words of Admiral Horatio Nelson (1758–1805), although an alternative version suggests they were 'Thank God I have done my duty']

kiss-me-quick *n.* [20C] **1** the penis. **2** a fool. [*kiss-me-quick* = prick]

kiss of life *n.* [20C] a wife.

kitchen range *n.* [20C] small change.

kitchen sink *n.* [20C] **1** a stink. **2** (*Aus.*) a drink. **3** (*derog.*) a Chinese person. [**3** *kitchen sink* = chink]

kitchen stoves *n.* [20C] (*Aus.*) cloves.

kit-kat *n.* [1960s+] a fool, a general term of abuse. [*kit-kat* = prat]

knife and fork *n.* [20C] pork.

knobbly-knee *n.* [20C] a key.

knocker and knob *n.* [20C] a job.

knock-me (*also* **knock-me-silly**) *n.* [20C] (*Aus.*) a billy (used to boil water).

knock-me-silly *n. see* KNOCK-ME.

knock on/at the door *n.* [20C] (*bingo*) the number four.

knotty ash *n.* [1980s] cash. [from Knotty Ash, the fictional residence of the comedian Ken Dodd, as used in his stand-up routines; the rhyme is underpinned by a reference to the comedian's one-time difficulties with the Inland Revenue; see KEN DODD]

kryptonite *n.* [2000s] a web site. [in Superman comics green kryptonite is the one element that can defeat the 'Man of Steel']

kung fu fighter *n.* [1990s+] a cigarette lighter.

Kuwaiti tanker *n.* [1990s+] **1** a masturbator. **2** a general term of abuse. [*Kuwaiti tanker* = wanker]

1

lace curtain *n.* [20C] beer, orig. specifically Burton's beer. [*lace curtain* = Burton]

la-di-dah *n.* [1970s] **1** a car. **2** a cigar.

Lady Berkeley *n.* [19C] the vagina. [from BERKELEY HUNT]

lady from Bristol *n.* [20C] (*Aus.*) a pistol.

Lady Godiva *n.* [20C] five pounds (sterling), a five-pound note. [*Lady Godiva* = fiver; from Lady Godiva (*c.*1040– 1080), who allegedly rode naked through the streets of Coventry in an attempt to persuade her husband Leofric to lower taxes on the citizenry]

lakes (of Killarney) *adj.* [20C] **1** mad, eccentric. **2** two-faced, untrustworthy. [*lakes of Killarney* = **1** barmy **2** carney (sl. 'hypocritical talk')]

Lal Brough (*also* **lally**) *n.* [1900s] snuff. [*Lal* is a diminutive of *Alice*; the image is of an old lady, 'Lal Brough', taking snuff]

lally *n. see* LAL BROUGH.

Lambeth Walk *n.* [20C] the chalk used in billiards. [from the 19C Lambeth Walk market, London SE11, but more recently the song-cum-dance 'Doing the Lambeth Walk', popularized by Lupino Lane in the 1937 musical *Me and My Gal*]

◆◆◆◆◆◆◆◆◆◆◆◆◆◆◆◆◆◆◆◆◆◆◆◆◆◆◆◆◆◆◆◆◆◆◆◆◆◆

Children's Hour

Andy Pandy	brandy
Bugs Bunny	money
george and zippy	nippy
Gonzo (the Great)	state
jackanory	story
Kermit the Frog	bog/snog
Mickey Mouse	house/Scouse
Minnie Mouse	house
Miss Piggy	ciggie
Pinky and Perky	turkey
Porky Pig	big
Rupert Bears	shares
Scooby Doo	screw
teletubby	hubby
Tom and Jerry	merry

◆◆

lamb fry *n.* [20C] (*US*) a tie. [*see* LAMB'S FRY]

lamb's fry *n.* [20C] (*Aus.*) **1** a necktie. **2** (*usu. pl.*) an eye. [from the Standard English *lamb's fry* lamb's testicles, as fried and eaten]

lame duck *n.* [20C] sexual intercourse. [*lame duck* = fuck; from the Stock Exchange sl. *lame duck* one who cannot meet his financial engagements, a defaulter, thus in politics an office-holder who is not, or cannot be, re-elected]

Lancashire lass *n.* [late 19C+] a drinking glass.

Lancashire lasses *n.* [20C] glasses, i.e. spectacles.

land of hope *n.* [20C] soap.

Lane Cove *n.* [20C] (*Aus.*) a stove. [from the town and National Park Lane Cove, near Sydney, Australia]

last card of the pack *n.* **1** [mid-19C–1910s] the back. **2** [20C] dismissal from employment. [**2** *last card of the pack* = the sack]

lath and plaster *n.* [mid-19C] a master, i.e. an employer.

laugh and joke *n.* [late 19C–1950s] a smoke.

laugh and titter *n.* [20C] a pint of beer. [*laugh and titter* = bitter]

laughs and smiles *n.* [20C] (*Aus.*) haemorrhoids. [*laughs and smiles* = piles]

Laurel and Hardy *n.* [20C] a Bacardi (rum). [from the comedians Stan Laurel (1890–1965) and Oliver Hardy (1892–1957)]

lay me in the gutter *n.* [1910s–20s] butter.

l.b.w. *n. see* LEG BEFORE WICKET.

leaky bladder *n.* [20C] a stepladder.

lean and fat *n.* [mid-19C] a hat.

lean and linger (*also* **long and linger**) *n*. [1920s–30s] (*US*) a finger.

lean and lurch *n*. [mid-19C] a church.

leaning fat *n*. [20C] (*US*) a hat.

Lee Marvin *adj*. [1960s+] starving. [from the US film star Lee Marvin (1924–87)]

Lee Van (Cleef) *n*. [1960s+] beef. [from the US film star Lee Van Cleef (1925–89)]

left and right *n*. [late 19C+] a fight. [referring to the punches with the left and right hands]

left in the lurch *n*. [late 19C+] a church.

leg before wicket (*also* **l.b.w.**) *n*. [20C] a ticket, both lit. and fig.; hence *not the l.b.w.* 'not the ticket'. [usu. in its abbreviated form; out 'leg before wicket' is one of the more complex forms of dismissing a batsman in cricket]

leg of beef *n*. [20C] a thief.

leg of mutton *n*. [20C] a button.

leg of pork *n*. [20C] a piece of chalk.

Leicester (Square) *n*. [20C] a chair. [from Leicester Square, London W1, a centre of popular entertainment for several centuries]

leisure hours *n*. [late 19C] flowers.

lemon *adj*. [1990s+] ostentatious. [*lemon squash* = flash; differing pronunciation means that the correspondence lies more in the spelling than in the rhyme]

lemon and dash *n.* [1950s+] a public lavatory. [*lemon and dash* = wash/slash]

lemon and lime *n.* [20C] time.

lemon (curd) *n.* [1960s+] **1** a piece of excrement. **2** a general term of abuse. **3** a woman. [*lemon curd* = **1, 2** turd **3** bird]

lemon (drop) *n.* [20C] a policeman. [*lemon drop* = cop]

lemon (flavour) *n.* [20C] a favour.

lemon squash *n.* [20C] (*Aus.*) a wash.

lemon-squeezer *n.* [1970s+] a man. [*lemon-squeezer* = geezer]

lemon-squeezy *adj.* [20C] easy. [from the rhyme 'Easy-peasy, lemon-squeezy']

lemon tea *n.* [20C] an act of urination. [*lemon tea* = pee/wee; but note the colour of both urine and weak tea]

Len Hutton *n.* [20C] a button. [from the cricketer Len Hutton (1916–90)]

lenny the lion *n.* [1950s–60s] a male homosexual. [*lenny the lion* = IRON (HOOF)]

Leo Sayer *n.* [1990s+] an all-day drinking session. [*Leo Sayer* = all-dayer; from the pop star Leo Sayer (b.1948)]

leslie *n.* [1990s+] the vagina. [*leslie ash* = gash; from the popular TV actress Leslie Ash (b.1960)]

let's rejoice *n.* [20C] (*Aus.*) the voice.

levy *v.* [20C] to masturbate. [*levy and frank* = wank; from the former London restaurateurs Levy and Frank]

Lewis and Witties *n.* [1940s–50s] (*Aus.*) the female breasts. [*Lewis and Witties* = titties; from the well-known Melbourne department store Lewis and Witty]

life and death *n.* [20C] breath.

Liffey water *n.* [late 19C+] porter. [the original reference was to Guinness, brewed near the River Liffey in Dublin]

light and dark *n.* [late 19C+] a park.

light of love *n.* [1940s–50s] (*UK prison*) a prison governor. [*light of love* = gov]

Lilley and Skinner *n.* [20C] **1** dinner. **2** a beginner. [from the London shoe shop Lilley and Skinner]

Lillian Gish *n.* [1920s+] (*Aus.*) **1** a dish. **2** a fish. [from the film star Lillian Gish (1899–1993)]

Lillian Gished *adj.* [20C] drunk. [*Lillian Gished* = pissed; *see* LILLIAN GISH; note Scots pronunciation of pissed as *pished*]

lily of lagoona *n.* [20C] (*Aus.*) **1** a schooner, a tall beer glass. **2** beer. [**2** *lily of lagoona* = schooner (used metonymically); from the popular song 'Lily of Laguna']

Limehouse Cut *n.* [20C] a paunch. [*Limehouse Cut* = gut; from Limehouse Cut, a 1½-mile-long canal linking the Regent's Canal (where it meets the Thames) to the Lee Navigation, running north into Hertfordshire]

Lincoln's Inn *n.* **1** [mid-19C+] a hand. **2** [late 19C] a five-pound note. **3** [late 19C+] gin. [*Lincoln's Inn* = **1** fin (sl. 'hand') **2** fin (sl. 'five-pound note'); from Lincoln's Inn, London WC2, one of London's four 'inns' of court, originally designed for the lodging of law students, now home to firms of solicitors and barristers' chambers]

linen (*also* **linen-draper**) *n.* [mid-19C+] a newspaper. [*linen-draper* = newspaper]

linen-draper *n. see* LINEN.

Lionel Bart *n.* [1960s] a breaking of wind. [*Lionel Bart* = fart; from the composer Lionel Bart (1930–99)]

Lionel Blair *n.* [1970s+] a chair. [from the entertainer Lionel Blair (b.1931)]

Lionel Blairs *n.* [1970s+] flared trousers. [*Lionel Blairs* = flares; *see* LIONEL BLAIR]

lion's lair *n.* [20C] a chair.

lion's roar *n.* [20C] a snore.

lisp and stutter *n.* [20C] (*Aus.*) butter.

little and large *n.* [20C] margarine. [*little and large* = marge]

Little Bo-Peep *n.* [late 19C+] sleep (*see* BO-PEEP).

little boy blue *n.* [20C] a prison warder. [*little boy blue* = screw; from the usual blue uniform plus the nursery rhyme 'Little Boy Blue']

little brown jug *n.* [20C] **1** an electric plug. **2** a bath plug. **3** a tampon. [**3** *little brown jug* = plug (ext. use); underpinned by the song 'Little Brown Jug']

little grey home in the west *n*. [1910s–50s] a vest. [from the popular Irish ballad 'Little Grey Home in the West']

Little Miss Muffet *v*. [20C] to get rid of, to ignore. [*Little Miss Muffet* = stuff it; from the nursery rhyme 'Little Miss Muffet']

Little Nell *n*. [20C] a bell, usu. a doorbell. [from the character Little Nell in Dickens's *Old Curiosity Shop* (1841), a maudlin figure whose mawkish death, as penned by Dickens, provoked Oscar Wilde's comment, 'One must have a heart of stone to read the death of Little Nell without laughing']

little peter *n*. [20C] a gas or electricity meter. [note sl. *peter* a safe]

little red ridings *n*. [1950s–60s] stolen goods. [*little red riding hoods* = stolen goods; from the fairy tale of Little Red Riding Hood]

little titch *n*. [20C] an itch; hence *little titchy* itchy. [from the music-hall comedian Harry Relph, nicknamed 'Little Titch' (1868–1928)]

live eels *n*. [mid-19C] fields.

L.K. Clark (*also* **Elkie Clark**) *n*. [20C] the mark, i.e. the beginning.

lloyd (*also* **Harold Lloyd**) *n*. [1910s+] a piece of celluloid used for picking Yale locks. [*Harold Lloyd* = loid (sl. 'piece of celluloid or plastic for picking locks'); from the silent-film star Harold Lloyd (1893–1971)]

Lloyd's (List) *adj*. [20C] drunk. [*Lloyd's List* = pissed; from

Lloyd's List, a news and information sheet published by the Lloyds conglomerate of insurance brokers, based in London]

load of hay *n*. [mid-19C] a day.

loaf (of bread) *n*. [1910s+] a head, esp. brains, intelligence; hence *use one's loaf* to act sensibly, often as imperative *use your loaf!*

loaf of bread *adj*. [1930s] dead.

locket *n. see* LUCY LOCKET.

locus *v*. [mid–late 19C] **1** to stupefy with drink; hence *locus away* to steal something when the victim is drunk. **2** to trick, to fool. **3** to render a victim unconscious with chloroform, usu. to rob them or carry them aboard a ship in need of crew. [*locus* = hocus, or from *locus(-ale)* an intoxicating drink made of the scum of the sugar cane]

lollipop *n*.[1] [20C] a monetary tip. [*lollipop* = drop (sl. 'bribe')]

lollipop (*also* **lolly**) *n*.[2] [20C] a policeman. [*lollipop* = cop]

lollipop *v*. [20C] to inform against, to betray. [*lollipop* = shop]

lolly *n*.[1] [mid-19C+] money. [*lollipop* = cop, i.e. copper (used generically)]

lolly *n*.[2] *see* LOLLIPOP *n*.[2].

lolly up *v*. [1950s+] to inform against, to betray. [LOLLIPOP *v*.]

Londonderry *n*. [mid-19C+] sherry.

London fog *n*. [late 19C–1910s] a dog.

London taxi *n*. [20C] the anus. [*London taxi* = jacksie]

Lone Ranger *n*. [1950s+] a chance, an opportunity, as in *there'll be no Lone Ranger of ...* there'll be no chance of ... [*Lone Ranger* = danger; from the 1950s *Lone Ranger* TV series]

Long Acre *n*. [mid-19C] a baker. [from Long Acre, London WC2, once a market garden, then a centre for coach-building and carpentry, now at the heart of London's refurbished Covent Garden]

long and linger *n*. *see* LEAN AND LINGER.

long and short *n*. [20C] port (wine).

looking glass *n*. [1960s] (*US*) the buttocks, the posterior. [*looking glass* = ass]

loop-the-loop *n*. (*US*) **1** [1910s+] soup. **2** [1920s] a finger ring or hoop.

loopy the loop *n*. [1910s+] (Aus.) soup.

loppy pop *n*. [1990s+] a shop. [var. on LOLLIPOP *v*.]

lord and mastered *adj*. [20C] drunk. [*lord and mastered* = plastered]

Lord John Russell *n*. [mid-19C] a bustle. [from the UK politician Lord John Russell (1792–1878)]

Lord Lovat *n*. [20C] to get rid of, to throw away. [*Lord Lovat* = shove it; from the aristocratic Scottish Lovat family]

Lord Lovell *n*. [mid-19C+] a shovel. [20C use is mainly US]

lord mayor *v.* [20C] to swear.

lord of the manor *n.* [mid–late 19C] a sixpence (2¹/₂ pence). [*lord of the manor* = tanner (early 19C–1970s sl. 'sixpence')]

Lord Sutch *n.* [20C] **1** the clutch. **2** the crutch, i.e. the groin. [from the pop star/politician David 'Screaming Lord' Sutch (1940–99)]

Lord Wigg *n.* [1960s] a pig. [from the UK politician George Wigg (1900–83)]

Loretta Young *n.* [1930s+] the tongue. [from the US film star Loretta Young (b.1913)

Lorna Doone *n.* [20C] a spoon. [from the novel *Lorna Doone* (1869) by R.D. Blackmore]

lost and found *n.* [20C] a pound (sterling).

loud and clear *adj.* [1940s+] dear, i.e. expensive.

Lou Reed *n.* [20C] (*drugs*) amphetamines. [*Lou Reed* = speed; from the rock star Lou Reed (b.1942)]

lousy lou *n.* [20C] influenza. [*lousy lou* = flu]

love and hate *n.* [20C] weight.

love and kisses *n. see* HUGS AND KISSES.

love and marriage *n.* [20C] a carriage. [underpinned by the song lyric 'Love and marriage / Go together like a horse and carriage']

lover's tiff *n.* [20C] venereal disease. [*lover's tiff* = syph]

lucky charm *n.* [20C] the arm.

lucky dip *n.* [20C] **1** a whip. **2** (*pl.*) chips.

Lucozade (*also* **luke**) *n.* [1950s+] (*derog.*) a Black person. [*Lucozade* = spade; from the tonic drink Lucozade]

Lucy Locket (*also* **locket**) *n.* [20C] a pocket.

luke *n. see* LUCOZADE.

Luke and Matt Goss *n.* [1980s] an infinitesimal amount, nothing whatsoever, as in *not give a Luke and Matt Goss* not care at all. [*Luke and Matt Goss* = toss; from the twin Goss brothers Luke and Matt (b.1968), who were the nucleus of the 'boy band' Bros]

lumberjack *n.* [20C] the back. [pun on Standard English *lumbar*]

lump and bump *n.* [late 19C–1930s] a fool, a simpleton. [*lump and bump* = chump]

lump of bread *n.* [1910s–20s] the head.

lump of coke *n.* [mid-19C] a man, a person. [*lump of coke* = bloke]

lump of ice *n.* [late 19C] advice.

lump of lead *n.* **1** [mid-19C] the head. **2** [20C] (*Aus.*) bread.

lump of school *n.* [late 19C] a fool.

m

mab *n.* [mid-19C] a taxi-cab.

macaroni *n.*[1] [mid-19C+] 25 pounds (sterling). [*macaroni* = pony (sl. '25 pounds')]

macaroni *n.*[2] [1920s+] (*Aus.*) nonsense, meaningless talk. [*macaroni* = PONY, plus a jocular use of Standard English, similar to US *apple sauce* rubbish]

macaroon *n.* [20C] (*derog.*) a Black person. [*macaroon* = coon]

MacGimp (*also* **MacGimper**, **magimp**, **McGimp**, **M'Gimp**) *n.* [1950s–60s] (*US*) a pimp.

MacGimper *n. see* MACGIMP.

Madame de Luce *n.* [1930s+] deceptive talk. [*Madame de Luce* = spruce (sl. 'fake')]

Madame Tussaud *adj.* [20C] bald. [from Madame Tussaud's Waxworks, Marylebone Road, London, founded in 1802; the original show included the death-masks of a number of French aristocrats, executed during the Revolution]

mad mick *n.* (*Aus.*) **1** [20C] the penis. **2** [1910s–30s] a pick. [**1** *mad mick* = prick]

Mae West *n.* [1930s–40s] a female breast. [from the Hollywood star Mae West (1892–1980)]

maggies *n.* [20C] (*Aus.*) women's underpants. [*maggie moores* = drawers]

magimp *n. see* MACGIMP.

magistrate's court *n.* [20C] a measure of spirits, as bought in a pub. [*magistrate's court* = a short]

Mahatma Gandhi *n.* [20C] **1** brandy. **2** shandy. [from the Indian nationalist and freedom fighter Mahatma Gandhi (1869–1948)]

maids adorning *n.* [mid-19C] the morning.

Maidstone jailer *n.* [mid-19C] a tailor.

Major Loder *n.* [late 19C] soda, usu. when mixed with whisky. [from Major Eustace Loder, owner of the race-horse Pretty Polly]

Major Stevens *n.* [20C] (*gambling*) evens.

mallee root *n.* [1940s+] (*Aus.*) a prostitute. [from Aboriginal *mallee* eucalyptus + *root* (Aus. sl. 'have sexual intercourse')]

man alive *n.* [20C] (*bingo*) the number five.

man and wife *n.* [1900s–10s] a knife.

Manchester cities (*also* **Manchesters**) *n.* [20C] (*Aus.*) the female breasts. [*Manchester cities* = titties]

Manchesters *n. see* MANCHESTER CITIES.

mangle and wringer *n.* [20C] a singer.

manhole cover *n.* [20C] a brother. [note Cockney pronunciation of brother as *bruvver*]

man in the moon *n.* [20C] a fool, an eccentric. [*man in the moon* = loon]

man on the moon *n.* [1960s+] a spoon.

man o' war *n.* [20C] a bore.

manto *n. see* MANTOVANI.

mantovani (*also* **manto**) *n.* [1980s+] women, girls. [*mantovani* = fanny; from the popular bandleader Annunzio Paolo Mantovani (1905–80)]

man-trap *n.* [late 19C–1900s] a piece of excrement. [*man-trap* = crap]

maracas *n.* [20C] the testicles. [*maracas* = knackers]

Marble Arch *n.* [20C] starch. [from Marble Arch, London W1, designed by John Nash on the model of Rome's Arch of Constantine and erected in 1827 near Buckingham Palace, before being moved to its present site in 1851]

marble halls *n.* [20C] the testicles. [*marble halls* = balls; presumably popularized by the popular song 'I Dreamed I Dwelt in Marble Halls']

marbles and conkers *adj.* [20C] eccentric, crazy. [*marbles and conkers* = bonkers]

Marcus Clark *n.* [20C] (*Aus.*) a shark.

Margaret (Rose) *n.* [1950s+] the nose.

Margate sands *n.* [20C] hands. [from the popular Essex resort of Margate, patronized by generations of Cockneys]

Maria Monk *n.* [late 19C+] **1** courage. **2** semen. [*Maria*

Monk = spunk; from the pornographic novel *The Awful Disclosures of Maria Monk* (1836)]

Marie Corelli *n.* [1970s] television. [*Marie Corelli* = telly; from Marie Corelli, pseudonym of the romantic novelist Marie Mackay (1855–1924)]

Mark Foy *n.* [1940s+] (*Aus.*) a boy. [from the name of the late-19C London firm of carters or from a well-known Sydney department store]

marquis *n. see* MARQUIS OF LORNE.

Marquis of Lorne (*also* **marquis**) *n.* **1** [mid-19C] the penis. **2** [1960s+] an erection. [*Marquis of Lorne* = horn; from the Marquis of Lorne, later the Duke of Argyll, who in 1871 married Princess Louise, daughter of Queen Victoria]

Mars and Venus *n.* [20C] the penis.

Mars bar *n.* [1970s+] a scar.

Martin-le-Grand *n.* [mid–late 19C] a hand. [*see* ST MARTIN'S (LE GRAND)]

Martin Place *n.* [1930s+] (*Aus.*) the face. [from Martin Place in Sydney]

Martin's *n. see* ST MARTIN'S (LE GRAND).

Marty Wilde *n.* [20C] mild (beer). [from the pop singer Marty Wilde (b.1936)]

Mary Ann *n.* [20C] **1** a fan. **2** a hand. [note standard sl. *mary ann* the female pubic hair]

Mary Blaine (*also* **Mary Blane**) *n.* **1** [mid–late 19C] a railway train. **2** [mid-19C–1900s] rain.

Mary Blaine (*also* **Mary Blane**) *v.* [mid–late 19C] to travel by train.

Mary Blane *n. see* MARY BLAINE *n.*

Mary Blane *v. see* MARY BLAINE *v.*

Mary Ellens *n.* [20C] the female breasts. [*Mary Ellens* = melons]

Mary Green *n.* [20C] in cards, the queen.

marylou *n.* [20C] glue.

Mary Rose *n.* [1950s+] the nose.

maud and ruth *n.* [1970s] the truth.

Max Factor *n.* [20C] one who fakes illness or injury, e.g. a footballer who 'dives' etc. [*Max Factor* = actor; from the brandname Max Factor, a leading producer of cosmetics and make-up]

Max Miller *n.* [20C] a pillow. [from the comedian Max Miller (1895–1963); note Cockney pronunciation of pillow as *piller*]

Max Walls *n.* [20C] the testicles. [*Max Walls* = balls; from the comedian Max Wall (1908–90)]

Maxwell House *n.* [1960s+] a mouse. [from the popular Maxwell House brand of instant coffee]

mazawattee *n.* [20C] a potty. [the reference to Mazawattee tea may tie in to the colour of the drink and of urine]

McGimp *n. see* MACGIMP.

me-and-you *n.* [20C] **1** (*bingo*) the number two. **2** sexual intercourse. [**2** *me and you* = screw]

meat pie *n.* [20C] **1** a fly. **2** a trouser fly. **3** (*usu. pl.*) an eye.

mechanical digger *n.* [20C] (*derog.*) a Black person. [*mechanical digger* = nigger]

Meg Ryan *n.* [1980s+] a male homosexual. [*Meg Ryan* = IRON (HOOF); from the US film star Meg Ryan (b.1962)]

Melbourne Pier (*also* **Port Melbourne Pier**) [1940s+] (*Aus.*) an ear.

melodies *n.* [20C] the fingers. [*melody lingers* = fingers]

Melvyn Bragg *n.* [1990s+] **1** sexual intercourse. **2** a promiscuous woman. **3** a cigarette. [*Melvyn Bragg* = **1** shag **2** slag **3** fag; from the UK broadcaster and author Melvyn Bragg (b.1939)]

merchant banker *n.* [1980s+] **1** a masturbator. **2** a general term of abuse. [*merchant banker* = wanker]

merry and bright *n.* [20C] (*usu. pl.*) a light.

merry-go-round *n.* [late 19C+] a pound (sterling).

merryheart *n.* [20C] a sweetheart.

merry old soul *n.* [20C] **1** coal. **2** a hole. **3** the anus. [**3** *merry old soul* = hole; from the song 'Old King Cole' beginning 'Old King Cole was a merry old soul and a merry old soul was he']

Meryl Streep *n.* [1970s+] sleep. [from the US film star Meryl Streep (b.1951)]

M'Gimp *n. see* MACGIMP.

Michael Caine *n.* [20C] **1** a pain. **2** an annoyance. [**2** *Michael Caine* = pain; from the actor Michael Caine (b.1933)]

Michael Miles *n.* [1950s–60s] haemorrhoids. [*Michael Miles* = piles; from the UK TV personality Michael Miles (1919–71)]

Michael Schumacher *n.* [1990s+] tobacco. [from the German motor racing champion Michael Schumacher (b.1969); note Cockney pronunciation of tobacco as *terbaccer*]

Michael Winner *n.* [1980s+] dinner. [from the film director (and food critic) Michael Winner (b.1935)]

mickey *n.* [late 19C+] (*UK tramp*) a casual ward. [*mike* = spike (sl. 'lodging house')]

mickey (*also* **micky**) *adj.* [late 19C] sick.

Mickey Bliss (*also* **Mike Bliss**) *n.* [20C] an act of urination; hence TAKE THE MICKEY. [*Mickey Bliss* = piss]

Mickey Duff *adj.* [1980s+] unwell, 'under the weather'. [*Mickey Duff* = rough; from the UK boxing promoter Mickey Duff (b.1929)]

Mickey Mouse *n.* [20C] **1** a house. **2** a Liverpudlian. [**2** = *scouse*; from Disney's animated rodent Mickey Mouse]

Mickey Mouse *adj.* [1930s+] (*Aus.*) excellent, wonderful, the best. [*Mickey Mouse* = grouse (Aus./N.Z. sl. 'excellent'); *see* MICKEY MOUSE *n.*]

Mickey Mouser *n.* [1990s+] a Liverpudlian. [*Micker Mouser* = scouser; *see* MICKEY MOUSE *n.*]

Mickey Rooney *n.* [20C] an eccentric, a mad person. [*Mickey Rooney* = loony; from the US film star Mickey Rooney (b.1920)]

Mick O'Dwyer *n.* [late 19C+] a domestic fire.

micky *adj. see* MICKEY *adj.*

Micky Spillane *n.* [1950s+] (*Aus.*) a game. [from the popular crime novelist Mickey Spillane (b.1918)]

micro-chip *n.* [20C] (*derog.*) a Japanese person. [*micro-chip* = Nip, plus a reference to Japanese technological expertise]

Midland Bank *n.* [1950s+] an act of masturbation. [*Midland Bank* = wank; from the former high-street banking chain Midland]

Mike Bliss *n. see* MICKEY BLISS.

Mike Malone *n.* [1950s+] the telephone.

mild and meek *n.* [20C] (*Aus.*) a cheek.

Mile End *n.* [20C] a friend. [from the East London suburb of Mile End]

milk jug *n.* [1920s+] (*Aus.*) a fool, a simpleton. [*milk jug* = mug]

milkman's horse *adj.* [late 19C+] cross, i.e. annoyed. [note Cockney pronunciation of cross as *crorss*]

milky way *adj.* [1970s+] homosexual. [*milky way* = gay]

Millennium Dome *n.* [1990s+] a comb.

miller's daughter *n.* [late 19C+] water. [a traditional mill is powered by water]

Millwall Reserves *n.* [1950s+] nerves.

Milton Keynes *n.* [1960s+] **1** beans, usu. baked beans. **2** a male homosexual. [**2** *Milton Keynes* = queen; from the new town of Milton Keynes, Buckinghamshire]

mince pies (*also* **minces**) *n.* [mid-19C+] (*also sing.*) the eyes.

minces *n. see* MINCE PIES.

Mini Moke *n.* [1960s] smoke. [from the once popular Mini Moke, a Mini-Minor with a 'jeep'-style body]

Minnie Mouse *n.* [1940s+] (*Aus.*) the house. [from the Disney character, Minnie Mouse, 'wife' to Mickey]

misbehave *n.* [20C] (*Aus.*) a shave.

Miss Fitch *n.* [20C] an unpleasant woman. [*Miss Fitch* = bitch]

Miss Piggy *n.* [1970s+] a cigarette. [*Miss Piggy* = ciggie; from the porcine prima donna, Miss Piggy, featured in the TV puppet series *The Muppet Show* (1976–80)]

Mr Chant *n.* [1920s–30s] an aunt.

Mr Hyde *n.* [20C] an unpleasant, untrustworthy person. [*Mr Hyde* = snide; from Mr Hyde, the maniacal alter-ego of Dr Jekyll in the novella *Dr Jekyll and Mr Hyde* (1886) by Robert Louis Stevenson]

Mister Mutch *n.* [20C] (*Aus.*) the crutch, i.e. the groin.

Mrs Chant's *n.* [1920s] (*euphemistic*) a lavatory; hence *visit*

Mrs Chant's. [*Mrs Chant's* = my aunt's; from Mrs Ormiston Chant (1848–1923), a well-known moralist]

Mrs Doyle *n.* [1990s+] a boil. [from the housekeeper character Mrs Doyle in the 1990s TV sitcom *Father Ted*]

Mrs Ducket (*also* **Mrs Duckett**) *n.* [20C] a bucket.

Mrs Duckett *n. see* MRS DUCKET.

Mrs Mopp *n.* [1940s+] a shop. [from the character Mrs Mopp created by Tommy Handley (1892–1949) for the radio comedy series *ITMA* (*It's That Man Again*, from 1939). Her catchphrase was 'Shall I do you now, sir?']

Mrs More *n.* [20C] the floor.

mix and muddle *n.* [20C] a cuddle.

moan and wail *n.* [1940s] a jail.

Moby Dick *n.* [late 19C+] **1** prison. **2** the penis. [*Moby Dick* = **1** nick **2** prick; from the novel *Moby Dick* (1850) by Herman Melville]

Moby Dick *adj.* [20C] ill, sick. [*see* MOBY DICK *n.*]

mods and rockers *n.* [1960s] the female breasts. [*mods and rockers* = knockers; from the Mods and Rockers, symbiotic UK youth cults of the early 1960s]

mogadored *adj.* [1930s+] beaten, defeated, confused. [*mogadored* = floored; *mogador* itself comes either from Irish *magadh* to mock, to jeer, to laugh at, or from Romani *mokardi/mokodo* tainted]

molly *adj.* [1960s–70s] (*Aus.*) drunk. [*molly the monk* = drunk]

Nursery Rhymes

buckle my shoe	Jew/two
dickory dock	clock/cock
ding-dong bell	hell
dish ran away	
with the spoon	hoon
hey-diddle-diddle	piddle/middle/fiddle
hickory-dock	clock
jack and jill	hill/bill/till/pill/dill
Jack Sprat	fat/brat
Little Bo-Peep	sleep
little boy blue	screw
Little Miss Muffet	stuff it
merry old soul	coal/hole
nursery rhyme	crime
nursery rhymes	*The Times*
Old King Cole	dole
pop goes the weasel	diesel
three bags full	load of bull
three blind mice	sack of rice
Wee Willie Winky	chinky

Molly Maguire *n.* [20C] (*Aus.*) a fire. [from the typically Irish proper name, but also possibly linked to the mid-19C Molly McGuires, a secret terrorist organization developed by Irish miners in Pennsylvania to fight exploitation by the mine-owners]

Molly Maguired *adj.* [20C] tired. [*see* MOLLY MAGUIRE]

Molly (Malone) *n.* [20C] the telephone.

Molly O'Morgan *n.* [late 19C+] an organ.

Mona Lisa *n.* [20C] **1** a freezer. **2** a pizza. [from the *Mona Lisa* or *La Gioconda* (1503–1506) by Leonardo da Vinci, arguably the world's best-known painting]

monkey's cousin *n.* [1940s+] (*bingo*) the number twelve. [*monkey's cousin* = dozen]

monkey spanker *n.* [1990s+] a masturbator. [*monkey spanker* = wanker]

monkey's tail *n.* [20C] (*usu. pl.*) a nail.

Monte Cairo *n.* [1990s+] a giro cheque.

montezumas *n.* [20C] bloomers. [from the Aztec emperor Montezuma II (1466–1520)]

moody *n.* [1930s+] deceit, lies, verbal trickery. [*moody & sankey* = hanky-panky; from the US evangelists Dwight Lyman Moody (1837–99) and Ivo David Sankey (1840–1908)]

moonlight flits *n.* [20C] the female breasts. [*moonlight flits* = tits]

mop and bucket! *excl.* [20C] an exclamation of annoyance or pain. [*mop and bucket!* = fuck it!]

more or less *n.* [20C] a dress.

Moreton (bay) *n.* [1950s+] (*Aus.*) **1** an informer. **2** a busybody. [*Moreton bay fig* = fizgig (Aus. sl. 'informer'); from the species of fig that grows at Moreton Bay, sited at the mouth of the Brisbane River, Queensland, and originally named Morton by its discoverer Captain Cook, after James Douglas, Earl of Morton FRS (1702–68). Between 1824 and 1939 Moreton Bay was the name of the penal settlement there, and the name of the whole area before Queensland was officially separated from New South Wales in 1859]

moriarty *n.* [20C] a party. [from the character Dr Moriarty, Sherlock Holmes's adversary in the books by Arthur Conan Doyle]

Morris Minor *n.* [20C] a black eye. [*Morris Minor* = shiner; from the once best-selling motor-car, the Morris Minor]

mortar and trowel *n.* [late 19C–1900s] a towel.

mother and daughter *n.* [mid–late 19C] water.

Mother Brown *n.* [20C] town, esp. the West End of London.

Mother Hubbard *n.* [late 19C+] a cupboard. [from the nursery rhyme 'Old Mother Hubbard']

Mother Kelly *n.* [20C] **1** jelly. **2** television. [**2** *Mother Kelly* = telly]

Mother Machree *n.* [20C] (*Aus.*) tea. [from Irish *mo chroí* my heart; best known as the title of Rida Johnson Young's 19C ballad]

mother of pearl *n.* [20C] a girl.

mother's joy *n.* [1900s] (*Aus.*) a boy.

mother's pride *n.* [20C] a bride.

mother's (ruin) *n.* [1930s+] gin. [from the spirit's long-reputed propensity for appealing to women and destroying life]

mountain passes *n.* [1900s–50s] glasses, i.e. spectacles.

mountains of Mourne *n.* [20C] an erection. [*mountains of Mourne* = horn; from the Mourne mountain range in Co. Down, Northern Ireland, the subject of a sentimental early-20C song 'Mountains of Mourne']

mouthwash *n.* [20C] food. [*mouthwash* = nosh]

Mozart and Liszt *adj.* [1920s+] drunk. [*Mozart and Liszt* = pissed; from the composers Wolfgang Amadeus Mozart (1756–91) and Franz Liszt (1811–86); var. on BRAHMS AND LISZT]

mozzle and brocha *n.* [20C] a door-to-door salesman. [*mozzle and brocha* = on the knocker; from Yiddish *mazel* good luck + *brocha* a blessing]

mud and ooze *n.* [20C] (*Aus.*) alcohol, liquor. [*mud and ooze* = booze]

muddy trench *adj.* [1910s+] French. [coined, unsurprisingly, during WWI]

mud in your eye *n.* [20C] a tie. [from the popular toast 'Here's mud in your eye']

mud pies *n.* [20C] (*Aus.*) the eyes.

mud's in your eye *n.* [late 19C–1940s] a tie. [playing on the popular toast 'Here's mud in your eye']

muffin *n.* [mid-19C; 1980s+] **1** a fool. **2** an incompetent, one who is awkward [*muffin the mule* = fool; from the popular children's TV puppet of the 1950s Muffin the Mule]

muffin baker *n.* [mid-19C] a Quaker.

mulligatawny *adj.* [20C] sexually aroused or arousing. [*mulligatawny* = horny; from mulligatawny soup, a highly seasoned product of the East Indies, itself from Tamil *milaku-tanni* 'pepper-water']

mum and dad *adj.* [20C] (*Aus.*) mad.

mum and daddo *n.* [20C] (*Aus.*) a shadow.

mumble and mutter *n.* [20C] butter.

mumblety-pegs *n. see* MUMBLY PEGS.

mumbly pegs (*also* **mumblety-pegs**) *n.* [1920s–40s] (*US*) the legs. [from the game mumblety-peg, in which each player in turn throws a knife from a series of positions, continuing until they fail to make the blade stick in the ground]

mustard (and cress) *n.* [20C] a dress.

mustard (pickle) *n.* [20C] a cripple.

mustard pot *n.* [late 19C+] the vagina. [*mustard pot* = twat; note also the many sl. terms that equate the vagina with a receptacle for semen]

mustard (pot) *adj.* [20C] hot.

must-I-holler *n.* [1980s+] (*US Black*) the vagina. [*must-I-holler* = collar; lit. 'do I have to shout']

mutt and jeff *adj.* [1930s+] deaf. [from by the US cartoon characters Mutt and Jeff, originated by H.C. 'Bud' Fischer in the 1930s]

mutter and stutter *n.* [20C] butter.

mutton-pies *n.* [19C] the eyes.

my gawd *n.* [late 19C] a sword.

my mother's away *phr.* [late 19C–1900s] (*Aus.*) the other day.

Myrna Loy *n.* [1930s–40s] a saveloy. [from the film star Myrna Loy (1905–93)]

Mystic Megs *n.* [1980s+] the legs. [from the popular TV fortune teller 'Mystic Meg']

my word *n.* [20C] a piece of excrement. [*my word* = turd]

n

nails and screws *n.* [20C] (*Aus.*) news.

Nancy Lee *n.* [mid-19C–1930s] **1** a flea. **2** tea.

nanny (goat) *n.* [20C] **1** a coat. **2** a boat. **3** the throat. **4** the totalizator. [**4** *nanny goat* = tote]

nanny goating *n.* [20C] courting. [a partial rhyme]

nap and double *n.* [1930s] trouble.

Napper Tandy *n.* [20C] (*Aus.*) a shandy (beer and lemonade). [from the Irish revolutionary James Napper Tandy (1740–1803)]

National Front *n.* [20C] a general term of abuse. [*National Front* = cunt; from the UK far-right, anti-immigration party the National Front, formed in 1967]

national hunt *n.* [20C] audacity, cheek. [*national hunt* = front]

Nat King Cole *n.* [20C] **1** the dole. **2** a mole (on the skin). **3** a bread roll. [from the US singer Nat King Cole (1919–65)]

Naughton and Gold *adj.* [20C] cold. [from Charlie Naughton (1887–1976) and Jimmy Gold (1886–1967), music-hall stars and members of the Crazy Gang (1935–62)]

naus (*also* **norz**) *n.* [1950s+] an unpleasant person. [NOAH'S (ARK); pronounced as if abbreviation of *nauseating* and commonly used with a derog. implication, but in fact representing a pronunciation of *Noah's*]

nautical miles (*also* **nauticals**) *n.* [20C] haemorrhoids. [*nautical miles* = piles]

nauticals *n. see* NAUTICAL MILES.

navigators *n.* [mid-19C] potatoes; hence the street cry *navigator scot* potatoes all hot. [note Cockney pronunciation of potatoes as *pertaters*; the connection with the predominantly Irish *navigators* (i.e. navvies), builders of Victorian Britain's railways and canals, whose stereotype consumed many potatoes, may or may not be coincidental]

Nazi spy *n.* [1940s+] (*Aus.*) a meat pie.

near and far *n.* [late 19C–1920s] a bar (in a pub).

near enough *n.* [20C] a male homosexual. [*near enough* = puff]

Ned Kelly *n.* **1** [1920s+] (*Aus.*) the stomach. **2** [1970s] the television. [*Ned Kelly* = **1** belly **2** telly; from the bushranger Ned Kelly (1855–80)]

Ned Skinner *n.* [late 19C] dinner.

needle and cotton *adj.* [20C] rotten.

needle and pin *n.* [1930s+] gin.

needle and pin *adj.* [1930s+] thin.

needle and thread *n.* [mid-19C–1930s] bread.

needles and pins *n.* [20C] twins.

Nell Gwyn *n.* [20C] gin. [from Nell Gwyn (1650–87), the mistress of Charles II]

nellie (*also* **nelly**) *n.* **1** [1910s+] an overtly homosexual, effeminate man. **2** [1970s+] (*US campus*) a lesbian. [NELLIE DUFF or *nellie dean* = queen]

Nellie Deans (*also* **Nelly Deans**) *n.* [20C] greens, i.e. vegetables. [from the popular song 'Nellie Dean']

Nellie Duff (*also* **Nelly Duff**) *n.* [20C] **1** breath, thus fig. life; hence NOT ON YOUR NELLIE! **2** a male homosexual. [*Nellie Duff* = **1** puff (sl. 'breath') **2** puff (sl. 'homosexual')]

nelly *n. see* NELLIE.

Nelly Bligh *n.* [1910s+] (*Aus.*) **1** a meat pie. **2** the trousers' fly. **3** (*usu. pl.*) an eye. **4** a tie. **5** a fly. **6** a lie.

Nelly Deans *n. see* NELLIE DEANS.

Nelly Duff *n. see* NELLIE DUFF.

Nelly Kelly *n.* [20C] (*Aus.*) the stomach. [female var. on NED KELLY]

Nelson Eddies *n.* [20C] money, cash. [*Nelson Eddies* = readies; from the US singer and actor Nelson Eddy (1901–67)]

Nelson Eddy *adv.* [20C] ready. [*see* NELSON EDDIES]

Nelson (Mandela) *n.* [1980s+] Stella Artois lager. [*Nelson Mandela* = Stella; from the former S Afr. president Nelson Mandela (b.1918)]

Nelson (Riddle) *n.* [1950s+] (*Aus.*) an act of urination. [*Nelson Riddle* = piddle; from the US composer and arranger Nelson Riddle (1921–85)]

nervo and knox *n.* **1** [1940s+] socks. **2** [1970s+] venereal disease, esp. syphilis. **3** [1970s+] television. [*nervo and knox* = **2** pox **3** the box; from Jimmy Nervo (1890–1975) and Teddy Knox (1896–1974), music-hall comedians and members of the Crazy Gang (1935–62)]

nervous wreck *n.* [20C] a cheque.

nescafé *n.* [1980s] a hand gesture used to indicate one's contempt. [from the popular brand of instant coffee Nescafé and a series of advertisements used to promote the brand in the 1980s; the ads featured various actors, most notably Gareth Hunt (b.1943), shaking a handful of coffee beans, a gesture widely adopted as an imitation of the male act of masturbation; the gesture thus implies both 'wanker' and the rhyme *Gareth Hunt* = cunt]

never again *n.* [20C] beer. [*never again* = Ben (Truman), a beer brewed in East London]

never better *n.* [20C] (*Aus.*) a letter. [from the often optimistic sentiments that end such missives]

never fear *n.* [mid-19C] a pint of beer.

New Delhi *n.* [20C] the stomach. [*New Delhi* = belly; from the capital of India, New Delhi]

Newgate gaol *n.* [20C] a tale, esp. of the 'hard-luck' variety. [Newgate was London's major prison from the

12C to the early 20C; it was demolished in 1902 and replaced by today's Central Criminal Court, the Old Bailey]

Newington Butts (*also* **newingtons**) *n.* [20C] the stomach. [*Newington Butts* = guts; from the north-east London suburb Newington Butts]

newingtons *n. see* NEWINGTON BUTTS.

Newton and Ridley *adj.* [20C] tipsy, drunk. [*Newton and Ridley* = tiddly; from the fictional brewer Newton and Ridley, which features in the popular TV soap opera *Coronation Street*]

New York nippers *n.* [20C] kippers.

Niagara Falls (*also* **Niagaras**) *n.* [1960s+] **1** the testicles. **2** rubbish, nonsense. [*Niagara Falls* = balls]

Niagaras *n. see* NIAGARA FALLS.

nice enough *n.* [20C] a male homosexual. [*nice enough* = puff]

nice one, Cyril! *n.* [1960s+] a squirrel. [from the football chant created to praise Cyril Knowles (1944–91), a Tottenham Hotspur player; more usually found in the rhymeless context of a general term of approval]

nickel and dime *n.* [1930s+] (*US*) time.

nicker bits *n.* [20C] diarrhoea. [*nicker bits* = the shits]

Nicky Butts *n.* [1990s+] **1** nuts (edible). **2** the testicles. [**2** *Nicky Butts* = nuts; from the UK footballer Nicky Butt (b.1975)]

nigger's lips *n.* [1970s–80s] (*US*) potato chips, i.e. crisps.

nigh enough *n.* [1920s–30s] a gay male prostitute.
[*nigh enough* = puff]

night and day *n.* [mid-19C] a play.

night and day *adj.* [20C] grey.

night and day *v.* [mid-19C] to see a play.

Niki Lauda *n.* [1980s+] cocaine. [*Niki Lauda* = powder
(sl. 'any powdered drug'); from the Austrian motor racing
champion Niki Lauda (b.1949)]

nits and lice *n.* [20C] (*esp. gambling*) a price.

Noah's ark *n.* **1** [late 19C] a lark, i.e. a game; crime.
2 [late 19C] a lark (the bird). **3** [late 19C+] a park.
4 [1940s+] (*Aus.*) a shark. [from the biblical story of
Noah's ark, a vessel that carried a small sample of every
living species to repopulate the earth after the great
flood (Genesis vi–viii)]

Noah's (ark) *n.* [late 19C+] an informer. [*Noah's ark*
= nark; *see* NOAH'S ARK]

Nobby Halls *n.* [20C] the testicles. [*Nobby Halls* = balls; from
Nobby Halls, the mono-testicled 'hero' of a music-hall song]

Nobby Stiles *n.* [1990s+] haemorrhoids. [*Nobby Stiles*
= piles; from the UK footballer Nobby Stiles (b.1942)]

no bottle *phr.* [20C] **1** lacking quality or style. **2** cowardly.
[*no bottle and glass* = **1** no class **2** no arse]

non-skid *n.* [1920s] (*derog.*) a Jew. [*non-skid* = Yid]

nook and cranny *n.* [20C] the vagina. [*nook and cranny* = fanny]

Normandy Beach *n.* [1950s+] a speech. [the Normandy beaches were the site of the 1944 D-Day invasion of German-occupied France]

no Robin Hood *phr.* [1910s+] (*orig. military*) no good. [from the mythical outlaw Robin Hood of Sherwood Forest]

north and south *n.* [mid-19C+] the mouth.

North Pole *n.* [20C] the anus. [*North Pole* = arsehole]

north Sydney *n.* [20C] (*Aus.*) the kidney.

norz *n. see* NAUS.

nose and chin *n.* **1** [mid-19C] a penny. **2** [late 19C] gin. **3** [20C] a win (on a wager). [**1** *nose and chin* = win (sl. 'penny')]

nosey-my-knacker *n.* [mid-19C] tobacco; hence the abbreviation *nose-my* baccy. [note Cockney pronunciation of tobacco as *terbaccer*]

no soap *phr.* [1920s+] (*orig. US*) nothing doing, not a chance, no hope of that. [*no bar of soap* = no dope, or from sl. *soap* money]

not much frocks *n.* [late 19C–1900s] socks.

not on your nellie! (*also* **not on your nelly!**) *excl.* [1940s+] not a chance! absolutely impossible! [*not on your nellie duff* = not on your puff; *see* NELLIE DUFF]

not on your nelly! *excl. see* NOT ON YOUR NELLIE!

not worth a tiger tank *phr.* [1970s] worthless, useless. [*not worth a tiger tank* = not worth a wank; from the German WWII Tiger tank, also influenced by the advertising slogan for Esso petrol, 'Put a tiger in your tank'; thus there is an oblique link to phrases such as *put lead in someone's pencil*]

now and never *adj.* [late 19C] clever.

nurembergs *n.* [1940s+] haemorrhoids. [*nuremberg trials* = piles; from the trials of the former leaders of Nazi Germany which took place in Nuremberg (1945–46)]

nursery rhyme *n.* [1990s+] a crime.

nursery rhymes *n.* [20C] *The Times* newspaper. [a jibe at *The Times's* much vaunted reputation as the UK's 'newspaper of record']

nutcrackers *n.* [20C] the testicles. [*nutcrackers* = knackers]

O

oak *n*. [late 19C] a joke.

oak and ash *n*. [20C] cash.

oars (and rollocks) *n*. [20C] nonsense, rubbish. [*oars and rollocks* = bollocks]

oats *n*. [1980s+] cocaine. [*oats and barley* = charlie (sl. 'cocaine')]

oats and barley *n*. [mid-19C] a watchman. [*oats and barley* = charley (17–19C sl. 'watchman')]

oats and chaff *n*. [mid-19C–1930s] a footpath.

obadiah *n*. [20C] a fire.

ocean liner *n*. [20C] (*Aus.*) a girl, a girlfriend. [*ocean liner* = cliner (19C–1940s Aus. sl. 'girlfriend')]

ocean pearl *n*. [late 19C+] a girl, i.e. a girlfriend.

ocean wave *n*. [1920s–30s] a shave.

Oedipus Rex *n*. [1970s] sex. [from Sophocles' play *Oedipus Tyrannus* (*c*.429 BC), in which Oedipus unknowingly kills his father and marries his mother; *rex* is the Latin for Greek *tyrannos* king]

office worker *n*. [20C] a shirker.

oh, my dear *n*. [mid-19C+] beer; hence POT OF O.

oh my God *adj.* [20C] bald. [note Cockney pronunciation of God as *gawd* and bald as *bawd*]

oil leak *n.* [1990s+] a Sikh.

oil slick *n.* [20C] (*derog.*) a Spaniard. [*oil slick* = spic/spick]

oil tanker *n.* [20C] a general term of abuse. [*oil tanker* = wanker]

oily *n.* [20C] a cigarette. [*oily rag* = fag]

Okker *n. see* OSCAR (ASCHE).

old black joes *n.* [20C] (*Aus.*) the toes.

old bubble *n. see* BUBBLE.

old dutch *n.* [late 19C+] a wife. [DUCHESS (OF FIFE) or DUTCH (PLATE)]

old fogey *n.* [20C] nasal mucus. [*old fogey* = bogey]

old grabem pudden *n.* [late 19C] an old woman; a wife or mother. [*pudden* = woman; the woman is seen as possessing a sweet tooth, i.e. she 'grabs the pudding']

old iron and brass *n.* [20C] grass.

old Jack Lang *n.* [1960s+] (*Aus.*) rhyming slang.

old Jamaica rum *n.* [20C] the sun.

Old King Cole *n.* [1920s+] the dole. [from the nursery rhyme 'Old King Cole']

old kit bag *n.* [20C] a cigarette. [*old kit bag* = fag]

old mick *adj.* [late 19C+] sick.

old nag *n*. [1910s–20s] a cigarette. [*old nag* = fag]

Old Oak *n*. [20C] London. [*Old Oak* = the Smoke]

old pot *n*. [late 19C+] (*usu. Aus.*) an old man, esp. a father. [*old pot and pan* = old man]

oliver *n*. **1** [late 19C] a fist. **2** [late 19C] (*Aus.*) the wrist. **3** [1970s] a deliberately incorrect entry, esp. by a book-maker in a ledger. [**3** *oliver twist* = fist (sl. 'handwriting'); from the eponymous young hero of Charles Dickens's *Oliver Twist* (1838)]

oliver *v*. [mid-19C] to understand, esp. in the phrase *do you oliver?* do you understand? [*oliver cromwell* = tumble; from Oliver Cromwell (1599–1658), Lord Protector of England; note pronunciation of cromwell as *crummle*]

Oliver Twist *adj*. [20C] drunk. [*Oliver Twist* = pissed; *see* OLIVER *n*.]

oller (boys) *n*. [late 19C+] a collar.

Ollie Beak *n*. [1970s] a Sikh. [from the children's puppet Olly Beak]

olly *n*. **1** [1960s+] marijuana. **2** [1980s] amphetamines. [*oliver reed* = **1** weed **2** speed; from the UK actor Oliver Reed (1938–99)]

on and off *n*. [20C] a cough.

once a week (*also* **oncer**) *n*. [20C] **1** a cheek. **2** a magis-trate. [**2** *once a week* = beak]

oncer *n*. *see* ONCE A WEEK.

one alone *n*. [20C] (*Aus.*) a moan.

one and eight *n*. [20C] a plate.

one and elevenpence three farden *n*. [late 19C+] a garden.

one and half *n*. [20C] a scarf.

one and t'other (*also* **one another**) *n*. **1** [late 19C+] a brother. **2** [20C] a mother.

one another *n*. *see* ONE AND T'OTHER.

one for his nob *n*. [20C] a shilling (five pence). [*one for his nob* = bob]

ones and twos *n*. [1920s+] (*Aus./US*) shoes.

onka *n*. *see* ONKAPARINGA.

onkaparinga (*also* **onka**) *n.* [1960s+] (*Aus.*) a finger. [from Onkaparinga, the brandname of a make of woollen blanket]

on one's Jack (Jones) (*also* **on one's Jack Malone**) *phr.* [20C] by oneself, alone. [*on one's Jack Jones* = on one's own]

on one's Jack Malone *phr. see* ON ONE'S JACK (JONES).

on one's Pat *phr.* [20C] (*Aus.*) by oneself, alone. [*on one's Pat Malone* = on one's own]

on one's Tod *phr.* [20C] by oneself, alone. [*on one's Tod Sloan* = on one's own; from the US jockey James Forman 'Tod' Sloan (1874–1933)]

on someone's ginger *phr.* [1960s+] (*Aus.*) following someone. [*on someone's ginger ale* = on someone's tail]

on someone's hammer *phr.* (*Aus.*) **1** [1920s+] very close behind someone. **2** [1940s+] hounding, pestering someone. [*on someone's hammer and tack* = on someone's back]

on the bottle *phr.* [20C] **1** working as a male prostitute. **2** (*US*) working in any form of prostitution. **3** working as a pickpocket. [*on the bottle and glass* = on the arse, referring to **1**, **2** the *arse* that one is selling, **3** the arse, i.e rear trouser pocket, from which one is stealing; *see* BOTTLE AND GLASS]

on the C and B *phr.* [mid-19C+] cadging. [from COAT AND BADGE]

on the cripple and crutch *phr.* [20C] looking for a loan. [*on the cripple and crutch* = on the touch]

on the cuff *adj.* [1940s+] (*N.Z.*) excessive, esp. in the phrase *a bit on the cuff.* [*on the cuff* = rough]

on the floor *adj.* [20C] poor. [the image is also of one who has 'fallen low']

on the Murray cod *phr.* [20C] (*Aus. gambling*) betting on credit. [*on the Murray cod* = on the nod]

on the ooze *phr.* [1920s+] drunk. [*on the ooze* = on the booze]

open the door *n.* [1940s+] (*bingo*) the number four.

orange pip *n.* [20C] (*derog.*) a Japanese person. [*orange pip* = Nip]

orange squash *n.* [20C] money. [*orange squash* = dosh]

orchestra stalls *n.* [20C] the testicles. [*orchestra stalls* = balls; note the false link between Greek *orchis* testicles and *orchestra*; in fact *orchestra* is from Greek *orchestra* the space on which the chorus danced in Greek drama]

orinoko *n.* [mid-19C–1920s] **1** cocoa. **2** a poker. [in **2** note Cockney pronunciation of orinoko as *orinoker*]

Orphan Annie *n.* [1930s+] the vagina. [*Orphan Annie* = fanny; from the cartoon (and later the musical based upon it) 'Little Orphan Annie', created by Harold Gray in 1922]

Oscar (Asche) (*also* **Okker**, **Oscar Nash**) *n.* [1910s+] (*Aus./N.Z.*) money. [*Oscar Asche* = cash, from the Aus. actor Oscar Asche (1871–1936)]

Oscar Hock *n.* [1920s–60s] (*US*) a sock.

Oscar Joes *n.* [20C] (*US*) the toes.

Oscar Nash *n. see* OSCAR (ASCHE).

ounce of baccy (*also* **ouncer**) *n.* [20C] (*derog.*) a British Asian. [*ounce of baccy* = paki]

ouncer *n. see* OUNCE OF BACCY.

out and in *n.* [20C] (*US*) the chin.

out the monk *phr.* [1940s+] (*N.Z.*) unconscious, asleep, often the result of drunkenness. [*out the monk* = drunk]

overcoat maker *n.* [20C] an undertaker. [the reference is to the 'wooden overcoats' or coffins that he makes]

over the stile *phr.* [mid–late 19C] committed for trial.

Owen Nares *n.* [20C] chairs. [from the UK actor Owen Nares (1888–1943)]

Oxford bag *n.* [1920s+] a cigarette. [*Oxford bag* = fag; the original Oxford bag was a voluminous, almost skirt-like trouser, popularized by Oxford undergraduates in the 1920s]

Oxford scholar *n.* **1** [late 19C+] a crown, five shillings (25 pence); hence HALF AN OXFORD (SCHOLAR). **2** [1900s] a collar. [**1** *Oxford scholar* = dollar]

Oxo cube *n.* [20C] the London Underground. [*Oxo cube* = tube]

p

paddy and mick *n.* [20C] a pick (axe). [referring to the stereotyping of the Irish as labourers]

paddy and mick *adj.* [20C] stupid. [*paddy and mick* = thick; referring to the stereotyping of the Irish as stupid]

Paddy O'Rourke *n.* [20C] talk, i.e. conversation.

Paddy Quick *n.* [mid–late 19C] **1** a stick. **2** a kick.

Paddy Quick *adj.* [mid-19C] stupid. [*Paddy Quick* = thick]

padlock *n.* [1960s–70s] the penis. [*padlock* = cock]

pain (in the neck) *n.* [20C] a cheque.

pair o' round-mys *n.* [late 19C] a pair of trousers. [*see* ROUND ME HOUSES]

Pall Mall *n.* [late 19C–1900s] **1** a woman. **2** a small amount, a 'damn', as in *not care/give a Pall Mall* not care at all. [*Pall Mall* = gal; in **2** the reference is to W.T. Steed's series on London prostitution, 'The Maiden Tribute of Modern Babylon' (1885); the 'gals' were presumably seen as 'damned']

pantomime cow *n. see* BULL AND COW.

pants and vest *n.* [20C] best, i.e. best bitter beer.

paper bag *v.* [20C] to nag.

paper doll *n.* [1960s+] a promiscuous, sexually available woman. [*paper doll* = moll]

paper hat *n.* [20C] a fool. [*paper hat* = prat]

paraffin *n.* [20C] (*S Afr.*) gin.

paraffin lamp *n.* [20C] a tramp.

Partick Thistle *n.* [20C] a whistle. [from the Scottish football team Partick Thistle]

pass in the pot *adj.* [late 19C–1900s] randy, amorous. [*pass in the pot* = hot]

pat and mick *n.* [late 19C+] the penis. [*pat and mick* = prick]

pat and mick *v.* [20C] (*Aus.*) **1** to lick. **2** to beat with the fists. [**2** *pat and mick* = lick]

pat and mike *n.* [late 19C+] a bicycle. [*pat and mike* = bike]

Pat Cash *v.* [1990s+] to urinate. [*Pat Cash* = slash; from the Aus. tennis star Pat Cash (b.1965)]

Pat Malone (*also* **Pat Maloney**) *adv.* [20C] (*Aus.*) alone.

Pat Maloney *adv. see* PAT MALONE.

patsy *adj.* [1930s–50s] (*US*) satisfactory, all right. [ety. unknown; possibly from a lost piece of rhyming slang]

Patsy Cline *n.* [1980s+] a line of cocaine.

pattie *n. see* PATTIE HEARST.

Pattie Hearst (*also* **pattie**) *n.* [1970s+] a first, i.e. a first-class degree. [*Pattie Hearst* = first; from the US heiress and former urban terrorist Pattie Hearst (b.1954)]

Paul Weller *n.* [1990s+] Stella Artois lager. [*Paul Weller* = Stella; from the singer-songwrighter Paul Weller (b.1958)]

pay me rent *n.* [20C] (*Aus.*) a tent.

peace and quiet *n.* [20C] a diet.

pear and quince *n.* [20C] (*Aus.*) a prince.

pearly gate *n.* [20C] a plate.

pearly king *n.* [20C] the anus; hence HAWK ONE'S PEARLY. [*pearly king* = ring; a Pearly King (or Queen) is, or more properly was, a leading London costermonger, dressed in festive costume covered with pearl-buttons]

pease pudding hot *n.* [20C] nasal mucus. [*pease pudding hot* = snot; from the nursery rhyme 'Pease pudding hot / Pease pudding cold / Pease pudding in the pot / Nine days old'; the colour and consistency also mimic mucus]

peas in the pot *adj.* [late 19C+] **1** hot. **2** sexy. [**2** *peas in the pot* = hot]

Pebble Mill *n.* [1960s+] (*drugs*) any form of pill, e.g. an amphetamine. [from the TV show *Pebble Mill at One*]

Peckham (Rye) *n.* [1920s+] a tie. [from Peckham Rye common, in the south-east London suburb of Peckham]

Pedigree Chum *n.* [20C] semen. [*Pedigree Chum* = come; from the Pedigree Chum brand of dog food]

pedlar's pack *n.* [1970s+] dismissal from a job. [*pedlar's pack* = the sack]

peep *v.* [late 17C–18C] (*UK Und.*) to sleep.

peg-legger *n.* [1930s–40s] a beggar. [a presumed reference to the many disabled WWI veterans reduced to beggary]

pen (and ink) *n.* **1** [mid-19C+] a stink. **2** [1960s] (*orig. Aus./N.Z.*) a drink.

pen and ink *v.* [late 19C+] **1** to stink. **2** to cause problems, to complain. [**2** *pen and ink* = (kick up a) stink]

pen and inker *n.* [1940s+] a suspicious person, esp. a possible informer. [*pen and inker* = stinker]

pencil, open, lost and found *n.* [late 19C] ten pounds (sterling).

penn'orth of bread *n.* [20C] the head.

penn'orth of chalk *n.* [late 19C+] a walk. [var. on BALL (AND/OF CHALK) *n.*]

penny-a-mile *n.* **1** [late 19C–1920s] a hat. **2** [late 19C–1920s] the head. **3** [20C] a smile. [**1, 2** *penny-a-mile* = tile (sl. 'hat', thus by extension 'head')]

penny-a-pound (*also* **penny-the-pound**) *n.* [late 19C+] the ground.

penny banger *n.* [20C] a mistake, a blunder. [*penny banger* = clanger]

penny black *n.* [20C] the back. [from the UK's first postage stamp, the penny black, issued in 1840]

penny brown *n.* [20C] (*Aus.*) a town.

penny bun *n.* [20C] **1** the number one. **2** the sun. **3** a son.

penny-come-quick *n*. [20C] a confidence trick.

penny for the guy *n*. [20C] a pie. ['penny for the guy' is the traditional demand of children on and around Guy Fawkes' Night, 5 November]

penny locket *n*. [late 19C] a pocket.

penny-the-pound *n*. *see* PENNY-A-POUND.

peppermint flavour *n*. [1960s] a favour.

peppermint rocks (*also* **peppermints**) *n*. [20C] socks. [var. on ALMOND ROCKS]

peppermints *n*. *see* PEPPERMINT ROCKS.

Percy Thrower *n*. [20C] the telephone. [*Percy Thrower* = blower; from the UK gardening expert Percy Thrower (1913–88)]

Perry Como *n*. [1950s] a homosexual. [*Perry Como* = homo; from the US singer Perry Como (b.1912)]

Pete Murray *n*. [1970s+] a curry. [from the UK DJ Pete Murray]

Peter and Lee *n*. [1990s+] a cup of tea. [from the singing duo Lennie Peters (1939–92) and Dianne Lee (b.1950)]

Peter O'Toole *n*. [1960s+] a (bar) stool. [from the UK actor and film star Peter O'Toole (b.1932)]

Peter Pan *n*. [20C] a van. [from J.M. Barrie's creation *Peter Pan* (1904), the ageless children's favourite]

Peters and Lee *n*. [1980s–90s] an act of urination. [*Peters and Lee* = pee/wee; *see* PETER AND LEE]

Pete Tong *adj.* [1980s] wrong. [from the UK dance DJ Pete Tong]

petrols *n.* [1970s] (*Aus.*) trousers. [*petrol bowsers* = trousers]

petrol tank *n.* [1950s+] an act of masturbation. [*petrol tank* = wank]

Petticoat Lane *n.* [20C] a pain. [from the East London street market, Petticoat Lane, properly Middlesex Street, London E1]

Peyton Place *n.* [1950s+] (*US*) the face. [from the best-selling novel (and later film and TV series) *Peyton Place* (1956) by Grace Metalious (1924–64)]

P.G. tips *n.* [20C] the lips. [from the popular P.G. Tips brand of tea]

philharmonic *n.* [20C] tonic water.

Phil McBee *n.* [mid-19C–1930s] a flea.

phil the fluter *n.* [20C] a gun. [*phil the fluter* = shooter; from the song 'Phil the Fluter's Ball' (1889)]

photo finish *n.* [20C] (a pint of) Guinness (stout).

Piccadilly *adj.* [20C] silly. [from Piccadilly, the major street in central London]

Piccadilly percy *n.* [1970s] mercy.

piccalilli *n.* [20C] the penis. [*piccalilli* = willie; from Heinz Piccalilli, a popular chutney-like condiment]

piccolo and flute *n.* [20C] a suit.

piccolo(s) and flutes *n*. [1930s+] boots.

pick and choose *n*. [20C] alcohol, liquor. [*pick and choose* = booze]

pickle and pork (*also* **pickled pork**) *n*. [1940s–50s] (*Aus.*) a walk.

pickled onion (*also* **Spanish onion**) *n*. [20C] a bunion. [possibly underpinned by the physical resemblance]

pickled pork *n*.[1] [late 19C–1930s] **1** talk, i.e. conversation. **2** chalk.

pickled pork *n*.[2] *see* PICKLE AND PORK.

pick up sticks *n*. [20C] the number six. [from the nursery/counting rhyme 'One two, buckle my shoe … five six, pick up sticks']

pie and liquor *n*. [20C] a vicar.

pie and mash *n*. [1970s+] **1** cash. **2** an act of urination. [**2** *pie and mash* = slash]

pie and mash *adj*. [1970s+] showy, ostentatious. [*pie and mash* – flash]

pie and one *n*. [20C] **1** a son. **2** the sun.

pieces of eight *n*. [20C] weight. [a *piece of eight* was the 17C Spanish dollar, or peso, of the value of eight reals; it was marked with the figure '8' and remains the classic currency of pirate stories]

pig and roast *n*. [20C] toast.

piggy bank *n.* [20C] an act of masturbation. [*piggy bank* = wank]

pig in the middle *n.* [20C] an act of urination. [*pig in the middle* = piddle]

pig's arse *n.* [20C] (*Aus.*) a glass.

pig's Christmas parcel! *excl.* [1960s+] (*N.Z.*) a general exclamation of annoyance. [*pig's Christmas parcel!* = arsehole!]

pig's (ear) *n.* [late 19C+] beer.

pig's fry *n.* [late 19C+] a tie. [from pig's fry, a dish made of fried pig's offal]

pig's fry *v.* [1930s+] to try. [*see* PIG'S FRY *n.*]

pig's trotter *n.* [1970s] a squatter.

pillar and post *n.* [20C] a ghost.

pimple and blotch *n.* [20C] Scotch whisky.

pimple and wart *n.* [late 19C–1950s] a quart, i.e. a quarter of a gallon (1.136 litres).

pineapple chunk *n.* **1** [20C] departure, escape. **2** [1990s+] (*Scot.*) semen. [*pineapple chunk* = **1** bunk **2** spunk]

pink lint *adj.* [20C] penniless, very poor. [*pink lint* = skint]

Pinky and Perky *n.* [1950s] a turkey. [from the puppets Pinky and Perky, popular children's TV characters (1957–72)]

pins and needles *n.* [20C] beetles.

pipe and drum *n.* [20C] the buttocks. [*pipe and drum* = bum]

pitch and fill *n.* [mid-19C] a nickname for a person called William. [*pitch and fill* = Bill]

pitch and toss *n.* [1940s+] the boss.

plain and gravy *n.* [late 19C–1900s] the Royal Navy.

plain and jam *n.* [1900s–20s] a tram.

plasterer's trowel and seringapatam *n.* [late 19C] a fowl and ham. [*plasterer's trowel* = fowl + *seringapatam* = ham; from the former capital of the Indian state of Mysore, Seringapatam (apparently used purely for assonance), home to Tipoo Sultan (*c.*1750–99), scourge of the English in southern India until they conquered and killed him]

plaster of Paris *n.* [20C] the buttocks. [*plaster of Paris* = ARRIS]

plate *v.* [1950s+] to fellate. [*plate of ham* = gam (sl. 'fellate')]

plate and dish *n.* [20C] a wish.

plate of meat *n.* [mid-19C] the street.

plate-rack *n.* [late 19C+] a horse. [*plate-rack* = hack]

plates and dishes *n.* [20C] kisses.

plates (of meat) *n.* [late 19C+] the feet.

pleasure and pain *n.* [20C] rain.

plinkity plonk *n.* [1910s+] (*Aus., orig. military*) white wine; cheap or second-rate wine. [*plinkity plonk* = vin blanc (French 'white wine')]

plough the deep *v.* [mid-19C] to go to sleep.

plum pud *adj.* [20C] (*Aus.*) good.

Plymouth Argyll *n.* [20C] a file, i.e. the tool. [from the English football team Plymouth Argyll]

poddy calf *n.* [20C] (*Aus.*) half-a-crown, two shillings and sixpence (12$\frac{1}{2}$ pence). [*poddy calf* = half; from Standard Aus. English *poddy* unbranded]

pogo *n.* [1970s+] (*Aus.*) the penis. [*pogo stick* = prick; plus a reference to 'bouncing up and down']

polish and gloss *v.* [20C] to masturbate. [*polish and gloss* = toss]

Polly Flinder *n.* [late 19C+] **1** a window. **2** a cinder. [from the nursery rhyme, 'Little Polly Flinders sat among the cinders'; note Cockney pronunciation of window as *winder*]

Polly Parrot *n.* [20C] a carrot.

polo mint *adj.* [1950s+] penniless, impoverished. [*polo mint* = skint]

pompey whore *n.* [1900s–40s] (*bingo*) the number four. [from *Pompey*, Royal Navalese for the home base of Portsmouth]

'pon my life *n.* [late 19C] a wife.

pony *n.* [late 19C+] **1** an act of defecation. **2** silver articles, e.g. cutlery. [*pony and trap* = crap; the inference in **2** is the relative worthlessness of such items as compared with gold]

poor relation *n.* [20C] the station.

popcorn *n.* [20C] an erection. [*popcorn* = horn]

Pope (of Rome) *n.* [mid-19C+] home.

popeye the sailor *n.* [20C] a tailor. [from the cartoon strip (and later film) 'Popeye', created in the 1930s by Elzie Segar]

pop goes the weasel *n.* [20C] diesel. [from the popular rhyme beginning 'Up and down the City Road, in and out the Eagle ...'; the etymology of 'pop goes the weasel' remains debatable; one feasible version suggests the image of *popping* or pawning a tailor's *weasel* or iron]

pork and bean *n.* [1960s+] (*Aus.*) a male homosexual. [*pork and bean* = queen]

pork chop *n.* [20C] a policeman. [*pork chop* = cop]

porky (pie) *n.* [20C] **1** a lie, often found in the pl. *porkies*. **2** an eye.

Porky Pig *adj.* [20C] generous. [*Porky Pig* = big; from the Warner Bros. cartoon character Porky Pig]

port and brandy *adj.* [20C] randy.

Port Melbourne Pier *n. see* MELBOURNE PIER.

Posh and Becks *n.* [2000s] sex. [from the celebrity couple David Beckham, the England footballer (b.1975), and his wife Victoria Adams ('Posh Spice', b.1975)]

postage stamp *n.* [20C] a bar (in a pub). [*postage stamp* = ramp (1930s sl. 'pub', 'bar')]

post-and-rail *n.* [1940s] (*Aus.*) a lie. [*post-and-rail* = fairy tale]

postman's knock *n.* [20C] a clock.

pot and pan *n.* [20C] a man.

potash and perlmutter *n.* [1910s–50s] butter. [from the play *Potash and Perlmutter* by Montague Glass, first performed in 1914]

potatoes in the mould *adj.* [20C] cold, esp. in the abbreviated form TATERS.

potato (peeler) *n.* [1950s+] (*Aus.*) a woman, a girlfriend. [*potato peeler* = sheila]

potato-pillin' *n.* [1930s] a shilling (five pence).

pot of glue *n.* [20C] **1** a Jew. **2** a queue.

pot of honey *n.* [late 19C+] money.

pot of jelly *n.* [20C] the stomach. [*pot of jelly* = belly]

pot of O *n.* [mid–late 19C] a glass or tankard of beer. [*see* OH, MY DEAR]

pots and dishes *n.* [1970s] wishes.

potted head *adj.* [20C] dead.

pound (of lead) *n.* [late 19C+] the head.

pound note *n.* [20C] a coat.

pound of butter *n.* [20C] an eccentric, a mad person. [*pound of butter* = nutter]

pound o' lead *n.* [late 19C–1900s] the head.

pounds and pence *n.* [20C] sense.

powdered chalk *n.* [late 19C+] a walk.

press and scratch *n.* [19C] a safety-match.

pride and joy *n.* [1930s–40s] (*Aus./US*) a boy.

prigg *n.* [1940s–50s] (*Aus.*) a busybody. [*wally prigg* = gig (sl. 'look', 'glance')]

Princess Di *n.* [1980s+] a pie. [from Diana, Princess of Wales (1961–97)]

prune and plum *n.* [20C] the buttocks, the behind. [*prune and plum* = bum]

prussian guard *n.* [1940s+] a card.

p's and q's *n.* [late 19C–1900s] shoes.

psychopathic *n.* [20C] traffic. [note Cockney pronunciation of psycopathic as *psychopaffic*]

pudding and gravy *n.* [1940s+] the Royal Navy.

pudding chef *adj.* [20C] deaf.

puddings and pies *n.* [mid-19C] the eyes. [var. on MINCE PIES]

puff and dart *n.* [late 19C–1930s] a start; as in *make a puff and dart* to begin, to make a start.

puff and drag *n.* [20C] a cigarette. [*puff and drag* = fag]

pull down the shutter *n.* [late 19C] butter.

pull rank *v.* [20C] to masturbate. [*pull rank* = wank]

pull-through *n.* [1970s] a Jew.

punch and judy *adj.* [20C] moody. [from the traditional children's puppet show 'Punch and Judy']

purple and mauve *n.* [20C] (*Aus.*) the stove.

push in the truck *n.* [1930s] sexual intercourse. [*push in the truck* = fuck]

pussy willow *n.* [20C] a pillow. [pussy willow is the name given to various types of willow tree on account of their fluffy catkins]

put and take *n.* [1920s+] a cake. [from the gambling game put and take, played with a six-sided top]

q

Quaker oat(s) *n.* [20C] a coat. [from the popular breakfast dish Quaker Porridge Oats]

quartern o' Bry *n.* [late 19C] a measure of gin. [Standard English *quartern* + BRIAN O'FLYNN]

quartern o' finger *n.* [late 19C] a measure of rum. [Standard English *quartern* + FINGER AND THUMB]

quarter to two *n.* [20C] a Jew.

quasimodo *n.* [20C] soda. [from the fictional Quasimodo, the Hunchback of Notre Dame, created in the novel *Notre Dame de Paris* (1831) by Victor Hugo; note Cockney pronunciation of quasimodo as *quasimoder*]

Queen of the South *n.* [20C] the mouth. [from the Scottish football team Queen of the South]

Queens Park Rangers *n.* [1960s+] (*also sing.*) strangers, esp. used as a warning by look-out men working with unlicensed street pitchmen. [from the West London football club Queens Park Rangers]

quiver and shake *n.* [20C] (*Aus.*) a steak.

r

rabbit *n.* [1940s+] a talk, a conversation. [*rabbit and pork* = talk]

rabbit *v.* [1940s+] to talk; hence *rabbit on* to chatter, to grumble, to complain. [*rabbit and pork* = talk]

rabbit hutch *n.* [20C] **1** the crutch, i.e. the groin. **2** a crutch.

rabbit's paw *n.* [20C] talk, conversation. [*rabbit's paw* = talk; note Cockney pronunciation of talk as *taw*]

racks (of meat) *n.* [20C] the female breasts. [*racks of meat* = teat/tit]

radio *adj.* [1970s+] insane, mad. [*radio rental* = mental; from the high-street rental chain Radio Rentals]

raffle ticket *n.* [20C] a mistake. [*raffle ticket* = ricket (1950s–60s sl. 'blunder')]

rag and bone *n.* [20C] the lavatory. [*rag and bone* = throne]

raging *n.* [1980s+] a first, i.e. a first-class degree. [*raging thirst* = first]

rain and pour *v.* [20C] to snore.

raleigh bike *n.* [20C] a lesbian. [*raleigh bike* = dyke]

Ralph Lynn *n.* [1920s–40s] gin. [from the UK actor Ralph

Lynn (1882–1964), best known from the Ben Travers farces of the 1920s]

rammy rousers *n.* [20C] (*Aus.*) trousers. [plus a link to Aus./S Afr. sl. *rammies* trousers]

Ramsgate sands *n.* [20C] the hands. [from the popular Kent resort of Ramsgate]

Randolph Scott *n.* [20C] a spot. [from the US film star Randolph Scott (1898–1987)]

rangoon *n.* [20C] a prune.

Raquel Welch *n.* [20C] a belch. [from the US film star Raquel Welch (b.1940)]

rasher and bubble *n.* [1970s] in darts, a throw between the two outer circles. [*rasher and bubble* = double]

raspberry *n.*[1] [late 19C+] **1** a coarse, dismissive, jeering noise. **2** a rejection, a dismissal. [*raspberry tart* = fart, the noise of which this resembles; **2** is an ext. use of **1**]

raspberry *n.*[2] [1970s+] **1** a nipple. **2** a disabled person. [**2** *raspberry ripple* = cripple]

raspberry tart *n.* **1** [late 19C+] the heart. **2** [1950s+] a breaking of wind. [**2** *raspberry tart* = fart]

rat and mouse *n.* **1** [late 19C+] a house. **2** [20C] an unpleasant person. [**2** *rat and mouse* = louse]

ratcatcher's daughter *n.* [20C] water (for drinking).

rats and mice *n.* **1** [1930s] a game of dice. **2** [1970s+] rice.

rattle and clank *n.* [20C] a bank.

rattle and hiss *n.* [20C] an act of urination. [*rattle and hiss* = piss]

rattle and jar *n.* [20C] (*US*) a car.

rattlesnakes *n.* [20C] delirium tremens. [*rattlesnakes* = the shakes]

rat trap *n.* [1940s+] a Japanese person. [*rat trap* = Jap]

raughty *adj. see* RORTY.

raw and ripe *n.* [20C] a tobacco pipe.

rawlpindi *adj.* [1940s–50s] of the weather, windy. [from the Pakistani city of Rawalpindi]

razor (blade) *n.* [1960s+] (*derog.*) a Black person. [*razor blade* = spade]

read and write *n.* [mid-19C] **1** an escape. **2** a fight. [**1** *read and write* = flight]

read and write *v.* [mid-19C] to fight.

read of tripe *n.* [mid-19C] transportation for life. [a partial rhyme from former Standard English *read* the stomach of an animal (from which comes tripe) + the '*tripe*' that is *read* out in court]

red hots *n.* [1950s+] (*Aus.*) **1** trotting races. **2** dysentery. [*red hots* = **1** trots **2** the trots]

red rum *adj.* [1970s+] dumb. [from the triple Grand National-winning horse Red Rum]

red steer *n.* [1940s] (*US*) beer.

◆◆◆

A Day at the Races

MEETINGS

Ascot races	races/braces
Epsom races	braces/faces
Flemington races	braces
Sheffield handicap	crap
Warwick Farm	arm

HORSES

derby winner	dinner
grey mare	fare
old nag	fag
red rum	dumb
shaun spadah	car

TRAINERS

Greville Starkey	darkie
Harry Wragg	fag

◆◆◆

red, white and blue *n.* [1970s] a shoe.

reeling *n.* [late 19C] a feeling.

reeling and rocking *n.* [1950s–60s] a stocking.

reels of cotton *adj.* [1970s] rotten.

reels of cotton 215

reggie and ronnie *n.* [1960s+] a condom. [*reggie and ronnie* = johnnie; from the UK gangsters Reggie Kray (b.1933) and his brother Ronnie (1933–95); they offered 'protection']

Reg Grundys (*also* **reggys, reginalds**) *n.* [1980s] (*Aus.*) underwear. [*Reg Grundys* = undies; from the Australian media executive Reg Grundy (b.1923)]

reggys *n. see* REG GRUNDYS.

Reginald Denny *n.* [1940s–50s] a penny. [from the UK film actor Reginald Denny (1891–1967)]

reginalds *n. see* REG GRUNDYS.

Reverend Ronald Knox *n.* [1950s] syphilis. [*Reverend Ronald Knox* = pox; from the Catholic clergyman Ronald Knox (1888–1957)]

rhubarb *n.* [20C] an advance on one's wages. [*rhubarb* = sub; note Cockney pronunciation of rhubarb as *rubbub*]

rhubarb pill *n.* [late 19C] **1** a bill. **2** a hill. [**1** involves a pun on the fact that both a bill and the consumption of rhubarb will require a 'giving out']

rhythm and blues *n.* [1950s+] shoes.

ribbon and curl *n.* [20C] a little girl.

Richard Burton *n.* [20C] a curtain. [from the Welsh actor Richard Burton (1925–84)]

Richard (the Third) *n.* **1** [late 19C+] a piece of excrement. **2** [20C] a word. **3** [1920s+] booing, barracking. **4** [1940s+] a young woman, a girlfriend. **5** [1980s+] a third, i.e. a third-class degree. [*Richard the Third* = **1** turd **3** the bird **4** bird]

rick and dick *adj*. [1960s] stupid. [*rick and dick* = thick]

rickety kate *n*. [20C] (*Aus*.) a gate.

riddle-me-ree *n*. [20C] an act of urination. [*riddle-me-ree* = pee/wee]

riff-raff *n*. [20C] **1** a Welsh person. **2** a café. [*riff-raff* = **1** taff **2** caff]

rifle range *n*. [20C] change.

rinky dink *n*. [20C] **1** the pink, i.e. the best of health, cicumstances etc., as in *in the rinky dink*. **2** in snooker, the pink ball.

rip and tear *v*. [20C] to swear.

rip rap *v*. [1930s+] to borrow money; hence *the rip-rap* the act of obtaining such a loan. [*rip rap* = tap]

Rip Van Winkle *v*. [20C] to urinate. [*Rip Van Winkle* = tinkle; from US writer Washington Irving's story *Rip Van Winkle* (1820)]

rise and shine *n*. [20C] wine.

rising damp *n*. [20C] cramp.

riverina *n*. [1920s–60s] (*Aus*.) a shilling (five pence). [*riverina* = deaner (19C–1960s sl. 'shilling')]

River Lea *n*. **1** [mid-19C] tea. **2** [1900s] the sea.

River Murry *n*. [20C] (*Aus*.) a curry.

River Nile *n*. [20C] a smile.

River Ooze *n. see* RIVER OUSE.

River Ouse (*also* **River Ooze**) *n.* [1930s+] alcohol, liquor. [*River Ouse* = booze; from the River Ouse, which runs through Bedfordshire]

River Tyne *n.* [20C] wine. [from the north-eastern British River Tyne]

roach and dace *n.* [20C] the face.

roaring horsetails *n.* [20C] (*Aus.*) the aurora australis.

roaring rain *n.* [20C] (*Aus.*) a train.

roast beef *n.* [20C] teeth. [note Cockney pronunciation of teeth as *teef*]

roasted duck *n.* [1930s] sexual intercourse. [*roasted duck* = fuck; unmentioned by Partridge or Franklyn, this may be a nonce-word, invented by Christopher Isherwood and W.H. Auden in their play *The Dog beneath the Skin* (1935): 'O how I cried when Alice died / The day we were to have wed! / We never had our Roasted Duck / And now she's a Loaf of Bread']

roastie *n. see* ROAST POTATO.

roast joint *n.* [20C] a pint of beer. [note Cockney pronunciation of joint as *jint*]

roast pork *n.* **1** [1910s+] a talk. **2** [1940s] a table fork.

roast potato (*also* **roastie**) *n.* [20C] a waiter.

Roberta Flack *n.* [1970s] (*Aus.*) bed; hence *hit the Roberta* to go to bed. [*Roberta Flack* = sack; from the disco diva Roberta Flack (b.1937)]

robert e. *n.* [20C] **1** a knee. **2** an act of urination. [*robert e. lee* = **1** knee **2** pee/wee; from General Robert E. Lee (1807–70), who led the Confederate armies during the American Civil War]

Robertson (and Moffat) *n.* [1940s+] (*Aus.*) a profit. [from the Aus. trading house Robertson and Moffat]

Robin Hood *adj.* [late 19C+] good. [from the mythical outlaw Robin Hood of Sherwood Forest]

Robin Hoods *n.* [20C] **1** (material) goods. **2** woods. [*see* ROBIN HOOD]

Robinson and Cleaver *n.* [20C] a fever. [from the defunct London department store Robinson and Cleaver]

Robinson Crusoe *v.* [late 19C–1940s] (*often imper.*) to do so. [from Daniel Defoe's novel *Robinson Crusoe* (1719), based on the real-life adventures of the castaway Alexander Selkirk]

rob my pal *n.* [20C] a woman. [*rob my pal* = gal]

Rob Roy *n.* [mid-19C–1920s] a boy. [from the Scots hero Rob Roy McGregor (d.1734)]

rock and lurch *n.* [20C] (*Aus.*) a church

rock and roll *n.* [20C] the dole.

rock and roll *v.* [1990s+] to have sexual intercourse. [*rock and roll* = get one's hole]

rocking horse *n.* [20C] **1** sauce (a condiment). **2** sauce, i.e. impudence, cheek.

rock 'n' roll *n.* [20C] **1** a hole. **2** the dole.

rock of ages (*also* **rocks**) *n.* [1930s+] wages.

rocks *n. see* ROCK OF AGES.

rocks and boulders *n.* [late 19C–1920s] the shoulders.

Roger Hunt *n.* [1960s+] the vagina. [*Roger Hunt* = cunt; from the former Liverpool and England footballer Roger Hunt (b.1938)]

rogue and villain *n.* [mid-19C] a shilling (five pence).

Roland Young *n.* [20C] the tongue. [from the UK character actor Roland Young (1887–1953)]

rollick *v.* [1920s+] **1** to tell off, to reprimand; hence *a good rollicking*. **2** to make a fuss, to complain loudly. [*rollick* = bollock]

rolling billow *n.* [late 19C+] a pillow.

rolling deep *n.* [20C] (*Aus.*) sleep.

roll me (in the dirt) *n.* [20C] a shirt.

roll me in the gutter *n.* [20C] (*Aus.*) butter.

Rolls Royce *n.* [20C] the voice. [from the Rolls Royce luxury marque of motor-car]

Roman candle *n.* [20C] a sandal.

romantic ballad *n.* [20C] salad.

Ronnie Biggs *n.* [20C] lodgings. [*Ronnie Biggs* = digs; from Ronald 'Ronnie' Biggs (b.1929), one of the Great Train Robbers of 1963]

ronson *n.*[1] [1950s+] a pimp. [*rons(on)* = ponce]

ronson *n.*[2] [1990s+] the anus; hence the dismissive exclamation *up your ronson!* [*ronson lighter* = shiter, i.e. shitter; from the popular brand of Ronson table-lighters]

rookery nook *n.* [1920s+] a book. [from the Ben Travers farce *Rookery Nook* (1926)]

rorty (*also* **raughty**) *adj.* [late 19C+] **1** fine, splendid, jolly. **2** boisterous, rowdy, noisy. **3** of drinks, intoxicating. **4** of behaviour, speech etc., coarse, earthy, crudely comic. [*rorty* = naughty or Yiddish *rorität* anything choice]

Rory (O'Moore) *n.* **1** [mid-19C+] the floor; hence *on the Rory (O'Moore)* in a bad way. **2** [late 19C+] a door. **3** [late 19C+] a prostitute. [**3** *Rory O'Moore* = whore]

Roseanne (Barr) *n.* [1980s+] a bra. [from the US TV star Roseanne Barr (b.1953)]

rosebuds *n.* [late 19C+] potatoes. [*rosebuds* = spuds]

roses red *n.* [20C] (*Aus.*) a bed.

Rosie (Lea) (*also* **Rosy (Lee)**, **Rosy Lea**) *n.* [1920s+] (*orig. military*) **1** tea. **2** a flea.

Rosie Loader (*also* **Rosie Loder**, **Rosy Loader**, **Rosy Loder**) *n.* [20C] a whisky and soda. [var. on MAJOR LODER]

Rosie Loder *n. see* ROSIE LOADER.

Rosie O'Grady's *n.* [20C] the ladies' (lavatory). [from the film *Sweet Rosie O'Grady* (1943), starring Betty Grable]

Rosy Lea *n. see* ROSIE (LEA).

Rosy (Lee) *n. see* ROSIE (LEA).

Rosy Loader *n. see* ROSIE LOADER.

Rosy Loder *n. see* ROSIE LOADER.

Rotten Row *n.* **1** [late 19C] a bow, i.e. for one's hair. **2** [20C] a blow. [from the riding track Rotten Row, used by fashionable 19C society, around Hyde Park, London; promenading on horseback 'in the Row' was a daily necessity for the smart]

round and square *adv.* [late 19C–1900s] everywhere.

round me houses (*also* **round the houses**) *n.* [mid-19C+] trousers; hence PAIR O' ROUND-MYS.

round the houses *n. see* ROUND ME HOUSES.

Rowton Houses (*also* **Rowtons**) *n.* [20C] trousers. [from the Rowton Houses, working men's lodging houses, established by Lord Rowton (Montagu Lowry), who opened the first, in Vauxhall, in 1892]

Rowtons *n. see* ROWTON HOUSES.

royal docks *n.* [20C] venereal disease. [*royal docks* = pox]

royal mail *n.* [20C] (*mainly Und.*) bail.

royal navy *n.* [20C] gravy.

Roy Castle *n.* [1970s+] the anus. [*Roy Castle* = arsehole; from the UK comedian and TV presenter Roy Castle (1932–94)]

Roy Rodgers *n.* [20C] second-rate builders. [*Roy Rogers* = bodgers; from the US film cowboy Roy Rogers

(1912–98); perhaps also a pun on the standard sl. *cowboys* unethical tradesmen]

rubadub *n. see* RUB-A-DUB.

rub-a-dub (*also* **rubadub, rub-a-dub-dub, rubbity dub**) *n.* [late 19C+] **1** a pub. **2** a drinking club. **3** a nightclub or social club. **4** an advance on wages. [**4** *rub-a-dub* = sub]

rub-a-dub-dub *n. see* RUB-A-DUB.

rubber duck *n.* [20C] sexual intercourse. [*rubber duck* = fuck]

rubbity dub *n. see* RUB-A-DUB.

Ruby Murray *n.* [1970s+] a curry. [from the popular singer Ruby Murray (1935–96)]

ruby red *n.* [1900s] the head.

ruby rose *n.* [20C] the nose.

ruck and row *n.* [20C] an unpleasant woman. [*ruck and row* = cow]

Rudolph (Hess) *n.* [1950s+] a mess. [from the Nazi leader Rudolph Hess (1894–87)]

ruin and spoil *n.* [20C] oil.

rumdadum *n.* [1910s–20s] the buttocks. [*rumdadum* = bum]

runner and rider *n.* [20C] cider.

Rupert Bears *n.* [1980s+] (business) shares. [from the children's cartoon strip *Rupert Bear*, launched in the *Daily*

Express in 1920 by Mary Tourtel; after her retirement in 1935 it was drawn by Alfred Betall]

Russell Harty *n.* [20C] a party. [from the UK TV personality Russell Harty (1934–88)]

Russian duck *n.* **1** [1910s–20s] dirt. **2** [1970s] sexual intercourse. [*Russian duck* = **1** muck **2** fuck]

Russian Turk *n.* [mid-19C–1900s] work.

Ruud Gullit *n.* [1980s+] a bullet. [from the Dutch footballer and manager Ruud Gullit (b.1962)]

Ryan Giggs *n.* [1990s+] lodgings. [*Ryan Giggs* = digs; from the Manchester United and Wales footballer Ryan Giggs (b.1973)]

S

sacks of rice *n.* [20C] mice.

sad and sorry *n.* [20C] a lorry.

Saddam Hussein *n.* [1990s+] a pain. [from the Iraqi dictator Saddam Hussein (b.1937)]

safe and sound *n.* [20C] the ground.

sailors on the sea *n.* [20C] tea.

saint and sinner *n.* [late 19C+] dinner.

St Louis blues *n.* [20C] (*Aus.*) shoes. [possibly from the US ice hockey team the St Louis Blues]

St Martin's (le Grand) (*also* **Martin's**) *n.* [mid-19C–1940s] the hand. [from the monastery and college St Martin's le Grand founded *c.*1050; its bells rang the nightly curfew, and prisoners on their way from Newgate to Tyburn regularly passed it; those who managed to escape were able to claim sanctuary within its walls – thieves and coiners were accepted, Jews and traitors were barred. The monastery was suppressed in 1540, and its only memorial is a street name]

Saint Moritz *n.* [1960s+] diarrhoea. [*Saint Moritz* = the shits; from the famous ski resort of Saint Moritz, Switzerland]

Salisbury Crag *n.* [1980s] (*drugs*) heroin. [*Salisbury Crag* = scag; from Edinburgh's famous geological landmark Salisbury Crags]

Sally Gunnell *n.* [1990s+] the Blackwall Tunnel. [from the UK athlete Sally Gunnell (b.1966)]

salmon and trout *n.* **1** [mid-19C+] (*esp. prison*) tobacco. **2** [mid-19C+] the mouth. **3** [20C] the snout, i.e. the nose. **4** [20C] stout (beer). **5** [1930s] a bookmaker's tout. **6** [1930s+] gout. [*salmon and trout* = **1** snout]

salt (junk) *adj.* [late 19C+] very drunk. [*salt junk* = drunk, although possibly a pun on *pickled*]

salty bananas *n.* [20C] (*Aus.*) sultanas.

salvation *n.* [late 19C–1910s] a station.

Salvation Army *adj.* [late 19C] **1** crazy, eccentric. **2** drunk. [*Salvation Army* = barmy; from the fervent and teetotal Christian group, the Salvation Army, founded in 1865 by William Booth as the Christian Mission]

Sammy Lee *n.* [20C] an act of urination. [*Sammy Lee* = pee/wee; possibly from the US diver Sammy Lee (b.1920)]

Samuel Pepys *n.* [20C] a sense of unease or distaste, a nervous feeling. [*Samuel Pepys* = the creeps; from the British diarist and civil servant Samuel Pepys (1633–1703)]

Sandy Macnab *n.* **1** [1910s+] (*usu. pl.*) a body louse. **2** [1920s+] (*Aus.*) a non-unionist. **3** [1940s+] a taxi-cab. [*Sandy Macnab* = **1** crab **2** scab]

Sandy Powell *n.* [1940s–50s] **1** a trowel. **2** a towel. [from the northern radio/music-hall comedian Albert 'Sandy' Powell (1898–1982)]

san toys *n.* [1930s] villains, criminals. [*san toys* = the boys; from San Toy, the brandname of a small cigar]

Sarah Soo *n.* [1920s+] a Jew. [the use of the popular Jewish name *Sarah* may be coincidental]

sargent's pie *n.* [1940s–50s] (*Aus.*) an eye. [from the popular Sargent's brand of meat pie, sold in Sydney]

satin and lace *n.* [20C] the face.

satin and silk *n.* [20C] milk.

saucepan lid *n.* **1** [late 19C] (*usu. pl.*) money. **2** [late 19C+] a tease. **3** [1950s+] (*derog.*) a Jew. **4** [1960s+] a child. [*saucepan lid* = **1** quid **2** kid **3** Yid **4** kid]

sausage (a goose's) *v.* [1920s] to cash a cheque. [SAUSAGE (AND MASH) + GOOSE'S NECK]

sausage and mash *n.* **1** [late 19C+] cash. **2** [1950s] a smash, a crash.

sausage (and mash) *v.* [1920s+] to cash (a cheque); hence SAUSAGE (A GOOSE'S).

sausage roll *n.* **1** [1920s+] the dole. **2** [1940s+] a Pole. **3** [1960s+] (*Aus.*) a goal.

saveloy *n.* [20C] a boy.

savoury rissole *n.* [20C] **1** a lavatory. **2** anywhere dirty or unpleasant. [*savoury rissole* = pisshole]

Scapa Flow *v.* [1910s+] to run away. [*Scapa Flow* = go; the immediate reference is geographical, i.e. to Scapa Flow, off northern Scotland, where in 1918 the defeated German fleet was scuttled; but note the mid-19C+ Parlari *scarper* (from Italian *scappare*) to escape, to run away]

Scarborough Fair *n.* [20C] hair.

Schindler's (List) *adj.* [1990s+] drunk. [*Schindler's List* = pissed; from the film *Schindler's List* (1993) and ultimately the novel *Schindler's Ark* (1982) by Thomas Kenneally (b.1935)]

Scooby Doo *n.* [1970s+] (*UK prison*) a warder. [*Scooby Doo* = screw; from the TV cartoon dog Scooby Doo]

Scotch eggs *n.* [mid-19C+] the legs. [var. on SCOTCH PEGS]

Scotch pegs *n.* **1** [mid-19C+] the legs. **2** [20C] eggs.

Scotland (the Brave) *v.* [20C] to shave.

scrambled eggs *n.* [20C] the legs.

scrum (*also* **scrummy**) *n.* [late 19C–1910s] (*Aus./N.Z.*) a threepenny piece. [*scrum* = thrums (17C–1960s sl. 'threepence')]

scrummy *n. see* SCRUM.

scuba (diver) *n.* [1950s+] a five-pound note. [*scuba diver* = fiver]

sealing wax *n.* [20C] (*Aus.*) tax.

seek and search *n.* [20C] a church. [presumably referring to the search for salvation or absolution]

seldom see *n.* [20C] (*US*) underwear. [*seldom see* = BVDs, a US brand of male underwear]

seldom seen *n.* [20C] the queen.

Selina Scott *n.* [20C] a spot. [from the UK TV personality Selina Scott]

semolina *n.* [20C] a cleaner, i.e. a charwoman.

sentimental *n.* [1920s–70s] (*Aus.*) a cigar or cigarette. [*sentimental bloke* = smoke]

seppo *n. see* SEPTIC.

September morn *n.* [1970s+] an erection. [*September morn* = horn; possibly linked to a man's early morning erection, but note 'September Morn' a painting by Paul Chabas of a young woman bathing nude, which was first exhibited at the 1912 Salon in Paris. Censors attempted to ban a reproduction of the picture from public exhibition in the US, a farcical effort, which led to the sale of more than 7 million reproductions – appearing on dolls, statues, umbrella handles, tattoos and many other places – and the assurance that Chabas need never work again]

septic (*also* **seppo**) *n.* [1970s+] an American. [*septic tank* = Yank]

Seven Dials *n.* [1970s+] haemorrhoids. [*Seven Dials* = piles; from Seven Dials, London WC2, the meeting place of seven small streets, marked by a seven-faced clock on a Doric pillar, originally erected in 1694]

seven-times-seven man *n.* [late 19C] a hypocritical

evangelist. [*seven-times-seven man* = heaven man, or from his repetitious praying]

Sexton Blake *n*. [late 19C+] **1** a cake. **2** a fake. [from the fictional detective Sexton Blake, created by 'Hal Meredith' (Harry Blyth) in *The Halfpenny Marvel* magazine (1893)]

shabba *v*. [1990s+] to masturbate. [*shabba rank* = wank; from the US reggae star Shabba Ranks, real name Rexton Gordon (b.1965)]

shake and shiver *n*. [20C] (*Aus.*) a river.

shandy *n*. [20C] a male homosexual. [*chandelier* = queer]

shank *v*. [20C] to masturbate. [*shank* = wank]

Sharon Stone *n*. [1980s+] a (usu. mobile) telephone. [from the US film star Sharon Stone (b.1957)]

sharp and blunt *n*. [20C] the vagina; hence *have a bit of sharp and blunt* to have sexual intercourse. [*sharp and blunt* = cunt]

sharper's tools *n*. [late 18C–19C] fools. [note standard sl. *sharper's tools* false dice]

shaun spadah *n*. [1920s] a motor-car. [from the racehorse Shaun Spadah, winner of the 1921 Grand National]

Sheffield handicap *n*. [20C] an act of defecation. [*Sheffield handicap* = crap]

shellmex *n*. [20C] sex.

Shepherd's Bush *n*. [20C] **1** the face. **2** dismissal. [*Shepherd's Bush* = **1** mush **2** the push; from the West London suburb of Shepherd's Bush]

Screen Goddesses

Betty Grable	table
Diana Dors	44
Goldie Hawn	prawn
Jane Russell	mussel
Loretta Young	tongue
Mae West	breast
Myrna Loy	saveloy
Raquel Welch	belch
Sharon Stone	mobile phone
Veronica Lake	steak

Something for the ladies ...

Alan Ladd	sad
Charles Dance	chance
Errol Flynn	chin
Gregory Peck	neck
Richard Burton	curtain
Steve McQueens	jeans
Stewart Granger	danger
Sylvester Stallone	alone
Tom Cruise	booze
Tyrone Power	shower

◆◆◆

shepherd's pie *n.* [20C] the sky.

shepherd's (plaid) *adj.* [mid-19C–1910s] bad.

sherbert (dab) *n.* [1990s+] a taxi-cab.

sherbert dip *n.* [20C] a tip.

sherman *n.* [1940s+] **1** an American. **2** an act of masturbation. [*sherman tank* = **1** Yank **2** wank]

shillings and pence *n.* [20C] sense.

shiny and bright *phr.* [20C] all right.

ship in full sail *n.* [mid-19C] a pot of ale.

ship under sale *n.* [1930s] a story used for begging or for a confidence trick. [*ship under sale* = tale]

shirt (and) collar *n.* [mid-19C–1930s] five shillings (25 pence). [*shirt and collar* = dollar]

shiver and shake *n.* [20C] a (slice of) cake.

shoes and socks *n.* [20C] venereal disease. [*shoes and socks* = pox]

shout and holler *n.* [20C] a collar.

shovel and broom *n.* [1920s–50s] (*Aus./US*) a room.

shovel and pick *n.* [20C] **1** a prison. **2** an Irishman. [*shovel and pick* = **1** nick **2** mick]

shovel and spade *n.* [20C] a blade, a knife.

shovel and tank *n.* [20C] a bank.

shovels and spades *n.* [1980s+] AIDS. [underpinned by the reference to a gravedigger's equipment]

shower bath *n.* [20C] ten shillings (50 pence); hence *showers to a shilling* (odds of) 10:1. [*shower bath* = half; note Cockney pronunciation of shower bath as *shahr barf*]

shower of rain *n.* [20C] (*Aus.*) a train.

sideways *n.* [1960s+] (*N.Z. prison*) suicide. [a marginal rhyme]

sighs and tears *n.* [1940s–50s] (*US*) ears.

sigmunds *n.* [1990s+] haemorrhoids. [*sigmund freuds* = haemorrhoids; from the Austrian pyscho-analyst Sigmund Freud (1856–1939)]

Sigourney Weaver *n.* [1990s+] the female genitals, esp. the pubic hair. [*Sigourney Weaver* = beaver; from the US film star Sigourney Weaver (b.1949)]

silent night *n.* [20C] light ale. [from the popular Christmas carol 'Silent Night']

silver (and gold) *adj.* [20C] old. [the image is of ageing hair]

silver spoon *n.* (*Aus.*) **1** [1940s+] the moon. **2** [1940s+] a pimp. [**2** *silver spoon* = hoon (Aus. sl. 'procurer of prostitutes')]

silvery (moon) *n.* **1** [1950s+] (*derog.*) a Black person. **2** [1970s] (*Aus.*) a pimp. [*silvery moon* = **1** coon **2** hoon (Aus. sl. 'procurer of prostitutes')]

simple simon *n.* **1** [1920s+] a diamond, usu. a diamond ring. **2** [1960s] (*drugs*) the hallucinogen psilocybin.

Sinbad the sailor *n.* [late 19C+] a tailor. [from the mythical Near Eastern adventurer Sinbad the Sailor]

Sir Anthony Blunt *n.* [1980s] a highly objectionable person. [*Sir Anthony Blunt* = cunt; from the UK art historian and traitor Anthony Blunt (1907–83)]

Sir Berkeley *n.* [1930s] **1** the vagina. **2** sexual intercourse. [*Sir Berkeley Hunt* = cunt]

Sir Walter Scott *n.* [mid-19C] a pot (usu. of beer). [from the Scottish novelist Sir Walter Scott (1771–1832)]

sit beside her *n.* [20C] a spider. [from the nursery rhyme of 'Little Miss Muffet': 'Along came a spider, who sat down beside her …']

six and eight *n.* [1960s+] a condition of emotional stress. [*six and eight* = state]

six-and-eight *adj.* [1930s+] honest. [*six-and-eight* = straight]

six months' hard *n.* [20C] a bingo card.

six to four *n.* [1930s] a prostitute. [*six to four* = whore]

skein of thread *n.* **1** [19C] a bed. **2** [late 19C–1930s] a loaf of bread.

skin-and-blister *n.* [1920s+] a sister. [never truncated]

skinny as a broom *n.* [20C] a bridegroom. [a jocular reversal of FAT AND WIDE and a possible reference to the fat-free Jack Sprat and his corpulent wife]

skip and jump *n.* [20C] the heart. [*skip and jump* = pump]

sky *n.* [1920s+] (*Aus. derog.*) an Italian. [*sky* = Eyetie]

sky-diver *n*. [20C] a five-pound note. [*sky-diver* = fiver]

skylark *n*. [20C] a park.

skylark *v*. [1950s+] to park (a vehicle).

sky-pocket *n*. [1940s] (*US Black*) an inside pocket. [a partial rhyme]

sky (rocket) *n*. [late 19C+] a pocket.

sky the wipe *n*. [1940s] (*US*) a hypodermic syringe. [*sky the wipe* = hype]

slap and tickle *n*. [20C] a pickle. [note standard sl. *slap and tickle* sexual embraces or intercourse]

slapsie maxie *n*. [1930s+] (*Aus./N.Z.*) a taxi. [from the US boxer 'Slapsie' Maxie Rosenbloom (*fl.*1930s)]

sleek wife *n*. [19C] a handkerchief. [probably rhyming slang]

slice of ham *n*. [20C] fellatio. [*slice of ham* = gam (sl. 'fellatio')]

slice of toast *n*. [20C] a ghost.

slide and sluther *n*. [20C] a brother.

sling one's daniel (*also* **take one's daniel**) *v*. [mid-19C] (*US*) to leave. [etymology unknown; possibly a lost rhyming link referring to some form of pack, although given the occasional synonym *sling one's dannet*, the link may be to dialect *donnot/dannet* a good-for-nothing]

slip in the gutter *n*. [20C] butter.

slippery-dip *n*. [20C] (*Aus.*) cheekiness. [*slippery-dip* = lip]

slippery (Sid) *n.* [1990s+] (*derog.*) a Jew. [*slippery Sid* = Yid, plus negative stereotyping]

slither *n.* [late 19C+] a lodge (e.g. of Freemasonry). [*slither and dodge* = lodge; underpinned by the continuing image of the Freemasons as a slightly dubious organization]

sloop of war *n.* [mid-19C] a prostitute. [*sloop of war* = whore; but note such standard sl. synonyms as *land carrack, frigate* and *pinnace*]

slop *n.* [mid-19C] a policeman. [*slop* = cop, or backslang from *police*]

slosh and mud *n.* [20C] a (collar or ear) stud.

slug and snail *n.* [20C] a (finger)nail.

slum of slops *n.* [1940s] (*US*) beer. [*slum of slops* = hops]

smack in the eye *n.* [20C] a pie.

smart and simple *n.* [1940s] (*US*) a dimple.

smash *n.* [mid-19C+] cash, usu. change. [note UK Und. sl. *smash* counterfeit money and *smasher* a counterfeiter]

smash and grab *n.* [20C] a taxi-cab.

smear and smudge *n.* [20C] a judge.

smile and smirk *n.* [20C] work.

smooth and coarse *n.* [1940s] (*US*) a horse.

snake in the grass *n.* [mid-19C+] **1** a looking glass, a mirror. **2** a drinking glass. [either of which might prove a 'treacherous friend']

snake's (hiss) *n.* [20C] (*Aus.*) **1** an act of urination. **2** a lavatory. [*snake's hiss* = piss]

sniffer and snorter *n.* [20C] a newspaper reporter.

snoop and pry *v.* [20C] to cry.

snoozing and snoring *adj.* [20C] boring.

snow and ice *n.* [20C] a price.

snow and rain *n.* [20C] (*US*) a railway train.

Snow Whites *n.* [1970s+] tights.

soap *n.* [1990s+] (*drugs*) cannabis. [*soap* = dope]

soap and flannel *n.* [1910s–40s] the drawing of sickness benefit. [*soap and flannel* = the panel, i.e. those doctors who accepted patients under the National Health Insurance Act (1913)]

soap and lather *n.* [late 19C+] a father.

soap and water *n.* [20C] a daughter.

soapy bubble *n.* [20C] trouble.

Sodom and Gomorrah *v.* [20C] to borrow. [from the biblical story of Lot and his hapless wife; note Cockney pronunciation of borrow as *borrer*]

soft as silk *n.* [20C] (*Aus.*) milk.

solder ants *n.* [20C] pants, i.e. underwear.

soldier bold *n.* [mid-19C–1930s] a (head) cold.

soldiers bold *adj.* [20C] cold.

Somerset (Maugham) *adj.* [1910s+] warm. [from the UK writer William Somerset Maugham (1874–1965)]

song and dance *n.* [1910s–30s] a male homosexual. [*song and dance* = nance]

song of the thrush *n.* [mid–late 19C] **1** a brush, a broom. **2** a brush-off, a rebuff.

songs and sighs *n.* [20C] (*US*) the thighs.

sorrowful tale *n.* [mid-19C] **1** a prison. **2** a three-month sentence. [*sorrowful tale* = jail]

sorry and sad *n.* [20C] a father. [*sorry and sad* = dad]

sorry and sad *adj.* [19C+] bad.

soup and gravy *n.* [20C] the Royal Navy.

Southend-on-Sea *n.* [20C] an act of urination. [*Southend-on-Sea* = pee/wee; from the popular Essex resort of Southend-on-Sea, much frequented by Cockneys]

Southend pier *n.* [20C] an ear. [*see* SOUTHEND-ON-SEA]

south of France *n.* [late 19C+] a dance.

south of the Equator *n.* [1940s] (*US*) an elevator.

South Pole *n.* **1** [19C] the vagina. **2** [20C] the anus. [*South Pole* = hole]

south Sydney *n.* [20C] (*Aus.*) a kidney.

spam fritter *n.* [1990s+] the anus. [*spam fritter* = shitter]

Spanish guitar *n.* [20C] (*US*) a cigar.

Spanish main *n.* [20C] a drain.

Spanish onion *n. see* PICKLED ONION.

Spanish waiter *n*. [20C] a potato. [note Cockney pronunciation of potato as *pertater*]

spare rib *n*. [20C] a lie. [*spare rib* = fib]

spinning top *n*. [1940s] (*US*) a policeman. [*spinning top* = cop]

spire and steeple *n*. [20C] (*Aus.*) people.

spit and a drag *n*. [late 19C+] (*orig. naval*) a surreptitious smoke. [*spit and a drag* = fag, or the result of a badly rolled cigarette, from which one spits out the odd strand of tobacco, while dragging or drawing down the smoke]

split asunder *n*. [mid-19C] a costermonger.

split pea *n*. [mid-19C] tea.

splodger *n*. [mid-19C] an old man. [*splodger* = codger]

Sporting Life *n*. [20C] a wife. [from the newspaper *Sporting Life*, widely read by racing enthusiasts]

spotted dick *adj*. [20C] sick.

spotty dog *n*. [20C] (*derog.*) any foreigner, irrespective of colour or race. [*spotty dog* = wog]

square rigger *n*. [20C] (*derog.*) a Black person. [*square rigger* = nigger]

squatter's daughter *n*. [20C] (*Aus.*) water.

Sri Lanka *n*. [1970s+] a general term of abuse. [*Sri Lanka* = wanker]

stage fright *n.* [20C] light ale.

stammer and stutter *n.* [20C] butter.

Stan and Ollie *n.* [1930s+] an umbrella. [*Stan and Ollie* = brolly; from the comedians Stan Laurel (1890–1965) and Oliver Hardy (1892–1957)]

stand an ale *v.* [1940s] (*US*) to go bail (for).

stand at ease *n.* [late 19C] **1** (*orig. military*) fleas. **2** cheese.

stand from under *n.* [20C] thunder.

stand to (attention) *n.* [20C] a pension.

Stanley knife *n.* [20C] a wife.

Starsky and Hutch *n.* [1970s] the crutch, i.e. the groin. [from the popular 1970s TV detective series *Starsky and Hutch*]

star's nap *n.* [20C] a loan; the act of borrowing. [*star's nap* = tap]

steak and kidney *n.* [20C] **1** the personal name Sidney. **2** (*Aus.*) the city of Sydney.

steamer *n. see* STEAM TUG *n.*[1].

steam-packet *n.* [mid-19C] a jacket.

steamroller *n.* [20C] a bowler hat.

steam tug (*also* **steamer**) *n.*[1] [1930s+] a fool, a gullible person. [*steam tug* = mug]

steam tug *n.*[2] [1930s+] (*Aus.*) **1** a prize-fighter. **2** an insect. [*steam tug* = **1** pug **2** bug]

Steele Rudds *n.* [20C] (*Aus.*) potatoes. [*Steele Rudds* = spuds; from the Aus. novelist Steele Rudd, real name Arthur Hoey Davis (1868–1935); *see* DAD AND DAVE]

Steffi Graf *n.* [1990s+] **1** a laugh. **2** a bath. [from the German tennis player Steffi Graf (b.1969); note Cockney pronunciation of bath as *barf*]

Stephenson's Rocket *n.* [20C] a pocket. [from the early railway engine, 'The Rocket', invented by engineer George Stephenson (1781–1848)]

Steve McQueens *n.* [1960s+] jeans. [from the US film star Steve McQueen (1930–80)]

Stevie Wonder *n.* [1970s+] thunder. [from the US singer Stevie Wonder, real name Steveland Judkins (b.1950)]

Stewart Granger *n.* [1980s] **1** danger. **2** a chance, an opportunity, as in *no Stewart Granger*. [**2** *Stewart Granger* = danger; from the UK film actor Stewart Granger (1913–93)]

stewed prune *n.* [20C] a tune.

stick of chalk *n.* [20C] (*Aus.*) a walk.

stick of rock *n.* [20C] the penis. [*stick of rock* = cock]

sticks and stones *n.* [20C] bones.

stick slingers *n.* [20C] (*US*) fingers.

sticky bun *n.* [20C] a son.

sticky toffee *n.* [1970s] coffee.

Stirling (Moss) *n.* [1950s+] an infinitesimal amount,

nothing whatsoever, as in *not give a stirling* not care at all. [*Stirling Moss* = toss; from the UK racing driver Stirling Moss (b.1929)]

stocks and shares *n.* [20C] stairs.

Stoke on Trent *n.* [1970s+] a male homosexual. [*Stoke on Trent* = bent; from the Midlands city of Stoke on Trent]

stone jug *n.* [1920s+] a fool, a gullible person. [*stone jug* = mug; note standard sl. *stone jug* Newgate Prison]

stop and go *n.* [20C] a toe.

stop and start *n.* [20C] the heart.

stop thief *n.* [mid-19C] beef. [a possible play on the sl. cry *hot beef!* stop thief!]

storm and strife *n.* [20C] a wife.

stormy dick *n.* [20C] (*US*) the penis. [*stormy dick* = prick]

strangely weird *n.* [20C] a beard. [underpinned by the image of bearded men as 'odd']

strangle and smother *n.* [20C] (*Aus.*) a mother.

strawberry tart *n.* [1960s+] the heart.

strike-me(-dead) *n.* [late 19C+] bread.

string and top *n.* [20C] a policeman. [*string and top* = cop]

string and twine *n.* [20C] (*US*) wine.

string beans *n.* [1970s+] jeans.

string vest *n.* [1960s+] an annoying person. [*string vest* = pest]

strong and thin *n.* [1940s] (*US*) gin.

struggle and strain *n.* [20C] a railway train.

struggle and strain *v.* [1980s+] to train, e.g. for a boxing match.

struggle and strainers *n.* [1980s+] trainers.

struggle and strife *n.* [20C] **1** a wife. **2** life.

strum and stroll *n.* [20C] (*Aus.*) the dole.

stump the chalk *v.* [20C] (*US*) to walk.

stutter and stammer *n.* [20C] a hammer.

St Vitus's dance *n.* [20C] (*Aus.*) trousers. [*St Vitus's dance* = pants; St Vitus's dance is an alternative name for Sydenham's chorea, a convulsive disorder in children, named after the Christian martyr St Vitus, the patron saint of epileptics]

sugar (and honey) *n.* [mid-19C+] money. [the etymologist G.L. Cohen (1989) suggests that on the basis of *honey* meaning gold, *sugar* means silver as well as the plain generic money]

sugar and spice *n.* [20C] ice.

sugar and spice *adj.* [20C] nice.

sugar-candy *n.* [mid-19C–1920s] brandy.

sugar-candy *adj.* [20C] handy.

suit and cloak *n.* [late 17C–19C] a drink, esp. brandy. [possibly the rhyme *suit and cloak* = soak, but if so, this is an exceptionally early use of rhyming slang]

Sunday best *n.* [20C] (*US*) a vest (undershirt).

Sunday morn *n.* [20C] an erection. [*Sunday morn* = horn; a var. on SEPTEMBER MORN]

sunny south *n.* [late 19C] the mouth. [var. on NORTH AND SOUTH]

suppose *n. see* I SUPPOSE

surgical truss *n.* [20C] a bus.

Surrey docks *n.* [1970s] venereal disease. [*Surrey docks* = pox; from Surrey Commercial Docks, the only enclosed docks on the south bank of the River Thames]

susie *n. see* SUSY.

susy (*also* **susie**) *n.* [1930s+] a sixpence (2^1/$_2$ pence). [*susy anna* = tanner (early 19C–1970s sl. 'sixpence')]

Suzie Wong *n.* [1970s+] **1** a smell. **2** a song. [**1** *Suzie Wong* = pong; from the novel *The World of Suzie Wong* (1976) by Richard Mason]

swallow and sigh *n.* [20C] a collar and tie.

Swan Lake *n.* [20C] a cake. [from the ballet *Swan Lake* (1877) by Tchaikovsky]

Swannee River *n.* [20C] the liver, whether human or animal. [from the Suwannee River which runs through Florida into the Gulf of Mexico, immortalized by the song 'Old Folks at Home' by Stephen Foster: 'Way down upon the Swannee River, far, far away …']

Swannee (Rivers) *n.* [20C] (*Aus.*) the shivers. [*see* SWANNEE RIVER]

swear and curse (*also* **swear and cuss**) *n.* [20C] a bus.

swear and cuss *n. see* SWEAR AND CURSE.

sweaty sock *n.* [20C] a Scot. [*sweaty sock* = jock, plus a reference to the old stereotype of the Scots as unwashed]

Sweeney (Todd), the *n.* [1930s+] the Flying Squad; hence *sweenies* members of the Flying Squad. [from the fictional and murderous Sweeney Todd, the 'demon barber of Fleet Street', whose victims ended up in the 'golopshious' pies he sold to innocent clerks]

sweetpea *n.* [19C] **1** whisky. **2** tea. **3** urine. **4** lysergic acid. [*sweetpea* = **3** pee/wee **4** LSD; **1** may refer to 'the colour of the resulting urine' (Partridge)]

swiftly flow *v.* [late 19C–1900s] (*Aus.*) to go.

Swiss Army (knife) *n.* [1980s] a wife. [yet another example of the stereotypical 'sharp' spouse]

switch and bone *n.* [1940s] (*US*) a telephone.

Sydney Harbour *n.* [1940s+] (*Aus.*) a barber.

Sydney harbor *n.* [1940s+] (*US*) a barber.

Sylvester (Stallone) *adj.* [1980s+] alone. [from the US film star Sylvester Stallone (b.1946)]

syrup (of figs) *n.* [20C] a wig.

t

take a fright *n.* [mid-19C] the night.

take a mike *v. see* TAKE THE MICKEY.

take and give *v.* [late 19C] to live, esp. as man and wife.

take one's daniel *v. see* SLING ONE'S DANIEL.

take the mick *v. see* TAKE THE MICKEY.

take the mickey (*also* **take a mike, take the mick, take the mike**) *v.* [1930s+] to tease; hence *mickey-take, mickey-taking* teasing. [*take the mickey bliss* = take the piss; *see* MICKEY BLISS]

take the mike *v. see* TAKE THE MICKEY.

take the vampire's *v.* [1980s+] to tease. [*take the vampire's kiss* = take the piss]

take your pick *adj.* [20C] stupid, foolish. [*take your pick* = thick]

tale of two cities *n.* [1950s] the female breasts. [*tale of two cities* = titties; from the novel *A Tale of Two Cities* (1859) by Charles Dickens]

tango and cash *n.* [1980s+] (*drugs*) the synthetic opiate fentanyl. [*tango and cash* = apache; from the film *Tango & Cash* (1989)]

tapioca *n*. [20C] in cards, a joker.

tar and feather *n*. [20C] leather, usu. a leather jacket.

tartan banner *n*. [1900s–70s] a sixpence (2^1/$_2$ pence). [*tartan banner* = tanner (early 19C–1970s sl. 'sixpence')]

Tate and Lyle *n*. [20C] cheek, audacity. [*Tate and Lyle* = style; from Tate and Lyle, best known as a sugar manufacturer]

tater-pillin' *n*. [20C] a shilling (five pence).

taters (*also* **taties**, **tatters**) *adj*. [20C] cold. [*taters in the mould* = cold; *see* POTATOES IN THE MOULD]

taties *adj*. *see* TATERS.

tatters *adj*. *see* TATERS.

taxicabs *n*. [20C] body lice. [*taxicabs* = crabs]

taxi rank *n*. [20C] a bank.

taxi-rank *v*. [1970s] to masturbate. [*taxi-rank* = wank]

tea and cocoa *n*. [20C] approval, sanction. [*tea and cocoa* = say-so]

tea-and-toast *n*. [20C] post, i.e. mail.

teabag *n*. [1990s+] a general term of abuse; a worthless, irrelevant person. [*teabag* = slag]

tea caddy *n*. [1990s+] (*derog*.) an Irish person. [*tea caddy* = paddy]

tea-for-two and a bloater *n*. [1900s–50s] a motor-car. [*tea-for-two and a bloater* = motor]

tea grout *n*. [20C] a Boy Scout.

tealeaf *n. see* TEA LEAF.

tea leaf (*also* **tealeaf**) *n.* [late 19C+] a thief; hence *tea-leafing* thieving.

teapot (lid) *n.* [20C] **1** (*derog.*) a Jew. **2** a child. **3** a pound (sterling). [*teapot lid* =**1** Yid **2** kid **3** quid]

teapot lid *v.* [late 19C+] to tease. [*teapot lid* = kid]

tears and cheers *n.* [20C] (*US*) tears.

tea strainers *n.* [1980s+] trainers.

teddy bear *n.* **1** [20C] a pear. **2** [1950s+] (*Aus.*) a show-off, esp. a cricketer who jokes around on the field and plays to the crowd. [**2** *teddy bear* = lair (Aus. sl. 'show-off')]

Ted Frazer *n.* [1960s+] a razor, always a cut-throat, 'open' model.

Ted Heath *n.* [1970s] **1** a thief. **2** teeth. [from the former UK Prime Minister Edward 'Ted' Heath (b.1916); in **1** note Cockney pronunciation of thief as *teef*]

teletubby *n.* [1990s+] a husband. [*teletubby* = hubby; from the popular children's TV show *Teletubbies*]

ten furlongs *n.* [20C] (*Aus.*) a daughter. [ten furlongs is 1¹/₄ miles, thus the rhyme is *mile and a quarter* = daughter]

tennis racket *n.* [20C] a jacket.

tens and twos *n.* [20C] (*Aus.*) shoes.

ten to two *n.* [1930s+] a Jew.

tent peg *n.* [late 19C+] an egg.

terrace *n.* [1940s+] (*Aus.*) trousers. [*terrace of houses* = trousers]

terrible Turk *n.* [20C] work.

terry toon *n.* [1970s+] (*Aus.*) a pimp, one who lives off a prostitute. [*terry toon* = hoon (Aus. sl. 'procurer of prostitutes')]

Terry Waite *adj.* [1990s+] late. [from the British religious emissary and one-time hostage in Lebanon Terry Waite (b.1939)]

Tex Ritter *n.* [1990s+] **1** bitter beer. **2** a lavatory. [**2** *Tex Ritter* = shitter; from the Country and Western star Tex Ritter (1905–74)]

that and this *n.* [20C] an act of urination. [*that and this* = piss]

Thelma (Ritter) *n.* [1940s–60s] **1** the anus. **2** a lavatory. [*Thelma Ritter* = shitter; from the US film actress Thelma Ritter (1905–69)]

Thelonius Monk *n.* [1940s+] semen. [*Thelonius Monk* = spunk; from the jazz pianist Thelonius Monk (1917–82)]

there first *n.* [late 19C] a thirst.

there you are *n.* [20C] **1** a bar (in a pub). **2** tea. [**2** *there you are* = char]

these and those *n.* [20C] **1** clothes. **2** toes.

Theydon Bois *n.* [20C] noise. [from Theydon Bois, a town in Essex; note pronunciation of Bois as *boyze*]

thick and thin *n.* [20C] **1** the chin. **2** gin. **3** (*Aus.*) the skin. **4** (*US*) a grin.

thief and robber *n.* [20C] (*Aus.*) a friend. [*thief and robber* = cobber (Aus. sl. 'friend')]

thimble and thumb *n.* [1940s] rum.

thimble and thumb *v.* [1940s] to run.

thirty-first of May *n.* [1920s+] (*Aus.*) a fool, a simpleton. [*thirty-first of May* = gay (Aus. sl. 'dupe', 'sucker')]

this and that *n.* [20C] **1** a hat. **2** a cricket bat.

thises and thats *n.* [1900s–10s] spats.

Thomas Cook *n.* [20C] a look, a glance. [from the pioneer travel agent Thomas Cook (1808–92) whose first tour, to Switzerland, was arranged in 1863]

Thomas Tilling *n.* [1920s–30s] a shilling (five pence). [from the 19C haulier Thomas Tilling]

thousand pities *n.* [late 19C–1900s] the female breasts. [*thousand pities* = titties]

three bags full *n.* [20C] (*Aus.*) a pack of lies. [*three bags full* = a load of bull]

three blind mice *n.* [20C] (a sack of) rice.

threepenny bits *n.* [late 19C+] **1** diarrhoea. **2** the female breasts. [*threepenny bits* = **1** the shits **2** tits]

three quarters of a peck *n.* [mid-19C] the neck, usu. written as 3/4.

three-wheel skid *n. see* FOUR-WHEEL SKID.

throw me in the dirt *n.* [mid-19C] a shirt.

thrupennies *n. see* THRUPS.

thrups (*also* **thrupennies**) *n.* [late 19C+] the female breasts. [from sl. *thrups* threepenny; *see* THREEPENNY BITS]

thunder and rain *n.* [20C] (*Aus.*) a train.

tibby drop *n.* [20C] hop, hence *on the tibby drop* on the hop, i.e. unprepared.

tickle your fancy *n.* [20C] a male homosexual. [*tickle your fancy* = nancy]

tick-tock *n.* [1950s] (*Aus.*) a clock or watch.

tic-tac *n.* [20C] a fact.

tiddler's bait *adj.* [20C] late.

tiddley (*also* **tiddly**) *n.* [20C] a drink. [TIDDLEYWINK]

tiddley (*also* **tiddly**) *adj.* [mid-19C+] slightly drunk, tipsy. [TIDDLEYWINK]

tiddleywink (*also* **tiddlywink**) *n.* **1** [mid-19C] a drink, usu. a spirit rather than beer or wine. **2** [1970s+] (*derog.*) a Chinese person. [**2** *tiddleywink* = chink]

tiddly *n. see* TIDDLEY *n.*

tiddly *adj. see* TIDDLEY *adj.*

tiddlywink *n. see* TIDDLEYWINK.

tidy and neat *v.* [20C] to eat.

tiger (tim) *n.* [20C] (*Aus.*) a swim.

Tilbury docks *n*. [late 19C+] **1** socks **2** venereal disease. [**2** *Tilbury docks* = pox; from the Gravesend-sited Tilbury docks, opened in 1886]

timothy *n*. [1950s+] (*Aus.*) a brothel. [*timothy grass* = arse, i.e. sexual intercourse, or *timothy titmouse* = house]

tin bath *n*. [20C] scarf. [note Cockney pronunciation of bath as *barf*]

tin flute *n*. [20C] a suit.

tin hat *n*. [20C] a fool. [*tin hat* = prat]

tin lid *n*. [20C] (*Aus.*) a child. **2** (*derog.*) a Jew. [*tin lid* = **1** kid **2** Yid]

tin of beans *n*. [1960s+] jeans.

tin plate *n*. [20C] a friend. [*tin plate* = mate]

tin-tack *n*. [late 19C+] dismissal from a job. [*tin-tack* = the sack]

tin-tacks *n*. [20C] facts.

tin tank *n*. [late 19C–1930s] a bank.

Tiny Tim *n*. [20C] a five-pound note. [*Tiny Tim* = flim (sl. 'five-pound note'); from the character Tiny Tim in Charles Dickens's novel *A Christmas Carol* (1843)]

titfa *n. see* TITFER.

titfer (*also* **titfa**, **tit-for**) *n*. [1920s+] a hat. [TIT-FOR-TAT]

tit-for *n. see* TITFER.

tit-for-tat *n.* [late 19C+] **1** a hat. **2** (*Aus.*) a non-trade unionist. [**2** *tit-for-tat* = rat]

tit willow *n.* [late 19C+] a pillow. [from the use of the phrase in Gilbert and Sullivan's hit operetta *The Mikado* (1885)]

to and fro *n.* [20C] snow.

to-and-from *n.* [1940s+] (*Aus.*) a British immigrant to Australia. [*to-and-from* = pom]

toasted bread *adj.* [1990s+] dead.

toby jug *n.* [20C] **1** a fool, a gullible person. **2** an ear. [*toby jug* = **1** mug **2** lug]

Tod Sloan *adj.* [20C] alone. [*see* ON ONE'S TOD]

toerag *n.* [mid-19C+] **1** a tramp. **2** any unappetizing old person. **3** (*UK prison*) any highly unpopular person, young or old. **4** a general term of abuse. [*toerag* = slag, or Standard English *toerag* the foot-bindings used by tramps]

toffee wrapper *n.* [20C] the head. [*toffee wrapper* = napper (sl. 'head')]

toilet roll *n.* [20C] the dole.

Tokyo rose *n.* [1940s–50s] the nose. [from the WWII pro-Japanese propagandist Tokyo Rose, real name Iva Toguri D'Aquino (b.1916)]

tom *n.*[1] [1950s+] jewellery. [TOMFOOLERY]

tom *n.*[2] *see* TOM MIX.

tom *n.*[3] *see* TOMTIT.

tom and dick *v.* [1970s+] to be sick.

tom and ed *n.* [1990s+] the head.

tom and funny *n.* [late 19C+] money.

Tom and Jerry *adj.* [20C] merry. [from the cartoon characters Tom (a cat) and Jerry (a mouse), although these in turn are rooted in Pearce Egan's best-selling *Life in London* (1821), whose heroes are thus named]

tom and sam *n.* [20C] (*Aus.*) jam.

tomato purée *n.* [1980s+] a jury.

tomato sauce *n.* [20C] a horse; hence *tomato sauces* the horses, i.e. horse-races.

tomcat *n.* [20C] a doormat.

Tom Cruise *n.* [1980s+] drink, a drink. [*Tom Cruise* = booze; from the US film star Tom Cruise (b.1962)]

Tom Doolies *n.* [1950s] the testicles. [*Tom Doolies* = goolies; from the popular song 'Hang Down Your Head, Tom Dooley' by the Kingston Trio (1958)]

Tom Finney *adj.* [1930s+] skinny. [from the UK footballer Tom Finney (b.1922)]

◆◆

Celebrity Body Parts

Holyfield's ear	year
Jagger's lips	chips

◆◆

tomfoolery *n*. [1930s+] jewellery.

tom, harry and dick *adj*. [20C] sick.

Tom Mix (*also* **tom**) *n*. [1930s+] **1** a fix, i.e. a problem, a predicament. **2** the number six. **3** an injection of heroin. [**3** *Tom Mix* = fix; from the US film cowboy Tom Mix (1880–1940)]

tommy *n*. [1920s+] (*Aus./N.Z.*) **1** a bookmaker. **2** a bookmaker's ledger. [*tommy rook* = book, or standard sl. *Tommy Rook* a cheat]

Tommy Dodd *n*.[1] **1** [late 19C] a general term of abuse. **2** [late 19C–1950s] God. **3** [1920s+] (*US*) a gun. [*Tommy Dodd* = **1** sod **3** rod]

Tommy Dodd *n*.[2] [mid-19C] **1** in coin-tossing, the 'odd man' who goes out. **2** the game of coin-tossing itself. **3** in coin-tossing, the winner or loser, the choice for the name having been allotted by previous agreement. [*Tommy Dodd* = odd]

Tommy Farr *n*. [20C] a bar (in a pub). [from the UK boxer Tommy Farr (1913–86)]

tommy guns *n*. [1940s+] diarrhoea. [*tommy guns* = the runs]

Tommy O'Rann *n*. [mid-19C] food. [*Tommy O'Rann* = scran]

Tommy Rabbit *n*. [late 19C] a pomegranate. [if this is rhyming slang it is a weak version]

Tommy Roller *n*. [late 19C+] a collar.

Tommy Rollocks *n*. [20C] the testicles. [*Tommy Rollocks* = bollocks]

Tommy Steeles *n*. [20C] eels. [from the UK actor and singer Tommy Steele (b.1936)]

Tommy Trinder *n*. [1940s+] a window. [from the UK comedian Tommy Trinder (1909–89); note Cockney pronunciation of window as *winder*]

Tommy Tripe *n*. [20C] a tobacco pipe.

Tommy (Tripe) *v*. [mid-19C] to examine, to survey, to keep a watch. [*Tommy Tripe* = pipe (sl. 'inspect')]

Tommy Tucker *n*. [20C] **1** a person. **2** (*UK Und.*) a gullible individual. [*Tommy Tucker* = **1** fucker **2** sucker; from the nursery rhyme 'Little Tommy Tucker']

Tommy Tupper *n*. [20C] supper.

Tom Noddy *n*. [20C] (*US*) a body, i.e. a corpse. [underpinned by Standard English *tom-noddy* a fool, a useless person]

tomorrow *v*. [20C] to borrow, esp. in the phrase *on the tommy* looking for a loan.

Tom Right *n*. [mid-19C] the night.

toms *n. see* TOMTITS.

Tom Sawyer *n*. [late 19C+] a lawyer. [from the book *Tom Sawyer* (1876) by Mark Twain (1835–1910)]

tom-tart *n*. [late 19C] (*Aus.*) a woman. [*tom-tart* = sweetheart, but note standard sl. *tart* a woman]

Tom Thacker *n*. [late 19C–1900s] tobacco. [note Cockney pronunciation of tobacco as *terbaccer*]

Tom (Thumb) *n.* **1** [late 19C–1900s] (*orig. Aus.*) rum. **2** [20C] the buttocks. **3** [1940s+] (*Aus.*) inside informa-tion. [*Tom Thumb* = **2** bum **3** the drum (Aus. sl. 'the facts'); from the famous dwarf 'General' Tom Thumb, real name Charles Sherwood Stratton (1838–83), who grew to a height of 25 inches and was exhibited around the US and Europe as a curiosity]

tomtit (*also* **tom**) *n.* [1940s+] an act of defecation. [*tomtit* = shit]

tomtit *v.* [late 19C+] to defecate. [*tomtit* = shit]

tomtits (*also* **toms**) *n.* [1960s+] (*Aus.*) diarrhoea. [*tomtits* = the shits]

Tom Tripe *n.* [mid-19C] a tobacco pipe.

Tom Tug *n.* **1** [19C] a fool, a victim. **2** [late 19C] a bedbug. [**1** *Tom Tug* = mug]

ton o' my rocks *n.* [20C] (*Aus.*) socks.

Tony Benn *n.* [1970s+] ten pounds (sterling). [from the UK politician Tony Benn (b.1925)]

Tony Blair *n.* [1990s+] hair. [from the UK Prime Minister Tony Blair (b.1953)]

Tony Hatch *n.* [1970s+] **1** the vagina. **2** a (young) girl. **3** a match. [*Tony Hatch* = **1** snatch; **2** is a generic use of **1**; from the UK songwriter Tony Hatch (b.1939)]

too bloody stew! (*also* **too Irish stew!**) *excl.* [20C] too true!

too Irish stew! *excl. see* TOO BLOODY STEW!

Tooting (Bec) *n.* [late 19C–1930s] **1** a light kiss. **2** food.

[*Tooting Bec* = peck; from the south-west London suburb of Tooting Bec]

top gun *n.* [1980s+] 100 pounds (sterling). [*top gun* = ton; from the hit film *Top Gun* (1984)]

top hat *n.* [20C] **1** a fool. **2** a rat (the rodent). [**1** *top hat* = prat]

top joint *n.* [mid-19C] a pint of beer. [note Cockney pronunciation of joint as *jint*]

top of Rome (*also* **top o' Rome**) *n.* [mid-19C–1920s] home.

top o' Rome *n. see* TOP OF ROME.

tosh and waddle *n.* [late 19C+] (*Aus.*) absolute nonsense. [*tosh and waddle* = twaddle, although the rhyme is essentially an intensification of sl. *tosh* nonsense]

total wreck *n.* [20C] a cheque.

touch and tap *n.* [20C] a cap.

touch-me *n.* [late 19C–1920s] a shilling (five pence). [*touch-me-on-the-nob* = bob]

Tower Bridge *n.* [20C] a fridge. [from Tower Bridge, London, opened in 1894, the only Thames bridge downriver from London Bridge]

Tower Hill *v.* [20C] to kill. [from Tower Hill, London, the former site of the imprisonment and execution – by beheading – of traitors]

town *n.* [late 19C] a halfpenny. [*town* = brown (19C sl. 'halfpenny')]

town crier *n*. [20C] a liar.

towns and cities *n*. [1900s–40s] the female breasts. [*towns and cities* = titties]

Trafalgar Square *n*. [20C] a chair. [from Trafalgar Square, London, named in 1835 as a memorial to the battle of Trafalgar (1805); Nelson's Column, in the centre of the Square commemorates the battle's victor, Admiral Lord Nelson]

train wreck *n*. [20C] (*US*) the neck.

trams *n*. [20C] the legs. [*trams* = gams (sl. 'legs')]

treacle tart *n*. [20C] a breaking of wind. [*treacle tart* = fart]

treasure hunt *n*. [20C] the vagina. [*treasure hunt* = cunt]

treble chance *n*. [20C] a dance.

tree and sap *n*. [20C] (*Aus.*) a tap.

T. Rex *n*. [1970s] sex. [from the 1970s pop group T. Rex]

trey-bits *n*. [1950s+] (*Aus./N.Z.*) **1** the female breasts. **2** diarrhoea. [*trey-bits* = **1** tits **2** the shits]

trilby hat *n*. [20C] a fool. [*trilby hat* = prat]

trolley and tram *n*. [20C] ham.

trolley (and truck) *n*. [1910s+] an act of sexual intercourse. [*trolley and truck* = fuck; note naval sl. *trolley-oggling* acting as a voyeur]

trolly-wags *n*. [19C] trousers. [*trolly-wags* = bags]

trombone *n*. [1930s] a telephone.

tropical fish *n.* [2000s] an act of urination. [*tropical fish* = piss; note Scots pronunciation of piss as *pish*]

trouble and fuss *n.* [20C] a bus.

trouble and strife *n.* **1** [1900s] life. **2** [20C] a wife.

troubles and cares *n.* [20C] stairs.

trunk and tree *n.* [20C] the knee.

tug o' war *n.* [20C] a prostitute. [*tug o' war* = whore]

tumble *n.* [1900s–30s] a drink. [*tumble down the sink* = drink]

tumble and trip *n.* [20C] a whip-round.

tumble and trips *n.* [1920s–30s] (*US*) the lips. [the image is of 'loose' lips causing a criminal to tumble, i.e. to betray himself]

tumbledown *n.* **1** [early–mid-19C] grog. **2** [late 19C+] alcohol, liquor. [*tumble down the sink* = drink]

Turkish bath *n.* **1** [20C] a laugh. **2** [2000s] someone or something amusing. [**2** *Turkish bath* = a laugh; note Cockney pronunciation of bath as *barf*]

Turkish (delight) *adj.* [20C] mean, grasping. [*Turkish delight* = tight]

turtle (dove) *n.* [mid-19C+] (*usu. pl.*) a glove, esp. those worn by housebreakers to hide fingerprints.

twelve-inch rule *n.* [20C] a fool.

twist *n.* **1** [20C] (*US Und.*) a girl, a woman. **2** [1950s+] the passive member of a lesbian relationship. [TWIST AND TWIRL]

twist and twine *v.* [20C] (*Irish*) to whine.

twist and twirl *n.* [1900s] a girl.

two and eight *n.* [1930s+] a condition of emotional stress. [*two and eight* = state]

two-bob bit *n.* [20C] **1** an act of defecation. **2** (*pl.*) diarrhoea. [*two-bob bit* = shit]

two by four *n.* [1950s–60s] a prostitute. [*two by four* = whore]

two eyes of blue! *excl.* [1920s+] too true!

two-foot rule *n.* [mid-19C] a fool.

twopenny *n.* [mid-19C–1930s] the head. [from *twopenny loaf* alluding to LOAF (OF BREAD)]

twos and threes *n.* [20C] keys.

two-slice *n.* [20C] an office.

two-thirty *adj.* [late 19C+] dirty.

two UEs *n.* [20C] (*Aus.*) fleas. [etymology unknown]

two-wheeler *n.* [20C] (*Aus.*) a woman. [*two-wheeler* = sheila]

typewriter *n.* [1920s+] a fighter (by profession or temperament).

Tyrone Power *n.* [1940s+] (*Aus.*) a shower of rain. [from the US actor Tyrone Power (1914–58)]

u

ugly sister *n.* [20C] a blister.

umbrella *n.* [20C] a man, esp. a husband, boyfriend or lover. [*umbrella* = fella]

uncle and aunt *n.* [20C] a plant.

Uncle Ben *n.* [1950s+] (*bingo*) the number ten. [from the popular Uncle Ben's brand of rice]

Uncle Bert *n.* [20C] a shirt.

Uncle Bob *n.* [20C] **1** the penis. **2** a job. [**1** *Uncle Bob* = knob; **2** is underpinned by the phrase *and Bob's your uncle*, with its roots in political nepotism]

Uncle Dick *n.* [20C] the penis. [*Uncle Dick* = prick, although note sl. *dick* penis]

Uncle Dick *adj.* [20C] sick, ill.

Uncle Dick *v.* [1970s+] to be sick.

Uncle Fred *n.* [20C] bread.

Uncle Lester *n.* [1990s+] a child molester.

Uncle Mac *n.* [1980s+] (*drugs*) heroin. [*Uncle Mac* = smack; possibly linked to the 1950s BBC radio 'Children's Hour' presenter 'Uncle Mac', although few heroin users of the 1980s would have heard him]

Uncle Ned *n.* **1** [1920s+] a bed. **2** [1950s+] the head. **3** [1950s+] (*Aus.*) bread.

Uncle Sam *n.* [20C] a cut of lamb.

Uncle Wilf *n.* [20C] the police. [*Uncle Wilf* = filth; note Cockney pronunciation of filth as *filf*]

Uncle Willie *adj.* **1** [mid-19C+] silly. **2** [1920s+] chilly.

underbeneaths *n.* [20C] (*US*) the teeth.

union jack *n.* [20C] the back.

up-and-down *n.* [20C] brown, i.e. brown ale.

up and under *n.* [20C] thunder.

up and under *v.* [1950s+] (*Aus.*) to vomit. [*up and under* = CHUNDER]

up a tree *n.* [1940s+] (*bingo*) the number three.

Uriah Heep *n.* [20C] an unpleasant person. [*Uriah Heep* = creep; from Uriah Heep, a villain in Charles Dickens's *David Copperfield* (1859)]

V

Valentine Dyalls *n.* [1930s+] haemorrhoids. [*Valentine Dyalls* = piles; from the UK film actor Valentine Dyall (1908–85)]

Vancouver *n.* [20C] a vacuum cleaner. [*Vancouver* = hoover; from the seaport of Vancouver, British Columbia]

Vanity Fair *n.* [20C] a chair. [from the book *Vanity Fair* (1848) by William Thackeray (1811–63) although the actual coinage is in John Bunyan's *Pilgrim's Progress* (1678)]

vera *n. see* VERA LYNN.

Vera Lynn (*also* **vera**) *n.* [1940s+] **1** gin. **2** skin. **3** (*Aus.*) the chin. [from the UK singer Vera Lynn (b.1917)]

Veronica Lake *n.* [1940s+] a steak. [from the US film star Veronica Lake (1919–73)]

Vicar of Bray *n.* [late 19C+] in cards, a three. [*Vicar of Bray* = tray (sl. 'three'); from the 18C popular song 'The Vicar of Bray', which details the career of a time-serving, malleable clergyman, bending with each prevailing cultural wind]

Victoria Monk *n.* [late 19C–1900s] semen. [*Victoria Monk* = spunk; from the music-hall star Victoria Monks (1884–1972), best known for her version of 'Won't You Come Home, Bill Bailey?']

Victor Trumper *n.* [20C] (*Aus.*) a cigarette butt. [*Victor Trumper* = bumper (Aus./N.Z. sl. 'cigarette end'); from the Aus. cricketer Victor Trumper (1877–1915)]

victory V *n.* [1940s+] an act of urination. [*victory V* = pee/wee; from WWI's 'V for Victory' sign and/or 'Victory V' cough sweets]

Vincent Price *n.* [1950s+] ice. [from the US film star Vincent Price (1911–93)]

Violet Crumble *v.* [20C] (*Aus.*) to understand. [*Violet Crumble* = tumble]

virgin bride *n.* [late 19C+] (*Aus.*) a ride. [presumably punning on sl. *ride* to have sexual intercourse]

W

wait and linger *n.* [20C] a finger.

Wallace and Gromit *v.* [1980s+] to vomit. [from the Oscar-winning animated plasticine characters Wallace and his dog Gromit]

Wallace Beery *n.* [1920s–40s] a query. [from the US film star Wallace Beery (1885–1949)]

Wally Grout *n.* [1960s+] (*Aus.*) one's turn to buy a round of drinks. [*Wally Grout* = shout; from the cricketer Arthur Theodore Wallace 'Wally' Grout (1927–68)]

walnut whip *n.* [20C] a sleep. [*walnut whip* = kip]

Walter Joyce *n.* [late 19C] the voice.

Walter Scott *n.* [20C] a pot (of beer). [*see* SIR WALTER SCOTT]

Wansteads *n.* [1920s–30s] spats. [*Wanstead Flats* = spats; from the East London area Wanstead Flats]

war and strife *n.* [1920s–30s] a wife. [var. on TROUBLE AND STRIFE]

warrior bold (*also* **warrior's hold**) *adj.* [20C] cold.

warrior's hold *adj. see* WARRIOR BOLD.

Warwick Farm *n.* [1940s–60s] (*Aus.*) an arm. [from the Sydney racecourse Warwick Farm]

wasp and bee *n.* [20C] (*Aus.*) tea.

watch and chain *n.* [20C] the brain.

waterbury watch *n.* [late 19C–1930s] Scotch whisky. [from the once popular watches made in Waterbury, Connecticut; *see* BOTTLE OF SCOTCH]

watercress *n.* [20C] a dress.

water hen *n.* [1960s] the number ten.

Waterloo *n.* [20C] stew. [from the London railway station Waterloo]

wattle *n.* [1940s–50s] (*Aus.*) a dirty, grubby person. [*wattle and daub* = warb (Aus. sl. 'dirty, unkempt person'); note Standard English *wattle and daub* interwoven twigs plastered with clay or mud, as a building material for huts, cottages]

weasel (and stoat) *n.* [20C] an overcoat.

Wee Georgie Wood *adj.* [20C] good; hence ANY WEE GEORGIE? [from the music-hall entertainer George 'Wee Georgie' Wood, popular in the 1920s–30s]

weep and wail *n.* [late 19C–1950s] a tale, esp. a beggar's tale of woe.

weeping willow *n.* [late 19C–1940s] a pillow.

Wee Willie Winky *n.* [20C] (*derog.*) a Chinese person. [*Wee Willie Winky* = chinky; from the nursery rhyme 'Wee Willy Winky']

well-hung *adj.* [20C] young.

wellington *n.* [1960s+] (*Aus.*) sexual intercourse. [*wellington boot* = root]

Wentworth Falls (*also* **wentworth's balls**) *n.* [1920s+] (*Aus.*) the testicles. [*Wentworth Falls* = balls; from the Wentworth Falls, near Katoomba in the Blue Mountains of New South Wales]

wentworth's balls *n. see* WENTWORTH FALLS.

werris *n.* [1960s+] (*Aus.*) a Greek. [*werris creek* = Greek; from the town of Werris Creek, New South Wales]

West Hams *n.* [20C] nerves. [*West Ham Reserves* = nerves; from the East London football team West Ham United]

Westminster Abbey *n.* [20C] a taxi driver. [*Westminster Abbey* = cabbie; from Westminster Abbey, London, which, after St Paul's Cathedral, is the city's most important church]

Westminster (Abbey) *adj.* [20C] shabby. [*see* WESTMINSTER ABBEY]

wheezy anna *n.* [20C] a spanner.

where the five 'n' arf? *phr.* [1920s–30s] where in God's name? [in pre-decimal measurement five-and-a-half yards was one rod, thus the rhyme is *rod* = God]

whip and lash *n.* [20C] a moustache.

whip and top *v.* [20C] to masturbate. [*whip and top* = strop]

whiplash *n.* [1940s+] **1** a rash. **2** an act of urination. [**2** *whiplash* = slash]

whippit quick *n.* [20C] the penis. [*whippit quick* = prick]

whisper (and talk) *n.* [late 19C+] a walk.

whistle (and flute) *n.* [1930s+] a suit of clothes.

whistle and toot *n.* [20C] money. [*whistle and toot* = loot]

Whitechapel *n.* [20C] an apple. [from Whitechapel, in the East End of London]

White Cliffs (of Dover) *adv.* [20C] over, i.e. finished, esp. in the phrase *(it's) all White Cliffs*.

Whitehaven docks *n.* [1970s] venereal disease. [*Whitehaven docks* = pox]

white mice *n.* **1** [1940s–50s] dice. **2** [20C] (*Aus.*) lice.

wicked rumours *n.* [20C] bloomers.

wicked witch *n.* [20C] an unpleasant, malicious woman. [*wicked witch* = bitch; although *witch* is in itself synonymous]

widow's mite *n.* [late 19C–1920s] a light. [from the biblical story of the widow's mite (Mark xii.42–44)]

widow's wink *n.* [1970s] (*derog.*) a Chinese person. [*widow's wink* = chink]

Widow Twankey *n.* [20C] **1** a handkerchief. **2** an American. [*Widow Twankey* = **1** hankie **2** Yankee; from the pantomime Aladdin, in which Widow Twankey is the hero's mother]

wilbur *n.* [20C] a flight. [*wilbur wright* = flight; from the US air pioneer Wilbur Wright (1867–1912)]

wild west *n.* [20C] a vest or undershirt.

A Rhyming Slang gazetteer

Barnet fair	hair
Bexley Heath	teeth
Camden Town	brown, i.e. halfpenny
chalk farm	arm
Charing Cross	horse
Covent Garden	farthing
Elephant and Castle	arsehole
Gospel Oak	joke
Hackney Marsh	glass
hampsteads	teeth
Hampton Wick	prick
Hanger Lane	pain
Hounslow Heath	teeth
Hyde Park	nark
Kennington Lane	pain
Kentish Town	brown, i.e. penny
Leicester Square	chair
Lincoln's Inn	gin
Long Acre	baker
Newington Butts	guts
Pall Mall	gal
Peckham Rye	tie

Shepherd's Bush	mush/push
Surrey docks	pox
Tilbury docks	socks/pox
Tower Hill	kill
Trafalgar Square	chair
Wansteads	spats
Westminster Abbey	cabbie/shabby
Whitechapel	apple
Woolwich and Greenwich	spinach

◆◆

Wilkie Bards *n.* [1920s–40s] playing cards. [from the music-hall comedy star Wilkie Bard (1874–1944)]

Wilkinson sword *adj.* [1950s+] bald. [from the Wilkinson Sword brand of safety razor; note Cockney pronunciation of bald as *bawd*]

william *n.*[1] **1** [mid-19C–1900s] a bill, esp. in the phrase *meet sweet William* to pay off a bill as soon as it is presented **2** [mid-19C–1920s] (*US*) a dollar bill. [partial rhyming slang, plus a use of *William* as the full form of the proper name *Bill*]

william *n.*[2] [1950s+] **1** excrement. **2** an act of defecation. [*william pitt* = shit; from the UK politician William Pitt the Younger (1759–1806)]

William Hill *n.* [1990s+] a pill, esp. an amphetamine, barbiturate etc. [from the William Hill chain of bookmakers]

William Pitts *n*. [1950s+] diarrhoea. [*William Pitts* = the shits; *see* WILLIAM *n*.²]

William Powell *n*. [20C] a towel. [from the US film star William Powell (1892–1984)]

William Tell *n*. [20C] a smell. [from the 15C Swiss hero William Tell, best known for shooting an apple from his son's head]

William the Third *n*. [1960s–70s] (*Aus.*) a piece of excrement. [*William the Third* = turd; from King William III of Orange (r.1689–1702)]

will o' the wisps *n*. [20C] crisps.

Will's Whiff *n*. [20C] syphilis. [*Will's Whiff* = syph; from the brandname Will's Whiff, a small cigar]

Willy Lees *n*. [1920s+] (*Aus.*) a flea, fleas.

Willy Wag *n*. [20C] (*Aus.*) a pack. [*Willy Wag* = swag]

Willy Wonka *n*. [1970s+] **1** the penis. **2** a fool. [*Willy Wonka* = plonker; from the character Willy Wonka in the children's book *Charlie and the Chocolate Factory* (1964) by Roald Dahl (1916–90)]

Wilson Pickett *n*. [1970s] a ticket. [from the US soul star Wilson Pickett (b.1941)]

Winchcombe Carson *n*. [20C] (*Aus.*) a parson. [presumably from the Aus. financial planners Winchcombe Carson]

wind do twirl *n*. [mid-19C] a woman. [*wind do twirl* = girl]

windjammer *n.* [20C] (*Aus.*) a hammer.

Windsor Castle *n.*[20C] the anus. [*Windsor Castle* = arsehole; from the Berkshire home of Britain's royal family, Windsor Castle]

wind-trap *n.* [20C] a flap, esp. of hair.

wind up *adj.* [late 19C–1920s] taut, usu. in fig. use, i.e. emotionally strained. [*wind up* = pinned up; the image is of a taut piece of cloth]

winkle *n. see* WINKLEBAG.

winklebag (*also* **winkle**) *n.* [1970s+] cigarette. [*winklebag* = fag]

Winona Ryder *n.* [1990s+] cider. [from the US film star Winona Ryder (b.1971)]

win or lose *n.* [20C] alcohol, liquor. [*win or lose* = booze]

wise monkey *n.* [20C] a condom. [*wise monkey* = flunkey (sl. 'condom')]

witchetty grub *n.* [20C] (*Aus.*) a boy scout. [*witchetty grub* = cub]

wombat *adj.* [20C] (*Aus.*) dead. [*wombat* = *hors de combat* (French, lit. 'out of the battle')]

woodener *n. see* WOODEN SPOON.

wooden leg *n.* [20C] an egg.

wooden pegs *n.* [20C] the legs. [var. on SCOTCH PEGS]

wooden plank *n.* [20C] an American. [*wooden plank* = Yank]

wooden spoon (*also* **woodener**) *n.* [1940s–50s] (*UK prison*) a one-month sentence. [*wooden spoon* = moon, plus a reference to the wooden spoon once issued to prisoners]

woolly vest *n.* [20C] a pest, i.e. an irritating person.

Woolwich and Greenwich *n.* [20C] spinach. [from the towns Woolwich and Greenwich, on the Thames estuary]

Woolwich ferry *n.* [20C] sherry. [from the Woolwich Free Ferry, crossing the Thames, which was opened in 1889]

Woolwich pier *n.* [20C] an ear.

working classes *n.* [20C] glasses, i.e. spectacles.

worms and snails *n.* [20C] fingernails.

worry and strife *n.* [1930s] a wife. [var. on TROUBLE AND STRIFE]

Wyatt Earp *n.* [20C] a burp. [from the US lawman Wyatt Earp (1848–1929)]

x y z

Xerox copy *n.* [1950s+] (*Aus.*) a Remembrance Day poppy. [from the brandname of the Rank Xerox Corporation, leading copier manufacturers]

X Files *n.* [1990s+] haemorrhoids. [*X Files* = piles; from the popular TV series *The X-Files*]

Yankee Doodles *n.* [20C] noodles. [from the popular song 'Yankee Doodle came to town …']

yard of tripe *n.* [mid-19C] a tobacco pipe.

Yarmouth bloater *n.* [1910s+] a motor-car. [*Yarmouth bloater* = motor]

yellow silk *n.* [late 19C–1900s] milk.

yet to be *adj.* [20C] free (in reference both to behaviour and to cost).

Yid (*also* **Yit**, **Yitt**) *n.* [1900s–10s] (*Aus.*) a sovereign; hence *half a Yid* a half sovereign, ten shillings (50 pence). [*Yid* = quid, but note also the stereotyped link of Jews and money]

Yit *n. see* YID.

Yitt *n. see* YID.

Yogi Bear *n.* [1960s+] (*Aus.*) a prison dandy. [*Yogi Bear* = lair (Aus. sl. 'show-off'); from the US cartoon character Yogi Bear]

Yorkshire penny bank *n.* [20C] an act of masturbation. [*Yorkshire penny bank* = wank]

Yorkshire rippers *n.* [1980s+] slippers. [from the serial killer Peter Sutcliffe (b.1946), who murdered 13 women in Yorkshire and Lancashire between 1975 and 1981 and became known as the 'Yorkshire Ripper']

Yorkshire tyke *n.* [20C] a microphone. [*Yorkshire tyke* = mike]

you and me *n.* **1** [late 19C–1910s] a flea. **2** [20C] tea. **3** [20C] an act of urination, urine. **4** [20C] (*Aus.*) a pea. **5** [1940s+] (*bingo*) the number three. [**3** *you and me* = pee/wee]

you know *n.* [1980s+] (*drugs*) cocaine. [*you know* = snow (sl. 'cocaine')]

young and frisky *n.* [20C] (*Aus.*) whisky.

yours and ours *n.* [20C] flowers.

Yuletide log *n.* [1970s] a dog.

Zachary Scotts *n.* [1940s–50s] diarrhoea. [*Zachary Scotts* = the trots; from the film star Zachary Scott (1914–65)]

Zane Grey *n.* [20C] (*Aus.*) pay, i.e. wages. [from the Western writer Zane Grey (1875–1939)]

Zasu Pitts *n.* [1930s–50s] diarrhoea. [*Zasu Pitts* = the shits; from the silent-film star ZaSu Pitts (1898–1963)]

zorba *v.* [1950s+] to urinate. [*zorba the greek* = leak; from the film *Zorba the Greek* (1964), itself from the novel (1946) by Nikos Kazantzakis]

zorba'd *adj.* [1950s+] annoyed, angry. [*zorba the greeked* = leaked, i.e. pissed (off); *see* ZORBA]

THE THESAURUS

Animals

Alsatian all stations

Cat brown hat

Dog
cherry hog
chock and log
Christmas log
golliwog
hollow log
London fog
Yuletide log

Donkey
moke Jerusalem artichoke

Horse
apple sauce
bottle of sauce
Charing Cross
tomato sauce
hack plate-rack

Mouse Maxwell House

Pig Lord Wigg

Rat top hat

Snake
George Blake
Joe
Joe Blake

Squirrel nice one, Cyril!

Bodily Functions

Break Wind
belch Raquel Welch
burp Wyatt Earp
fart apple tart
beef-heart
broken heart
bullock's heart
D'Oyly Carte
gooseberry tart
heart and dart
horse and cart
Lionel Bart
raspberry tart
treacle tart

Excrement
crap game of nap
horse and trap
man-trap
poop ali oop
shit big hit
bob and hit
brad
eartha
Edgar Britt
florin
william
turd Douglas Hurd
Henry III
Henry the Third
lemon

turd continued

                lemon curd
                my word
                Richard
                Richard the Third
                William the Third

Defecate

crap	Andy Capp
shit	tom
	tom tit

Defecation

crap	pony
	Sheffield handicap
dump	Forrest Gump
pony	Egon
	Egon Ronay
shit	banana
	banana split
	big hit
	brad
	eartha
	Edgar Britt
	hard hit
	tom
	tomtit
	two-bob bit
	william

Diarrhoea

runs	tommy guns
shits	banana

shits continued

                banana splits
                Edgar Britt
                Jim Britts
                jimmies
                Jimmy Britts
                nicker bits
                Saint Moritz
                threepenny bits
                toms
                tomtits
                trey-bits
                two-bob bit
                William Pitts
                Zasu Pitts

trots	Zachary Scotts

Urinate

go for a slash	
	go for a leslie
leak	zorba
piddle	dicky diddle
	hi-diddle-diddle
piss	apple and pip
slash	Pat Cash
tinkle	Rip Van Winkle

Urination

leak	bubble and squeak
pee	Christopher Lee
	Jack Dee
	lemon tea
	Peters and Lee

pee continued
   riddle-me-ree
   robert e.
   Sammy Lee
   Southend-on-Sea
   victory V
   you and me
piddle Gerry Riddle
   hey-diddle-diddle
   hi-diddle-diddle
   Jenny Riddle
   Jerry Riddle
   Jimmy Riddle
   Nelson
   Nelson Riddle
   pig in the middle
piss comical chris
   cousin sis
   cuddle and kiss
   gipsy's
   gipsy's kiss
   goodnight kiss
   gypsy's
   gypsy's kiss
   hit
   hit and miss
   hit or miss
   Johnny Bliss
   Mickey Bliss
   Mike Bliss
   rattle and hiss
   snake's
   snake's hiss
   that and this

slash bangers
   bangers and mash
   Frazer Nash
   Jackie
   Jackie Dash
   J. Carroll Naish
   Johnny Cash
   pie and mash
   whiplash

Urine
pee sweetpea
   you and me

Clothing

Boots burdetts
   daisy recroots
   daisy recruits
   daisy roots
   fiddles and flutes
   German flutes
   King Canutes
   piccolo(s) and flutes

Cap baby pap
   baby's pap
   butter flap
   game of nap
   touch and tap
cheeser Julius Caesar

Clothes	these and those	**Fan**	Mary Ann

Coat	all afloat
	billy goat
	bucket afloat
	bucket and float
	city tote
	Dover boat
	Glasgow boat
	I'm afloat
	ivory float
	John O'Groat
	nanny
	nanny goat
	pound note
	Quaker oat

Collar	Arty Roller
	Charlie Rawler
	half-a-dollar
	holla
	holla boys
	holler
	holler boys
	oller
	oller boys
	Oxford scholar
	shout and holler
	Tommy Roller
collar and tie	
	swallow and sigh
collar stud	
	slosh and mud

Glove	turtle
	turtle dove

Hat	ball and bat
	barrel of fat
	bladder of fat
	lean and fat
	leaning fat
	this and that
	titfa
	titfer
	tit-for
	tit-for-tat
bowler	bottle of cola
	bottle of Kola
	steamroller
cady	Charley Brady
lid	God forbid
tile	battle of the Nile
	penny-a-mile

Jacket	steam-packet
	tennis racket
leather	tar and feather

Pocket	chain and locket
	Davy Crockett
	locket
	Lucy Locket
	penny locket
	sky
	sky-pocket

Pocket continued

	sky rocket
	Stephenson's Rocket
poke	Barney Moke

Purse   doctor and nurse
grey nurse

Scarf   centre half
cry and laugh
one and half
tin bath

Shirt   dickey
dickey dirt
dicky
dicky dirt
dig and dirt
dinky dirt
roll me
roll me in the dirt
throw me in the dirt
Uncle Bert

Shoe(s)   five to twos
howd'ye dos
ones and twos
p's and q's
rhythm and blues
St Louis blues
tens and twos

Sock(s)   almond rocks
almonds
army rocks
Bobby Rocks
curly locks
East India docks
Grimsby Docks
Joe Rocks
Katharine Docks
nervo and knox
not much frocks
Oscar Hock
peppermint rocks
peppermints
Tilbury docks
ton o' my rocks

Suit   bag of fruit
box of fruit
whistle
whistle and flute

Tie   fourth of July
lamb fry
lamb's fry
mud in your eye
mud's in your eye
Nelly Bligh
Peckham
Peckham Rye
pig's fry
swallow and sigh

Tights   fly-by-nights
Snow Whites

Trousers	council houses
	dead wowsers
	Johnny Rousers
	Johnny Rowsers
	pair o' round-mys
	petrols
	rammy rousers
	round me houses
	round the houses
	Rowton Houses
	terrace
bags	harolds
	trolly-wags
cords	House of Lords
flares	Dan Dares
	Grosvenor Squares
	Lionel Blairs
fly	Nelly Bligh
pants	bull-ants
	insects
	insects and ants
strides	Herbie Hides
	Jekyll and Hydes

Underwear

	do and dare
bags	harolds
bloomers	montezumas
	wicked rumours
BVDs	seldom see
drawers	early doors
	maggies
knickers	Alan Whickers
	Brenda Frickers

knicks	clickety-clicks
pants	insects
	insects and ants
undies	Reg Grundys
	reggys
	reginalds
vest	brigg's rest
	east and west
	little grey home in the west
	Sunday best
	wild west

Conversation

all right harbour light
shiny and bright

any good?
any Wee Georgie?

arsehole!
pig's Christmas parcel

be my guest
be my Georgie Best

fuck it! mop and bucket!

I'm all right
dieu et mon droit

I should say so!
I should coco!
I should cocoa!

Insults

berk	Joe Erk		toerag
bum	date	*sod*	Tommy Dodd
cunt	joe	*turd*	lemon
	Joc Hunt		lemon curd
	National Front	*wanker*	Kuwaiti tanker
fucker	feather-plucker		merchant banker
prat	kit-kat		oil tanker
slag	teabag		Sri Lanka

♦♦

later! alligator!

no good chump of wood
no Robin Hood

not bad chesapeake shad

not on your life!
not on your nellie!
not on your nelly!

on your way!
edna!

steal the lot!
ding the tot!

too true! too bloody stew!
too Irish stew!
two eyes of blue!

where in God's name?
where the five 'n' arf?

you understand?
dry land?

Crime and Punishment

Bail Daily
Daily Mail
ginger ale
holy nail
royal mail

Burgle
crack a crib
eat a fig

Cell flowery dell

Cheat   daisy beat

Child Molestor
        Uncle Lester
nonce   bacon-bonce

Criminal(s)
crook   bab
        babbler
        babbling brook
        Joe Hook
        Joe Rook
the boys   san toys

Confidence Trick
        penny-come-quick
con   Elton
        Elton John
tale   Binnie Hale
        hill and dale
        ship under sale

Electric Chair
        I don't care

Fine   Calvin Klein

Go Bail   stand an ale

Parole   jam roll

Petty Crime
earner   Anthea
        Anthea Turner

Pickpocket
boost   fowl roost

Prison
chokey   hokey
jail   bucket
        bucket and pail
        ginger ale
        jug and pail
        moan and wail
        sorrowful tale
nick   cow's lick
        Moby Dick
        shovel and pick
stir   Joe
        Joe Gurr
treadmill   can't-keep-still
treadwheel
        fillet of veal

Prison Officers
chief   bully beef
        corned beef
        ham and beef
gov.   light of love

Sentence
drag   carpet
moon   woodener
        wooden spoon
stretch   Jack Ketch
time   bird
        bird lime

◆◆

Weapons

Blade	shovel and spade	**Knife**	charming wife
			drum and fife
Bullet	Ruud Gullit		Duke of Fife
			husband and wife
Gun	hot cross bun		man and wife
gat	fly flat		
shooter	phil the fluter	**Razor**	House of Fraser
rod	Tommy Dodd		howser
			Ted Frazer

◆◆

Thief corned beef
leg of beef
tealeaf
tea leaf
Ted Heath
hook in the book

Villain Harold Macmillan

Warder Harry Lauder
screw flue
four by two
kanga
kangaroo
little boy blue
Scooby Doo

Disease and Disability

AIDS shovels and spades

Blind bacon
bacon rind
golden hind

Cancer jack the dancer
Jimmy Dancer

Chill frock and frill

Cold soldier bold

Cough Darren Gough
horse and trough
on and off

Cripple mustard
              mustard pickle
              raspberry

Deaf a.i.f.
              mutt and jeff
              pudding chef

Diarrhoea

the runs tommy guns
the shits bananas
              banana splits
              Edgar Britts
              Jim Britts
              jimmies
              Jimmy Britts
              nicker bits
              Saint Moritz
              threepenny bits
              toms
              tomtits
              trey-bits
              two-bob bits
              William Pitts
              Zasu Pitts
the trots red hots
              Zachary Scotts

Dumb red rum

Fever Robinson and Cleaver

Gout in-and-out
              salmon and trout

Influenza

flu inky blue
       lousy lou
wog chocolate frog

Malinger

sham abraham
         abram

Pain Hanger Lane
         Kennington Lane
         Michael Caine
         Petticoat Lane
         Saddam Hussein

Sick bob and dick
         bob, harry and dick
         harry, tom and dick
         mickey
         micky
         moby dick
         old mick
         spotted dick
         tom, harry and dick
         Uncle Dick
crook butcher's hook
         Captain Cook
lousy housey-housey
queer Brighton pier
rough Mickey Duff

Venereal Disease

clap handicap
       hat and cap

Veneral disease continued

	horse
	horse and trap
pox	band in the box
	boots and socks
	cardboard box
	coachman on the box
	Collie Knox
	goldilocks
	jack, the
	jack in the box
	nervo and knox
	Reverend Ronald Knox
	royal docks
	shoes and socks
	Surrey docks
	Tilbury docks
	Whitehaven docks
	bang and biff
	lover's tiff
	Will's Whiff

Vomit	Wallace and Gromit
be sick	tom and dick
	Uncle Dick
chunder	up and under
spew	chunder

Minor ailments, injuries and infestations

Bad Breath king death

Bed Bug hearth rug
Tom Tug

Black Eye
shiner Morris Minor

Boil can of oil
canov
Conan Doyle
Jack Doyle
Mrs Doyle

Bunion pickled onion
Spanish onion

Cramp rising damp

Flea(s) Crocodile Dundee
Jack Rees
Jennie Lea
Jenny Lee
Nancy Lee
Phil McBee
Rosie
Rosie Lea
Rosy
Rosy Lea
Rosy Lee
stand at ease
two UEs

Flea(s) continued
Willy Lees
you and me

Haemorrhoids
emmas
sigmunds
piles chalfonts
farmer Giles
farmers
Johnny Giles
laughs and smiles
Michael Miles
nautical miles
nauticals
Nobby Stiles
nurembergs
Seven Dials
Valentine Dyalls
X Files

Lice boys on ice
white mice
crabs beattie and babs
dibs and dabs
dribs and drabs
hansom cabs
taxicabs

Scar Mars bar

Spot Randolph Scott
Selina Scott

Wind Jenny Lind

Drinking

Alcohol General
beers Britney Spears
bevvy Don Revie
booze mud and ooze
pick and choose
River Ooze
River Ouse
Tom Cruise
win or lose
drink bit of blink
blink
cuff link
Engelbert
Engelbert Humperdinck
kitchen sink
pen
pen and ink
tiddley
tiddly
tumble
tumbledown
glass Hackney Marsh
Jack Surpass
lush comb and brush
soak suit and cloak
short magistrate's court

Bar balloon
bazaar
jack
Jack Tar
near and far

Bar continued

> there you are
> Tommy Farr

ramp postage stamp

Bar Stool

> Peter O'Toole

Public House

boozer battle and cruiser
> battle-cruiser
> battleship and cruiser

corner Johnny Horner

pub rubadub
> rub-a-dub
> rub-a-dub-dub
> rubbity dub

Beer Charlie Freer
> crimea
> far and near
> Germaine Greer
> never fear
> oh, my dear
> pig's
> pig's ear
> red steer

ale Daily
> Daily Mail
> ship in full sail

Bass beggar boy's
> beggar boy's arse

Ben (Truman)
> Jenny Wren

Ben (Truman) continued
> never again

best pants and vest

bitter apple fritter
> chirrup and titter
> Gary Glitter
> giggle and titter
> laugh and titter
> Tex Ritter

brown up-and-down

Burton lace curtain

drink one's beer
> chew one's ear
> chew one's lug

glass of beer
> pot of O

Guinness photo finish

hops slum of slops

keg Auntie Meg

lager Forsyte Saga

light day and night
> silent night
> stage fright

mild Jimmy Wilde
> Marty Wilde

pint roast joint
> top joint

pot Sir Walter Scott
> Walter Scott

schooner lily of lagoona

shandy Mahatma Gandhi
> Napper Tandy

Stella (Artois)
> Nelson (Mandela)

Stella (Artois) continued	Paul Weller
stout	in-and-out
	salmon and trout
toss	Jonathan Ross

Brandy Amos and Andy
Andy Pandy
Charley Randy
fine and dandy
jack-a-dandy
Jack Dandy
Mahatma Gandhi
sugar-candy
soak suit and cloak

Cider runner and rider
Winona Ryder

Drinking Session

all-dayer Leo Sayer

Drunk bullaphants
elephant's
elephant's trunk
jumbo's trunk
molly
out the monk
salt
salt junk
barmy Salvation Army
drink tiddley
tiddly
pissed Adrian

pissed continued
Adrian Quist
booed and hissed
Brahms and Liszt
hand and fist
hit and missed
Lillian Gished
Lloyd's
Lloyd's List
Mozart and Liszt
Oliver Twist
Schindler's
Schindler's List
full John Bull
on the booze
on the ooze
plastered lord and mastered
tiddly Newton and Ridley
tight high as a kite
tipsy kisky

Get Drunk

go on the piss
go on the cousin sis

Get Someone Else Drunk

hocus locus

Gin Brian O'Flynn
Brian O'Linn
bung it
bung it in
Huckleberry Finn
Lincoln's Inn

Gin continued
　　　　mother's
　　　　mother's ruin
　　　　needle and pin
　　　　Nell Gwyn
　　　　nose and chin
　　　　paraffin
　　　　Ralph Lynn
　　　　thick and thin
　　　　vera
　　　　Vera Lynn
measure of gin
　　　　quartern o' Bry

Hangover
the shakes
　　　　ducks and drakes
　　　　Joe Blakes
　　　　rattlesnakes

Hung over
shaky　currant-cakey
sick　　bob and dick
　　　　bob, harry and dick

Port　didn't ought
　　　　long and short

Round of Drinks
shout　Wally Grout

Rum　dad and mum
　　　　finger and thumb
　　　　kingdom come

Rum continued
　　　　thimble and thumb
　　　　Tom
　　　　Tom Thumb
Bacardi　kiss me hardy
　　　　Laurel and Hardy
measure of rum
　　　　quartern o' finger

Soda　Major Loder

Spirits
short　magistrate's court
drink　tiddleywink
　　　　tiddlywink

Whisky　Charley Frisky
　　　　frisky
　　　　gay and frisky
　　　　highland frisky
　　　　I'm so
　　　　I'm so frisky
　　　　sweetpea
　　　　young and frisky
corn　　Kentucky horn
Scotch　gold watch
　　　　pimple and blotch
　　　　waterbury watch

Whisky and Soda
　　　　Rosie Loader
　　　　Rosy Loader
　　　　Rosie Loder
　　　　Rosy Loder

Wine   Calvin Klein
             rise and shine
             River Tyne
             string and twine
plonk   honky tonk
vin blanc plinkity plonk

Drugs and Smoking

Cannabis

dope   Bob Hope
        soap
grass   brass
hash   Jack Flash
        Johnny Cash
marijuana
        blue de hue
quarter bottle of water
        janet
weed   olly

Cigar

Cigar   la-di-dah
        Spanish guitar
smoke sentimental

Cigarette

        forgive and forget
cig   Irish jig
ciggie Miss Piggy
fag   Harry Wragg
        Melvyn Bragg
        oily

fag continued
        old kit bag
        old nag
        Oxford bag
        puff and drag
        spit and a drag
        winkle
        winklebag
smoke sentimental
snout in-and-out
wood   do me good

Cigarette Butt

bumper Victor Trumper

Cocaine

charlie barley
        gianluca
        oats
coke   big bloke
        Billie Hoke
line   Patsy Cline
powder Niki Lauda
snow   you know

Comedown

bummer John Selwyn

Crack

Crack applejack
        half-track
        hubba, I am back
        I am back

Drugs General

dope	bar of soap
pill(s)	Jenny Hills
	Jimmy Hills
	Pebble Mill
tablet	Gary Ablett

Fentanyl

apache	tango and cash

Hallucinogens

LSD	sweetpea
PCP	busy bee
	green tea
psilocybin	
	simple simon

Heroin

fix	Jimmy Hicks
	Jimmy Hix
	tom
	Tom Mix
pill	jack
	jack and jill
scag	Salisbury Crag
smack	hammer
	hammer and tack
	Uncle Mac

Light

fly my kite

Lighter

kung fu fighter

Pipe

cherry-ripe
raw and ripe
Tommy Tripe
Tom Tripe
yard of tripe

Snuff

blindman's buff
hang bluff
Harry Bluff
Lal Brough
lally

Tobacco

hi jimmy knacker
Michael Schumacher
nosey-my-knacker
Tom Thacker

chew	kanga
	kangar
snout	salmon and trout

Uppers

pill	Damon
	Damon Hill
	William Hill
speed	Lou Reed
	olly

Woodbine

wood	do me good

Emotions, Intelligence and Mental States

Angry
crook butcher's hook

Bravery
arse bottle
  bottle and glass

Coward Charley Howard

Cowardice
no arse no bottle

Fear cauliflower
shivers Hawkesbury rivers

Fool lump of school
  muffin
  twelve-inch rule
  two-foot rule
berk Charlie Smirke
  Joe Erk
chump lump and bump
cunt berk
  Berkeley hunt
  Berkshire hunt
  Burlington hunt
  burk
  burke
  charlie
dill Beecham's pill
  jack and jill

dope Joe Soap
gay thirty-first of May
gets nutten
  Billy Button
goon egg and spoon
loon man in the moon
muff beery buff
mug hearth rug
  milk jug
  steamer
  steam tug
  stone jug
  toby jug
  Tom Tug
muggins Harry Huggins
plonker Willy Wonka
prat kit-kat
  paper hat
  tin hat
  top hat
  trilby hat
prick Hampton
  Hampton Wick
  kiss-me-quick
twat dillypot
  dollypot
wank J. Arthur
wanker ham shanker

Huff cream puff

Mad mum and dad
barmy lakes
  lakes of Killarney

batty	carlo
mental	radio
yarra	cock-sparrow

Mad Person

loony	Mickey Rooney
nutter	bread and butter
	pound of butter

Moody   punch and judy

Nerves   hors d'oeuvres

	Millwall Reserves
	West Hams
shakes	joes
shits	Jim Britts
	jimmies
	Jimmy Britts

Sad   Alan Ladd

Silly   daffadown dilly

	daffydown dilly
	daffy-down dilly
	harry
	Piccadilly
	Uncle Willie

State   Harry Tate

	six and eight
	two and eight

Stupid   Eros and Cupid

bats	Kilkenny cats
thick	king dick
	paddy and mick
	Paddy Quick
	rick and dick
	take your pick

◆◆◆

Books and reading

Book   Captain Cook

	Joe Hook
	Joe Rook
	King Farouk
	rookery nook

Catalogue

cattle dog

Newspaper

	Johnny Raper
	linen
	linen-draper
Herald	Jim Gerald
Sun	currant bun
The Times	
	Captain Grimes
	nursery rhymes

◆◆◆

Tense

pinned up wind up

Entertainment

Cinema

pictures dolly mixtures
fleas and itches
flies and itchers

Dance Isle of France
kick and prance
south of France
treble chance
tap cellar-flap
varsovienne
arse over header

Nightclub

rubadub
rub-a-dub
rub-a-dub-dub
rubbity dub

Sing highland fling

Song dinky-dong
Suzie Wong
sing-song ding-dong

Television

box nervo and knox

telly custard and jelly
Marie Corelli
Mother Kelly
Ned Kelly

Theatre Box
artful fox
Charles James

Food

Apple Whitechapel

Banana Gertie Gitana

Baked Beans
kings
kings and queens
Milton Keynes

Beans Aberdeens

Beef Lee Van
Lee Van Cleef
stop thief

Bread lump of lead
needle and thread
skein of thread
strike-me
strike-me-dead
Uncle Fred
Uncle Ned

Bread roll
      Nat King Cole

Butter Calcutta
      chuck me in the gutter
      cough and stutter
      Danny Rucker
      Dan Tucker
      Gordon Hutter
      Johnny Rutter
      kerb and gutter
      lay me in the gutter
      lisp and stutter
      mumble and mutter
      mutter and stutter
      potash and perlmutter
      pull down the shutter
      roll me in the gutter
      slip in the gutter
      stammer and stutter

Cabbage Joe Savage

Café   riff-raff

Cake   give and take
      Joe
      Joe Blake
      put and take
      Sexton Blake
      shiver and shake
      Swan Lake

Carrot Polly Parrot

Cheese Annie Louise
      balmy breeze
      bended knees
      cough and sneeze
      flying trapeze
      John Cleese
      stand at ease

Chips   Jagger's lips
      jockey's whips
      lucky dips
      nigger's lips

Chop   Keystone cop

Cocoa orinoko

Coffee Everton toffee
      sticky toffee

Coke   holy smoke

Crisps will o' the wisps
potato chips
      nigger's lips

Curry   Pete Murray
      River Murry
      Ruby Murray

Diet   peace and quiet

Dinner Charley Skinner
      derby winner

Dinner continued
glorious sinner
Jimmy Skinner
Jim Skinner
Joe Skinner
Johnny Skinner
Lilley and Skinner
Michael Winner
Ned Skinner
saint and sinner

Dripping
Doctor Crippen

Eat tidy and neat

Eels Tommy Steeles

Egg(s) borrow and beg
clothes-peg
Doctor Legg
Scotch pegs
tent peg
wooden legs

Fat Jack Sprat

Fish Andy McNish
dirty dish
Lillian Gish

Food in the mood
in the nude
nosh mouthwash

peck Tooting
Tooting Bec
scran Johnny Rann
Tommy O'Rann

Gravy army and navy
royal navy

Greens God save the queens
has-beens
Nellie Deans
Nelly Deans

Ham hop it and scram
Jean-Claude
Jean-Claude Van
Damme
trolley and tram

Kipper(s)
bronze figure
Jack the Ripper
New York nippers

Lamb Uncle Sam

Lunch judy and punch
kidney punch

Meat hands

Meat Pie
dog's eye
Nazi spy
Nelly Bligh

Milk	Charley Dilke
	satin and silk
	soft as silk
	yellow silk
Mussel	Jane Russell
Mutton	Billy Button
Noodles	Yankee Doodles
Pasty	cheap and nasty
Pear	teddy bear
Pie	Captain Bligh
	penny for the guy
	Princess Di
	smack in the eye
Piecrust	dirt, grime and dust
Potatoes	navigators
	Spanish waiters
spuds	Captain Bloods
	rosebuds
	Steele Rudds
Prawn	Goldie Hawn
Prune	rangoon
Salad	romantic ballad

Sandwich	
sarnie	Giorgio Armani
Saveloy	girl and boy
	Myrna Loy
Soup	bowl the hoop
	iron hoop
	loop-the-loop
	loopy the loop
Spinach	Woolwich and Greenwich
Steak	ben-flake
	Joe
	Joe Blake
	quiver and quake
	Veronica Lake
Stew	battle of Waterloo
	bonnets so blue
	boy in blue
	Waterloo
Sultanas	salty bananas
Supper	Tommy Tupper
Tea	Betty Lea
	Betty Lee
	Dicky Lee
	George Bohee
	glory be

tea continued

      Gypsie Lee
      hay lee
      Jennie Lee
      Jenny Lea
      Jimmy Lee
      Mother Machree
      Nancy Lee
      peter and lee
      River Lea
      Rosie
      Rosie Lea
      Rosy
      Rosy Lea
      Rosy Lee
      sailors on the sea
      split pea
      sweetpea
      wasp and bee
      you and me
char   there you are

Winkle granny's wrinkle

Gambling

Bet   give and get
         house to let
flutter grumble and mutter

Bet on Credit

bet on the blue
      bet on the Mary Lou

on the nod
      on the Murray cod

Bettor/Customer

punter Billy Bunter
        gezunter
        hillman hunter

Bookie Joe Rookie
book   tommy

Evens   Major Stevens

Football Pools
      April Fools

Greyhound Races

dogs   cherries
       cherry oggs
       golliwogs

Horse-races
      airs and graces
      Ascot races
      Ascots
trots   red hots

Ledger

book   docker's hook
      tommy

Place a Bet
      cast a net

♦♦♦

Cards, darts and dice

Ace	cat's face	Heart	jam tart
Card(s)	bladder of lard	Joker	tapioca
	prussian guard	King	highland fling
	Wilkie Bards	Queen	Mary Green
Darts	horses and carts		

Six (in craps)
    Captain Hicks
    Jimmy Hicks
    Jimmy Hix

Dice	cats and mice
	rats and mice
	white mice

Double (in darts)
    rasher and bubble

Three (in cards)
tray   Vicar of Bray

Flush	barmaid's blush

♦♦♦

Price	nits and lice	Win	nose and chin
Stake	joe		
	Joe Blake		

Bingo

Tip	egg flip	One	buttered bun
	sherbert dip		buttered scone
Tipster	eggflipper	Two	buckle my shoe
			dink-do
Tote	canal boat		dirty old Jew
	giddy goat		me-and-you
	nanny goat		
Tout	in-and-out	Three	up a tree
	salmon and trout		you and me

Four	door to door
	knock on/at the door
	open the door
	pompey whore
Five	man alive
Six	chopping sticks
	chopsticks
	clickety-click
	Joynson-Hicks
Seven	God in heaven
	God's in heaven
Eight	garden gate
	Harry Tate
Nine	Brighton Line
Ten	Uncle Ben
Twelve	
dozen	monkey's cousin
20	horn of plenty
30	Burlington Bertie
33	Gertie Lee
34	dirty whore
44	
all the fours	
	Diana Dors
66	clickety-click

Home

Bed	roses red
	skein of thread
	Uncle Ned
hay	Botany Bay
kip	feather and flip
	jockey's whip
sack	Robert Flack
Chair(s)	Fred Astaire
	here and there
	I declare
	I'll be there
	Leicester
	Leicester Square
	Lionel Blair
	lion's lair
	Owen Nares
	Trafalgar Square
	Vanity Fair
Cupboard	
	Mother Hubbard
Curtain	Richard Burton
Door	Bobby Moore
	George Bernard Shaw
	Rory
	Rory O'Moore
Doormat	tomcat

Fire Andy Maguire
Anna Maria
Aunt Maria
Barney Maguire
I desire
jeremiah
Mick O'Dwyer
Molly Maguire
obadiah

Floor Auntie Flora
Charlie Clore
Jane Shore
Mrs More
Rory
Rory O'Moore

Home gates of Rome
Pope
Pope of Rome
top of Rome
top o' Rome

House cat and mouse
flea and louse
Mickey Mouse
Minnie Mouse
rat and mouse

Lodger artful dodger
jolly roger

Room birch broom
bride and groom
shovel and broom

Stairs apple and pears
apples
apples and pears
Fred Astaires
stocks and shares
troubles and cares

Table Betty Grable
Cain and Abel
Cain and Able

Wall bat and ball

Window burnt
burnt cinder
Jenny Linda
Jenny Linder
Polly Flinder
Tommy Trinder

Bathroom

Basin Charley Mason
Fortnum and Mason
Jimmy Mason

Bath hat and scarf
Steffi Graf

tub bib and bub

Bath Plug
little brown jug

Chamber Pot

jerry	Ellen Terry
potty	mazawattee

Razor
Dawn Frazer
Frankie Fraser
howser
House of Fraser

Shave
dad and dave
dig a grave
dig in the grave
misbehave
ocean wave
Scotland
Scotland the Brave

Shower bag of flour

Soap
bander
band of hope
Bob Hope
Cape of Good Hope
Charley Pope
Jimmy Hope
Joe Hope
land of hope
frisk and frolic

Toilet

bog	captain's log
	Kermit the Frog
carsey	Ilie Nastase

crapper	Frank Zappa
dunny	don't be funny
ladies'	Rosie O'Grady's
my aunt's	
	Mrs Chant's
pisshole	savoury rissole
shitter	banana fritter
	Tex Ritter
	Thelma
	Thelma Ritter
piss	snake's
	snake's hiss
throne	rag and bone
wash	lemon and dash

Towel
Bob Powell
enoch
mortar and trowel
Sandy Powell
William Powell

Wash
Bob Squash
lemon squash

Water
didn't oughter
dirty daughter
miller's daughter
mother and daughter
squatter's daughter

Law and Order

At Large
on the run
    hot cross bun

Dock   Brighton rock

Handcuffs
shackle block and tackle

Inform
shop   garden hop
           lollipop
           lolly up
speak   bubble and squeak
squeal conger
           conger eel

Informer
dog   chocolate frog
fizgig Moreton
         Moreton bay
nark   carpark
         grass in the park
         Hyde Park
         Noah's
         Noah's ark
rat   cabbage-tree hat
         cocked hat
shopper grass
stinker pen and inker
talker Johnny Walker

word   dicky-bird
         dickey-bird

Judge   Barnaby Rudge
         inky smudge
         smear and smudge

Lawyer Tom Sawyer

Police ducks and geese
boss   Joe Goss
cop   dime a pop
         ginger-pop
         greasy
         greasy mop
         John Hop
         Johnny Hop
         lemon
         lemon drop
         lollipop
         lolly
         pork chop
         slop
         spinning top
         string and top
copper bottle
         bottle and stopper
         clodhopper
         grasshopper
         Johnny Hopper
dick   club and stick
filth   Uncle Wilf
john   hot scone

officer of the law
       hammer and saw
Old Bill blueberry
       blueberry hill
sarge   half of marge

Scotland Yard
       bladder of lard

Security
bouncer half-ouncer

Life and Death

Born   got out of porn

Dead   brown bread
       buttered bread
       currant bread
       fried bread
       gone to bed
       loaf of bread
       potted head
       toasted bread
hors de combat
       wombat

Kill   Tower Hill
nix   eight six
       eighty-six

Life   fork and kinfe

Life continued
       struggle and strife
       trouble and strife
puff   Nellie Duff
       Nelly Duff

Suicide sideways

Men and Women

Boy   hipsy hoy
       Mark Foy
       mother's joy
       pride and joy
       Rob Roy
       saveloy

Experienced Man
man of the world
       flag unfurled

Girl   ivory pearl
       mother of pearl
       ocean pearl
       ribbon and curl
       twist
       twist and twirl
       wind do twirl
gal   bob my pal
       bob's my pal
       fal
       Pall Mall
       rob my pal

Man (General)

	heavenly plan
	pot and pan
bloke	bag of coke
	bushel of coke
	heap o' coke
	heap of coke
	heapy
	lump of coke
dope	Joe Soap
fella	umbrella
geezer	fridge freezer
	ice-cream freezer
	lemon squeezer

Old Man

	frying pan
	old pot
codger	splodger

Old Woman

	old grabem pudden
old hag	boiled rag

Sexually Objectified Woman

	manto
fanny	mantovani
moll	paper doll
polone	eau-de-Cologne
snatch	Tony Hatch

Woman (General)

	gooseberry pudden
	gooseberry pudding

bird	lemon
	lemon curd
	Richard
	Richard the Third
bitch	Miss Fitch
	wicked witch
cherry ripe	
	cherry-pipe
cow	ruck and row
miss	cuddle and kiss
sheila	Charlie Wheeler
	potato
	potato peeler
	two-wheeler
slag	Melvyn Bragg

Money

Bank	arthur
	cab rank
	chain and crank
	clink and blank
	fish and tank
	frank and hank
	iron tank
	J. Arthur
	rattle and clank
	shovel and tank
	taxi rank
	tin tank

Banker's Draft	George Raft

Bill Beecham's pill
jack and jill
rhubarb pill
william

Borrow Sodom and Gomorrah
tomorrow
cadge coat and badge
tap cellar-flap
rip rap

Bribe
bung Jimmy Young

Cash (a Cheque)
sausage
sausage a goose's
sausage and mash

Crown
dollar Oxford scholar

Dollar Charlie Roller
hoot and holler
bill william

Eight Pounds
garden gate

800 Pounds
golden gate

Farthing Covent Garden

50 Pence
half calf
cow and calf
cow's
cow's calf

Five Pounds
beehive
jack's
jack's alive
jax
fin Lincoln's Inn
fiver deep-sea diver
Lady Godiva
scuba
scuba diver
sky-diver
flim Tiny Tim
half a ten half-a-cock

Five Shillings
dollar shirt and collar
shirt collar

Four Pounds
rouf French loaf

Giro Monte Cairo

Half-Crown
half poddy calf
half a dollar
half an Oxford
half an Oxford scholar

Halfpenny

brown Camden Town
town

100 Pounds

ton top gun

Loan

tap star's nap

Money bees
beesum
bees and honey
bread
bread and honey
Bugs Bunny
Easter bunny
Gene Tunney
honey
pot of honey
sugar
sugar and honey
tom and funny
brass beggar boy's
beggar boy's arse
cash dot and dash
Harry Nash
Henry Nash
knotty ash
oak and ash
Oscar
Oscar Asche
Oscar Nash
Okker

cash continued
pie and mash
sausage and mash
smash
copper lolly
dough Bromley
Bromley by Bow
cod's roe
dosh orange squash
loot whistle and toot
quids saucepan lids
readies Nelson Eddies
screw kanga
sovereigns
Jemmy O'Goblins
Jimmy O'Goblins
wad Ken Dodd

Penny Abergavenny
Jack Benny
kilkenny
Reginald Denny
brown Kentish Town
copper clod
stiver coal heaver
heaver
win nose and chin

Pension stand to
stand to attention

Poor on the floor
broke coal and coke
coals and coke

broke continued

	heart of oak
	hearts of oak
skint	After Eight Mint
	boracic
	brassic
	brassick
	brassic lint
	pink lint
	polo mint

Pound hole in the ground

	lost and found
	merry-go-round
nicker	cherry-picker
	cow's licker
quid	fiddley-did
	teapot
	teapot lid
sovereign	frog
	frogskin

Seeking a Loan

on the cadge
    on the C and B

on the touch
    on the cripple and crutch

Shares Rupert Bears

Shilling abraham's willing

	Barney Dillon
	I'm willing
	John Dillon
	potato-pillin'

Shilling continued

	rogue and villain
	tater-pillin'
	Thomas Tilling
bob	doorknob
	kettle
	kettle on a hob
	one for his nob
	touch-me
deaner	riverina

Sixpence

tanner	goddess Diana
	lord of the manor
	susie
	susy
	tartan banner
zac	hammer
	hammer and tack

Sovereign

	Jemmy O'Goblin
	Jimmy O'Goblin
quid	Yid

Ten Pounds

	Big Ben
	cock and hen
	cockle
	cockle and hen
	pencil, open, lost and found
	Tony Benn
tenner	ayrton

Unemployment & industrial action

Claiming Unemployment Benefit

on the labour
beggar my neighbour

Dismissal

the push Shepherd's Bush
the sack big mac
last card of the pack
pedlar's pack
tin-tack

Non-unionist

rat   tit-for-tat
scab hansom cab
jack
Sandy Macnab

Shirk   burk

shirker office worker
skiver   backseat driver

Unemployment Benefit

dole   cob o' coal
con and coal
horse and foal
jam roll
Kid Creole
Nat King Cole
Old King Cole
rock and roll
rock 'n' roll
sausage roll
strum and stroll
toilet roll

Ten Shillings

half   calf
cow and calf
cow's
cow's calf
shower bath

Thousand Pounds

grand bag of sand

Threepence

thrums currants and plums
scrum
scrummy
tray   Alma Gray
Dolly Gray
Dora
Dora Gray

Three Pounds

drag   carpet

Till   Benny Hill
            jack and jill

Tip   sherbert dip
drop   lollipop

20 Pounds
score apple core

25 Pounds
pony   macaroni

Wages greengages
            greens
            rock of ages
            rocks
pay   Zane Grey
sub   rhubarb
            rubadub
            rub-a-dub
            rub-a-dub-dub
            rubbity dub

Occupations

Baker Long Acre

Barber coffs harbour
            Sydney Harbour
            Sydney harbor

Beggar peg-legger

Boss edmundo
          Joe Goss
          pitch and toss
chief chunka beef
          chunk of beef
          joint of beef

Bricklayer
brickie king dickie

Brokers engineers and stokers

Builders
bodgers Roy Rodgers

Cleaner semolina

Cook bab
          babbler
          babbling brook

Doctor king's proctor
           Gamble and Proctor

Engineer ginger beer

Fighter typewriter
pug   steam tug

Foreman
          Joe O'Gorman

Job doorknob

◆◆◆

University degrees

First	Geoff Hurst	**Third**	Douglas Hurd
	Pattie Hearst		George the Third
	raging		Richard
			Richard the Third

Lower Second

2:2	desmond

◆◆◆

Job continued
knocker and knob
Uncle Bob
caper brown paper

Jockey hickey hockey

Master lath and plaster

Reporter sniffer and snorter

Salesman
door-to-door
forty-four
knocker mozzle and broccha

Singer dona highland-flinger

Stripper herring and kipper

Tailor Maidstone jailer

Tailor continued
popeye the sailor
Sinbad the sailor

Taxi-driver
cabbie Westminster abbey

Tram Conductor
girl abductor

Waiter cheese grater
cold potato
hot potato
roastie
roast potato

Work dodge and shirk
Russian Turk
smile and smirk
terrible Turk
graft George Raft

Parts of the Body

Anus

arsehole	elephant and castle
	Roy Castle
	Windsor Castle
bum	date
erse	chorus and verse
hole	merry old soul
	north pole
	south pole
jacksie	London taxi
ring	pearly king
shiter	ronson
shitter	council gritter
	Gary Glitter
	spam fritter
	Thelma
	Thelma Ritter

Arm(s)

Arm(s)	burglar alarm
	chalk
	Chalk Farm
	Emmerdale
	Emmerdale Farm
	false alarm
	fire alarms
	five-acre farm
	Indian charm
	lucky charm
	Warwick Farm

Breast(s) (female)

	cabman's rests
	Mae West
knockers	mods and rockers
melons	Mary Ellens
sheilas	Charlie Wheelers
	charlies
teat	racks
	racks of meat
tits	brace and bits
	bradleys
	Bristol bits
	Bristols
	fainting fits
	moonlight flits
	threepenny bits
	thrups
	thrupennies
	trey-bits
titties	Bradford cities
	Bristol City
	cats and kitties
	Jersey City
	jerseys
	Lewis and Witties
	Manchester cities
	Manchesters
	tale of two cities
	thousand pities
	towns and cities

Buttocks

arris	April in Paris
	plaster of Paris

arse	ala
	April in Paris
	ari
	aristotle
	arris
	arry
	bottle
	bottle and glass
	harris
	Khyber
	Khyber Pass
	looking glass
	plaster of Paris
bottle	ari
	aristotle
	arris
	arry
	harris
bum	bubble gum
	date
	fife and drum
	kingdom come
	pipe and drum
	prune and plum
	rumdadum
	Tom
	Tom Thumb
plaster of Paris	
	ala
tail	Daily
	Daily Mail

Chin Andy McGinn
  Errol Flynn

chin continued
  Gilbey's gin
  Gunga Din
  Jerry McGinn
  out and in
  thick and thin
  vera
  Vera Lynn

Ear(s) bottle of beer
  fifth gear
  glass of beer
  King Lear
  Melbourne Pier
  Port Melbourne Pier
  sighs and tears
  Southend pier
  Woolwich pier
lug toby jug

Erection general election
blue veined root-on
  crouton
bone full-blown stallone
horn Colleen Bawn
  frog
  frog spawn
  hail smiling morn
  marquis
  Marquis of Lorne
  mountains of Mourne
  popcorn
  September morn
  Sunday morn

Eye(s)	baby's cries	**Feet**	dogs
	jam pies		plates
	kidney pies		plates of meat
	lamb's fries	*trotters*	Gillie Potters
	meat pies		
	mince pies	**Fingernail(s)**	
	minces		slug and snail
	mud pies		worms and snails
	mutton-pies		
	Nelly Blighs	**Finger(s)**	bees wingers
	porky		bell ringers
	porky pie		lean and linger
	puddings and pies		long and linger
	sargent's pie		melodies
			onka
Face(s)	airs and graces		onkaparinga
	boat		stick slingers
	boat-race		wait and linger
	cherry ace		
	chevy chase	**Forehead**	centre lead
	chips and chase		
	deuce and ace	**Hand(s)**	brass band
	Epsom races		German bands
	glass case		Margate sands
	handicap chase		Martin's
	Jem Mace		Martin-le-Grand
	kipper and plaice		Mary Ann
	Martin Place		Ramsgate sands
	Peyton Place		St Martin's
	roach and dace		St Martin's le Grand
	satin and lace	*fin*	Lincoln's Inn
mush	Shepherd's Bush	*forks*	duke

Head alive or dead
ball of lead
cherry red
crust of bread
gingerbread
Judge Dread
Judge Dredd
Kelly Ned
loaf
loaf of bread
lump of bread
lump of lead
ned
penn'orth of bread
pound
pound of lead
pound o' lead
ruby red
tom and ed
twopenny
Uncle Ned
napper toffee wrapper
thinkbox bundle of socks
tile penny-a-mile

Jaw jackdaw
Johnny Raw

Knee(s) biscuits and cheese
bugs and fleas
Cecil Gee
chips and peas
Christmas tree
high seas

Knee(s) continued
robert e.
trunk and tree

Leg(s) bacon and eggs
clothes-pegs
cribbage-peg
Dutch pegs
Easter egg
fried eggs
Gregory Peg
ham and eggs
mumbly pegs
mumblety-pegs
Mystic Megs
Scotch eggs
Scotch pegs
scrambled eggs
wooden pegs
gams trams

Lips apple-pips
P.G. tips
tumble and trips

Mouth dip south
east and south
Queen of the South
salmon and trout
sunny south

Neck Gregory Peck
half a peck
three quarters of a peck
train wreck

♦♦♦

Vitals

| **Brain(s)** | down the drains |
| | watch and chain |

| | | | strawberry tart |
| *pump* | skip and jump |

Heart	gooseberry tart
	grocer's cart
	horse and cart
	jam tart
	raspberry tart
	stop and start

| **Kidney** | north Sydney |
| | south Sydney |

| **Liver** | bow and quiver |
| | cheerful giver |

♦♦♦

| **Nipple** | raspberry |

Nose	Irish rose
	I suppose
	Margaret
	Margaret Rose
	Mary rose
	ruby rose
	suppose
	Tokyo rose
conk	glass of plonk
snout	in-and-out
	salmon and trout

Penis	good ship Venus
	Mars and Venus
bean	haricot
chopper	gobstopper
cock	almond

cock continued	
	dickery
	dickory dock
	grandfather
	grandfather clock
	Hampton rock
	padlock
	stick of rock
corie	gruesome and gory
	Jolson story
pecker	Black and Decker
plonker	Willy Wonka
prick	bob and dick
	donkey
	donkey's
	gigglestick
	Hackney wick
	Hampton
	Hampton Wick

prick continued

	kiss-me-quick
	mad mick
	Moby Dick
	pat and mick
	pogo
	stormy dick
	sugar-stick
	Uncle Dick
	whippit quick
tadger	fox and badger
willy	piccalilli

Pubic Hair (Female)

beaver	Sigourney Weaver
Skin	thick and thin
	vera
	vera Lynn

Stomach

belly	Auntie Nelly
	cape kelly
	Darby Kelly

◆◆

Hair

Bald	Madame Tussaud
	oh my God
	Wilkinson sword
Beard	Charley Sheard
	just as I feared
	strangely weird
Bow	Rotten Row
Hair	barnet
	barnet fair
	bonny fair
	Dublin fair
	Fanny Blair
	Fred Astaire
	here and there

	Scarborough Fair
	Tony Blair
barnet	Alf Garnett
flap	wind-trap

Moustache

	dot and dash
	whip and lash

Pudding Basin

	Fortnum and Mason

Wig

Wig	guinea pig
	Irish jig
	syrup
	syrup of figs

◆◆

belly continued

          Derby Kelly
          Ned Kelly
          Nelly Kelly
          New Delhi
          pot of jelly
gut(s)   comic cuts
          comics
          Limehouse Cut
          Newington Butts
          newingtons

Testicles

balls   cobblers
          cobbler's
          cobblers' awls
          cobbler's stalls
          coffee stalls
          Henry Halls
          marble halls
          Max Walls
          Niagara Falls
          Niagaras
          Nobby Halls
          orchestra stalls
          Wentworth Falls
          wentworth's balls
bollocks flowers and frolics
          fun and frolics
          Jackson Pollocks
          Jimmy Rollocks
          Tommy Rollocks
cods   Ken Dodds

goolies Tom Doolies
knackers cheese and crackers
          Christmas crackers
          cream crackers
          maracas
          nutcrackers
nuts   General Smuts
          Nicky Butts

Throat hairy goat
          nanny
          nanny goat
neck   bushel and peck

Thumb Jamaica rum

Toe(s) buttons and bows
          old black joes
          Oscar Joes
          stop and go
          these and those

Tongue heart and lung
          Jimmy Young
          Loretta Young
          Roland Young
say   first of May

Vagina

bum   date
collar   must-I-holler
cunt   all quiet
          Berkeley hunt
          Berkshire hunt

cunt continued

Burlington hunt
Birchington hunt
Burchington hunt
gasp and grunt
grumble and grunt
groan and grunt
growl and grunt
Lady Berkeley
Roger Hunt
sharp and blunt
Sir Berkeley
treasure hunt

fanny   jack an' danny
nook and cranny
Orphan Annie

gash   leslie
hole   south pole
pit   bob and hit
snatch   Tony Hatch
twat   dillypot
gluepot
honeypot
mustard pot

Race and Nationality

American

Yank   board and plank
hamshank
seppo
septic
sherman

Yank continued

wooden plank
Yankee   Widow Twankey

Black, Asian, Chinese etc.

chink   kitchen sink
chinky   Wee Willie Winky
coon   harvest moon
silvery
silvery moon
darkie   Feargal Sharkey
Greville Starkey
nigger   grave digger
mechanical digger
square rigger
paki   half-ounce of baccy
Joe Daki
spade   Lucozade
razor
razor-blade
wog   chocolate
hedgehog

Englishman

pom   to-and-from

Foreigner

wog   spotty dog

French   muddy trench

Frenchman

frog   jiggle and jog

Greek   bubble and squeak
          werris

Immigrant
          Jimmy Grant

Irishman

paddy   goodie and baddie
          tea caddy
mick   shovel and pick

Italian

eyetie   sky
wop   grocer's shop

Japanese

Nip   micro-chip
          orange pip
Jap   five star nap
          rat-trap

Jew   box of glue
          buckle my shoe
          fifteen and two
          fifteen-two
          five by two
          five to two
          four by two
          half past two
          kangaroo
          pot of glue
          pull-through
          quarter to two

Jew continued
          Sarah Soo
          ten to two
ikey-mo eskimo
Yid   back-wheel skid
          Cisco Kid
          four-wheel skid
          front-wheel skid
          God forbids
          non-skid
          saucepan lid
          slippery
          slippery Sid
          teapot
          teapot lid
          three-wheel skid
          tin lid

Pole   sausage roll

Scot
jock   sweaty sock

Sikh   oil leak
          ollie beak

Spaniard
spic   oil slick

Turk   Captain Kirk

Welshman
taff   riff-raff

Relationships

Aunt   garden plant
           Mr Chant

Baby   basin of gravy
nipper   fly
           fly tipper

Boyfriend
fella   umbrella

Brother   manhole cover
              one and t'other
              one another
              slide and sluther

Child
brat   Jack Sprat
kid   dixie lid
          saucepan lid
          teapot
          teapot lid
          tin lid
sod   haddock and cod

Cousin   baker's dozen

Courting   nanny goating

Daughter
           bottle of water
           bricks and mortar
           didn't oughter

Daughter continued
           holy water
           soap and water
           ten furlongs

Father   soap and lather
dad   good and bad
             sorry and sad
old man old pot

Friend   Mile End
chum   finger and thumb
cobber   thief and robber
mate   china
             china plate
             Dutch
             Dutch plate
             garden gate
             tin plate

Girlfriend
bird   Richard
           Richard the Third
cliner   ocean liner
girl   ocean pearl
sheila   potato peeler
sweetheart
           jam tart
           merryheart

Husband
fella   umbrella
hubby   teletubby

Mother   God love her
           one and t'other
           one another
           strangle and smother
mum   finger and thumb
old woman
           old grabem pudden

Sister   black man kissed her
           blister
           blood blister
           kid blister
           skin-and-blister

Son   bath bun
           Chelsea bun
           hot cross bun
           penny bun
           pie and one
           sticky bun

Wife   bit of tripe
           bubble
           old bubble
           carving knife
           duchess
           Duchess of Fife
           drum and fife
           fork and knife
           joy of my life
           old dutch
           'pon my life
           Sporting Life
           Stanley knife

wife continued
           storm and strife
           struggle and strife
           Swiss Army (knife)
           trouble and strife
           war and strife
           worry and strife
missus   cheese and kisses
           cow-and-kisses
           hugs and kisses
           love and kisses
old woman
           gooseberry pudding
           gooseberry pudden
           old grabem pudden

Religion

Catholics   cattle ticks

Church   chicken-perch
           in the lurch
           lean and lurch
           left in the lurch
           rock and lurch
           seek and search

Devil   Henry Melville

God   Tommy Dodd

Heaven   fifteen and seven

Hell   ding-dong bell

Hypocrite

heaven man
           seven-times-seven man

Hymns hers and hims

Mormon Jerry O'Gorman

Parson Winchcombe Carson

Quaker muffin baker

Vicar half-a-nicker
        half-nicker
        pie and liquor

Sex

Aroused/Arousing

horny mulligatawny
hot pass in the pot
      peas in the pot
randy port and brandy

Brothel

house flea and louse
       timothy

Condom

johnnie reggie and ronnie
flunkey wise monkey

Fellatio

gam slice of ham
go down Divine Brown

Have Anal Sex

arse bottle
go up the shitter
      go up the council

Have Sex

arse bottle
charver balaclava
get one's hole
      rock and roll

Homosexual

bent bottle of scent
gay C&A
     howard's way
     milky way
queer gear

Homosexual Man

bent Duke of Kent
     Stoke on Trent
catamite dyna
cock hock
fairy Julian Clary
homo Perry Como
iron lenny the lion
     Meg Ryan
nance song and dance
nancy tickle your fancy

poof	horse's hoof
	iron
	iron hoof
poofter	cloven hoofter
puff	collar and cuff
	jam duff
	near enough
	Nellie
	Nelly
	Nellie Duff
	Nelly Duff
	nice enough
queen	haricot
	in between
	Milton Keynes
	Nellie
	Nelly
	pork and bean
queer	Brighton pier
	buccaneer
	ginger
	ginger beer
	jeer
	jere
	King Lear
	shandy

Lesbian

dyke	raleigh bike
girl	twist
queen	Nellie
	Nelly

Male Prostitute

| *rent boy* | burton |
| *puff* | nigh enough |

Masturbate

choke the chicken

	drain Charles Dickens
strop	whip and top
toss	polish and gloss
wank	bang the plank
	levy
	pull rank
	shabba
	shank
	taxi-rank

Masturbation

wank	Allied Irish
	barclay's
	ham shank
	J. Arthur
	jodrell
	Midland Bank
	petrol tank
	piggy bank
	sherman
	Yorkshire penny bank

Masturbator

wanker	ham shanker
	Kuwaiti tanker
	merchant banker
	monkey spanker

Oral Sex

French tricks
        flying sixty-six

Perform Anilingus

arse   bottle

Perform Fellatio

gam   plate
plate   garden
        garden gate

Petting

snog   Kermit the Frog

Pimp   fish and shrimp
        MacGimp
        MacGimper
        magimp
        McGimp
        M'Gimp
hoon   blue moon
        dish ran away with the
          spoon
        egg and spoon
        silver spoon
        silvery
        silvery moon
        terry toon
ponce alphonse
        candle
        candle-sconce
        Charlie Ronce
        dillydonce

ponce continued
        Harry Ronce
        Joe Bonce
        Joe Ronce
        ronson

Promiscuous Woman

moll   paper doll
slag   Melvyn Bragg

Prostitute mallee root
brass   champagne glass
moll   kewpie
tail   brass
        brass-nail
wanker jodrell
whore boat and oar
        broken oar
        early door
        forty-four
        Jane Shore
        Rory
        Rory O'Moore
        six to four
        sloop of war
        tug o' war
        two by four

Sex   Oedipus Rex
        Posh and Becks
        shellmex
        T. Rex
cunt   groan and grunt
        growl and grunt
        grumble and grunt

Tools

Transport

Bicycle

bike   clever Mike
        do as you like
        iron Mike
        pat and mike

Boat   frog in the throat
        hat and coat
        I'm afloat
        nanny
        nanny goat

Brake   Charlie Drake

Bus   camerer cuss
        don't make a fuss
        surgical truss
        swear and curse
        swear and cuss
        trouble and fuss

Bus Shelter helter-skelter

Car   jam
        jam jar
        la-di-dah
        rattle and jar
        shaun spadah
motor haddock and bloater
        kipper and bloater
        tea-for-two and a
          bloater

motor continued
        Yarmouth bloater
Rolls Camilla Parker
        Camilla Parker Bowles
wheels jellied eels

Carriage love and marriage

Charabanc
        bow and arrow

Coach cockroach

Fare   grey mare

Garage horse and carriage

Honda Henry Fonda

Station aggravation
        poor relation
        salvation

Sulky big and bulky

Tax (Disc)
        ajax

Taxi Joe Baxi
        Joe Maxi
        slapsie maxie
cab   flounder
        flounder and dab
        mab

cab continued

	Sandy Macnab
	sherbert
	sherbert dab
	smash and grab

Ticket Wilson Pickett

Tram bread and jam
jar of jam
plain and jam

Trap butter flap

Tyre Billy Liar

Weather

Cold brave and bold
Cheltenham
Cheltenham bold
Naughton and Gold
potatoes in the mould
soldiers bold
taters
taties
tatters
warrior bold
warrior's hold
chilly Uncle Willie
nippy George and Zippy

Fog golliwog

Hot mustard
mustard pot
peas in the pot

Rain alacompain
allacompain
Andy Cain
France and Spain
King of Spain
Mary Blaine
Mary Blane
pleasure and pain

Shower David Gower
Eiffel Tower
fairy bower
happy hour
Tyrone Power

Snow to and fro

Thunder stand from under
Stevie Wonder
up and under

Warm Somerset
Somerset Maugham

Wind Jenny Lind

Windy Jenny Lindy
rawlpindi